D-DAY
IN HISTORY AND MEMORY

*The Normandy Landings
in International Remembrance and Commemoration*

Edited by Michael R. Dolski, Sam Edwards, John Buckley

UNT
PRESS

Denton, Texas

©2014 University of North Texas Press

10 9 8 7 6 5 4 3 2 1

Permissions:
University of North Texas Press
1155 Union Circle #311336
Denton, TX76203-5017

The paper used in this book meets the minimum requirements of the American National Standard for Permanence of Paper for Printed Library Materials, z39.48.1984. Binding materials have been chosen for durability.

Library of Congress Cataloging-in-Publication Data

D-Day in history and memory : the Normandy landings in international remembrance and commemoration / edited by Michael Dolski, Sam Edwards, John Buckley. -- Edition: 1
    pages cm
  Includes bibliographical references and index.
    ISBN 978-1-57441-548-3 (cloth : alk. paper) -- ISBN 978-1-57441-558-2 (ebook)
    1. World War, 1939-1945--Campaigns--France--Normandy. 2. World War, 1939-1945--Campaigns--France--Normandy--Social aspects. 3. World War, 1939-1945--Historiography. 4. Nationalism and collective memory. I. Dolski, Michael, 1978- editor of compilation. II. Edwards, Sam, 1981- editor of compilation. III. Buckley, John (John D.), editor of compilation. IV. Dolski, Michael, 1978- "Portal of liberation". V. Title: "Portal of liberation".
  D756.5.N6D23 2014
  940.54'21421--dc23
                    2013043836
The electronic edition of this book was made possible by the support of the Vick Family Foundation.

For the combatants of D-Day and the people of Normandy;
Those whose lives and experiences lie behind all of this memory work.

CONTENTS

List of Figures

Acknowledgments

As those who commanded the D-Day invasion knew all too well, collaborative, transatlantic, ventures are a challenging enterprise in both planning and execution. This book was no exception. Admittedly, as editors our endeavor was of a rather different sort and scale to that of Ike in June 1944 (we used far fewer ships and hardly any aircraft at all…). But there were, on reflection, some uncanny connections. Our supreme commander throughout was American, Michael Dolski, and his lieutenants were both British: Sam Edwards and John Buckley (one is tempted to push the analogy as far as it will go and mark the former as a sort of Tedder figure, and the latter as a Monty; although it must be acknowledged that not once did John attempt to suggest we all join him in a dynamic drive through Belgium). And much like Overlord, there were the obligatory confusions and differences to overcome (what to do with that so troubling issue in Anglo-American relations, vowels). But, as we hope our readers will agree, the result of this transatlantic endeavor is an engaging and rewarding assessment of how one event—D-Day—has been appropriated, adapted, and assimilated into six distinct national cultures.

The project began as a conference panel exploring comparative perspectives on the Normandy landings organized by Michael and Sam for the Society of Military History's conference in 2010 (always a stimulating occasion) at the Virginia Military Institute (a fascinating venue). Soon after, Ron Chrisman of UNT Press contacted

Michael expressing an interest in the panel and inviting us to submit a proposal for a book-length comparative study if we thought there was scope for it. We did, and leapt at the opportunity. But, as relatively junior scholars, we needed experience and wisdom to guide us, and we found both in Professor John Buckley, eminent military historian, scholar, and gentleman. With John's involvement, we were ready to begin our search for the expert contributors necessary to the project's successful completion. Michael, an authority when it comes to D-Day's place in American memory, was to deal with the American-focused chapter, while Sam, with interests in all aspects of war commemoration, was to take the British chapter. John, meanwhile, was to exercise a detached overview of the project, prompting and advising where necessary. But that still left four chapters in need of suitable authors, those dealing with Canadian, French, German, and Russian memory. Our approach to finding these authors was simple: we looked for those with the requisite knowledge and expertise to examine their subject matter with skill, care, and flare. Hence Terry Copp and Matt Symes for the Canadian chapter, Kate Lemay for the French chapter; Günter Bischof and Michael Maier for the German chapter (which, due to Günter's unique skills and knowledge, also includes a consideration of Austrian memory), and Olga Kucherenko for the chapter exploring the view of D-Day from beyond the Urals.

As editors, we would like to take this opportunity to thank all these experts for agreeing to be involved in the project, and for the dedication and diligence with which they have undertaken their research and writing. Not once have we had to cajole, hurry, or encourage: our authors completed their assignments in good time, and in good order, and for this, our sincere thanks. On behalf of all of us (editors included) our thanks must also go to all those staff of the many different archival facilities in the United States, United Kingdom, Canada, France, Germany, Austria, and Russia whose documents and sources are recorded in the footnotes and bibliography. Our gratitude and appreciation must also go to our editor at UNT Press, Ron Chrisman, who has been unfailingly supportive throughout, guiding us through the challenges and pitfalls of edited collections. In so many respects, this project was his initiative, and for this, we thank him. For all of us too, family and friends have been understanding and accepting of the demands of scholarship, especially that which is, like this book, transatlantic and transnational. For their patience, indulgence, and interest, we thank them all.

It seems apt here to conclude with the words of GEN Eisenhower, words written on a scrap of paper on 5 June 1944, and thrust into his breast pocket where they stayed, never to be used for their original purpose. The words were for communication to his respective superiors should the invasion he had just ordered fail. He finished this brief note with the statement that "If any blame or fault attaches to the attempt, it is mine alone." Likewise, therefore, while any success attributed to this project is certainly due to the efforts and expertise of our contributors, and to the help and guidance of Ron, any failings or faults, errors or inaccuracies, are ours, and ours alone.

Sam Edwards, Michael R. Dolski, John Buckley
August 2013

INTRODUCTION

MICHAEL R. DOLSKI, SAM EDWARDS,
JOHN BUCKLEY

Over the past seventy years, the Allied invasion of Northwestern France in June 1944 has come to stand as something more than a major battle in an increasingly distant war. The assault itself formed a vital component of Allied victory in the Second World War. The hard-fought invasion on that sixth day of June opened a new European battlefront that would expand during the ensuing eleven months into the heart of Germany and thereby help ensure the eventual destruction of Hitler's Nazi regime. Together, the military signifi-cance of the invasion and the broader social, political, and economic changes which accompanied European liberation and the end of the war, have ensured that D-Day—as the initial landing is tradition-ally termed (following military convention)—has developed into a sign and symbol, especially in North America and Western Europe. Most importantly, as a word it carries with it a series of ideas and associations all of which, while linked, nonetheless have a degree of national and cultural specificity. This book, therefore, offers a study of these specificities. It explores the construction and reconstruction in the period since 1944 of at least six different D-Days: the stories of the landings as told by North Americans, Western Europeans, and Russians. As the subsequent chapters amply demonstrate, from high statesmen to everyday individuals, many different people have spent the post-war period invoking, interpreting, and (re)inventing D-Day for a variety of reasons. As with all instances of collective memory, there is a politics at play because the past serves to help make sense of the ever-changing present (an issue we examine in more depth below).

This book, then, examines the commonalities and differences in national collective memories of D-Day. With separately authored chapters devoted to individual nations, readers will encounter a range of different ways and means of commemorating D-Day. The chapters cover the main belligerent forces on the day of battle, including the United States, Great Britain, Canada, France, and Germany. In addition, a chapter on Russian engagement with the invasion explores other views of the battle. At its broadest, this book shows that memories of the past vary over time, are linked to present-day needs, and, despite the effects of transnational globalization that have challenged the economic structures and political sovereignty of the traditional nation state, such memories are still circumscribed by issues of language and location. Simply put, memories of D-Day have diverged according to time, place, and national culture. The powerful expressions of this memory work arise in a multitude of locations such as films, books, monuments, anniversary celebrations, and news media representations, and germinate from a variety of individuals, organizations, and even political institutions. Rather than simply drawing on a series of facts about the past, the attribution of specific meanings and themes to this battle shows how individuals, groups, and even the imagined community of the nation state draw on the past to validate the present and chart a course for the future. In the end, therefore, the constructed and re-created interpretations of D-Day explored by the contributors to this book tell us a great deal about the changes, challenges, and circumstances of these various societies in the decades since the battle itself concluded.

D-Day and the Battle for Normandy

Operation Overlord, the code name for the Normandy invasion in June 1944, was an important component in the Allied march toward victory in the Second World War. The Allied disputes over the need for the invasion of German-occupied France offered a degree of uncertainty and high drama even before the killing on the beaches began. An enormous level of difficulty, on the day of battle and in the campaign that followed, further attracts attention to this operation. Former US Army officer and D-Day historian Capt. Flint Whitlock reminds us that "an amphibious operation is the most difficult and complex of military maneuvers. And no amphibious operation was more difficult or complex than the invasion of Normandy on 6 June 1944."[1] The invasion included intricate naval and aerial support plans, far-flung bombardment activities, airborne assaults, and multiple amphibious landings—all this happening far from base areas in the face of an entrenched and experienced enemy. Unlike island hopping in the Pacific, once ashore the Allies had to face the real prospect of losing the race to reinforce any beachhead if the *Wehrmacht* reacted rapidly enough. To overcome the challenges facing them, Allied military forces had to display a tremendous level of ingenuity.

The threat of failure was real. German defensive preparations had strengthened what their military planners deemed the most likely invasion route. They focused on the Pas-de-Calais area of France, which was the shortest in distance from England and offered the greatest air coverage for the invading fleet. Privy to German plans due to a series of intelligence successes, the Allies decided to avoid that more accessible, and more dangerous, landing area. Meanwhile, they added to the likelihood for initial gains by spreading out the defenders through deception operations. Double agents, false signals traffic, fake armies, and deliberately scattered aerial bombing operations all confounded the defense. The Allies, on the other hand, focused their attention on preparing for the inevitably difficult task of landing on hostile shores. The preparatory planning agency, Chief of Staff to the Supreme Allied Command (COSSAC) headed by British Lt. Gen. Frederick Morgan, selected the location based on an array of factors. Tide tables, beach composition, transportation routes inland, distance from air and sea bases in England, and the German defensive preparations all factored into the choice. Southwest of Calais, Normandy became the optimal site based on all these calculations.[2]

Normandy was optimal, but it also was far from an easy landing location. Learning from the disastrous Dieppe Raid experience in 1942, military planners sought to avoid the formidable defenses built up around any major port. Still, the Normandy area was hardly bereft of defensive features by mid-1944. Hitler had assigned Gen. Fd. Mar. Erwin Rommel as head of Army Group B, underneath Gen. Fd. Mar. Gerd von Rundstedt's German Army Command in the West (OB West), early in the year. With typical energy, Rommel instituted a program for quickly strengthening existing fortifications, leading to millions of mines, flooded river regions, and a host of nasty surprises for potential invaders throughout France and the Low Countries.[3] By June 1944, the Norman landscape contained a number of what the Germans called defense points (*Wiederstandsnesten*), anti-tank obstacles, reinforced gun emplacements, and pre-sighted weapons ranging over potential air or seaborne landing sites. Manning the defenses stood several infantry divisions of varying quality and the hope of rapid reinforcement if needed by reserve units that included more mobile forces. Aerial reconnaissance, along with covert fact-finding missions and information provided from the French Resistance, painted an increasingly grim picture for Allied planners.[4] Chances for a successful landing decreased each day that German preparations continued.

With several years of intensive combat operations behind them, though, Allied military leaders could face such a daunting task with a reasonable sense of confidence. By the early part of 1944, when the final planning for the invasion came together, the Western Allies had fought in tandem across the globe: in North Africa, in the Mediterranean, in Asia, and in the Pacific. In doing so, there had been more than enough setbacks and fiascos along the way. But so too were there successes achieved and lessons learned. Global warfare demanded tremendous industrial output and logistical organization, areas that these countries displayed a great deal of skill in mastering. Not everything was a glowing success story. Production bottlenecks in vital equipment like the Landing Ship Tank (LST) pushed cautious leadership to postpone the original landing date in Normandy from May to June, which acutely displeased the Red Army and Stalin. Yet the underlying point is that Americans, Canadians, British, and even their subordinate partners in this venture *did* produce thousands of naval craft, planes, tanks, motor vehicles, and sufficient food, equipment, and ammunition to equip a multi-million man force ready to invade and expand inland. For some soldiers, like the members of the US Army's 29th Infantry Division, the training had consumed years of their lives—and many were ready to make their contribution to victory. Others, such as the battle-hardened veterans of the US 1st Infantry Division or the British 50th Division, glumly anticipated the carnage and bloodletting that awaited them in France. All throughout the belligerent countries people waited, watched for news, and prayed for those they loved to make it through the coming storm.

The one thing all the planning, training, and preparations could not conclusively settle was how nature itself would influence the coming battle. As it turned out, environmental factors intervened in a near disastrous manner, as the oft-recounted tale of US GEN Dwight D. Eisenhower's lonely hours in command prior to the invasion readily maintains.[5] After delaying a month for more shipping, the operation had to start soon to leave sufficient clear weather months for the following campaign. The weather took a drastic turn for the worse late on 4 June, threatening one of the two acceptable windows to launch in that month. Eisenhower had to make the tough choice of starting in a less than opportune moment—and risking disaster in an already challenging maneuver—or stalling for a few more weeks and hopefully clear weather. After reconvening his top subordinates for a more up-to-date forecast, Ike's response was simply to go for it, thus setting the sixth of June as D-Day. If Eisenhower had delayed, the next invasion window opened two weeks later. That period witnessed one of the most powerful Channel storms of the past century, which surely would have foundered any attempted invasion. More than one commentator noted the incredible fortune, or, as sometimes expressed, divine assistance, that pushed Eisenhower to act in early June despite the dire weather.[6]

His go order pushed the vast machinery of invasion into action. Ships milling about filled to the brim with a soaking, miserable cargo of amphibious forces began moving to rendezvous points for the landings to start that Tuesday morning. The potential for a naval attack or aerial harassment by the Germans ratcheted up tensions. The main dangers that the vast Allied armada faced, however, came from the large number of mines strewn throughout these waters and the dislocation that nighttime operations necessary to get the amphibious forces to the beaches for the rising tide at dawn on such a vast scale threatened. As it turned out, a small squadron of German motor torpedo boats did attack the fleet, sinking the Norwegian destroyer HNoMS *Svenner* in the process.[7] In the aftermath of the battle, many Allied personnel expressed wonderment that the Germans did not take a proactive defense and try to disrupt seaborne operations more forcefully. Due to ceaseless defensive preparation, their German opponents had whittled away operational strength and possessed few naval or aerial resources available to confront the armada's protection. Those units the Germans had in place were lulled into a false sense of security because of inclement weather in the Channel.

The first Allied soldiers to face sustained hostile fire on D-Day were the airborne forces and those that transported them to France. As historian Ronald J. Drez asserted, "The great invasion started on the wings of the troop carriers."[8] The initial airborne assault employed three specially trained divisions: the British 6th and the US 82d and 101st. To quote the title of another book on their exploits, these were "the first men in."[9] Aside from the intensity of dropping into battle, behind enemy lines, to face a determined foe with the mere *hope* that your follow-up comrades will make it in to you in time, these divisions had important missions to fulfill in the fleeting hours before the seaborne landings. The British superbly secured their planned-for objectives, succeeding in a *coup de main* blow that took control of two important bridges on the eastern flank of the invasion area shortly after midnight.[10] Holding onto those bridges, while reducing another threatening artillery battery and other targets, produced some confused reactions from the Germans. Local commanders assumed that major landings were taking place even farther to the east. Their misapprehension was minimal, however, compared to the German bewilderment over the American landings in the Cotentin Peninsula. The two American divisions had the difficult task of securing ingress routes from the beaches inland for the westernmost seaborne forces. Unfortunately for them, the lay of the land beckoned an airborne landing, and flooded rivers, deadly anti-landing obstacles, and stout defenders awaited the men as they floated to ground in the dark amid a hail of gunfire. German anti-air activity had been so intense that it, combined with heavy clouds and less than fully trained pilots, led to a muddled dispersion of the airborne forces across multiple drop zones and occasionally well beyond them. An unintended benefit came with the Allied confusion as local pockets of Germans dealt with smatterings of Americans in their midst. Despite misdrops and deadly opposition, certain key sites like the town of Sainte-Mère-Église and the causeways in from the beaches fell to American control.[11]

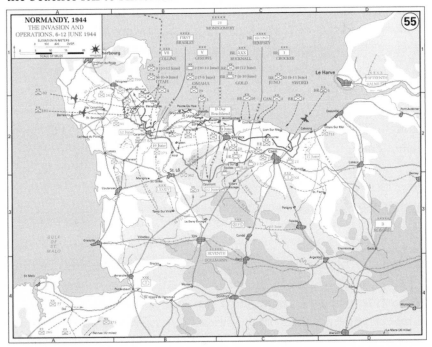

Figure 1: Map of the Normandy invasion area. The Cotentin Peninsula is to the left. The beaches, running west to east, include Utah (US), Omaha (US), Gold (UK), Juno (Canada), and Sword (UK). The American airborne forces landed behind Utah beach on the Cotentin (dashed lines approximate the area). The British air landings, of Pegasus Beach fame, occurred on the eastern flank of the invasion zone shown on the right here. Map adapted from Gordon A. Harrison, *Cross Channel Attack* (1951).

Due to the particulars of tides and coastal conditions, the American beaches (Utah and Omaha) had earlier start times than the three British-Canadian beaches (Gold, Juno, and Sword). The American amphibious forces had a 6:30 a.m. kick off, whereas their fellow combatants would start roughly one hour later. Preceding the waterlogged men themselves, a furious naval and aerial bombardment of the beach area served to ease the way in for the amphibious units. The battle of D-Day serves as ample proof for the old axiom that the plan never survives contact with the enemy. The breakdown between plan and reality with this initial bombing effort threatened to derail the entire operation. Although the opening arpeggio of fire from huge battlewagons and smaller naval craft of all sizes proved heartening to the amphibious troops as they dutifully headed to shore, the sad fact is that this storm of shells accomplished little. Coupled with ineffectual aerial bombardment, caused in large part by the cautious bomb release delays to avoid friendly fire incidents, the defenses remained fairly intact, manned by stunned but still very much active opponents.[12]

Naval support proved important in several different ways, though. First, accompanying ships occupied and distracted German defenders in a series of duels spread across the invasion area. This attention came at a cost, as indicated by LTJG Howard A. Anderson's description of the final minutes on the USS *Corry*, which sank after hitting a mine while maneuvering to avoid battery fire. Anderson helped treat men horribly burned "from swimming in burning oil or . . . scalded by hot steam escaping from ruptured boilers."[13] The second contribution of naval forces came as the meticulous landing schedule broke down in the chaos of battle. When essential tanks and artillery failed to materialize on the beaches, several destroyer skippers ordered their ships in to act as invaluable close-order support for the men on the beaches. Beholding this vital assistance, MG Leonard Gerow, who commanded the US V Corps assaulting Omaha Beach, exulted "Thank God for the US Navy!"[14]

The men on the beaches fortunate to remain among the living by that evening certainly had good reason to be in an appreciative mood. A clear indicator of the fighting's intensity comes from the jarring fact that, in the years since the war, for Americans the storming of Utah Beach pales alongside the far more famous action at Omaha because "only" several hundred men lost their lives for the former strip of sand. The Utah assault force caught a major break when tides and battlefield smoke led it away from the intended landing area to a section of beach with weaker defenses. Rather quickly, MG Raymond O. Barton's 4th Infantry Division streamed inland, joined up with airborne forces, and began a slow thrust across the Cotentin Peninsula.[15] Omaha Beach, "Bloody Omaha" as it is often remembered, presented a more sobering view of the D-Day invasion. In contrast to Utah's low casualty rate and relatively easy advance, Omaha exacted the highest number of losses and demanded the hardest fighting of the five landing beaches. Due to a recent German redeployment involving the 352d Division and some deadly defensive fieldworks that took excellent advantage of the concave beach and its high bluffs, the 1st Infantry Division (with attached elements of the 29th) faced a tough day. As SSG John J. Moglia, 16th Infantry, 1st Division, wrote years later, "It's still hard to believe that we were able [to] fight through it."[16] Moglia and his comrades did fight through the hard shell of German defenses, at the cost of approximately 3,000 casualties, and they held on grimly to a small bubble of territory by nightfall.[17] PVT Heinrich Severloh, opposing this 1st Infantry Division at *Wiederstandsnest* 62 on Easy Red Beach, later admitted, "I don't know how many I killed . . . Many."[18] Situated roughly between Utah and Omaha Beaches, the Pointe du Hoc promontory also witnessed intense fighting on D-Day as the soldiers of the 2d Ranger Battalion clambered up the cliffs to neutralize a battery of heavy artillery guns located there.[19] Even though the commander of the invasion's American component, LG Omar N. Bradley, briefly considered halting operations in the Omaha sector at noon, the primary mission of landing, and staying, was successful.

The British, Canadians, and small groups of other nationalities were just as determined, and experienced the same mix of achievement and frustration on D-Day. Running west to east, the three beaches of Gold, Juno, and Sword led to a more densely settled area of the Norman coastline. Mixing in with the buildings provided some coverage for the defense while beach obstacles added to Allied difficulties. Of the three British Commonwealth divisions, the Canadian 3d Division had the roughest landing at Juno, where the early assault looked eerily similar to the near-catastrophe at Omaha. Determined to avenge the humiliation at Dieppe, this force with attached British units smashed through the German resistance and made notable advances inland before halting that night in the area west of the Norman town of Caen.[20] Despite these successes, the Canadian 3d Division halted its inland advance short of its D-Day goal of Carpiquet Airfield, to the west of Caen.[21] Recriminations would fly in the coming weeks and years, but on the day of battle itself this stall was important for two reasons: 1) yet another aspect of the complex D-Day plan came unhinged by the inevitable frictions of war, and 2) the Canadians were held up in the relatively flat ground that proved the most likely locus of any major armored activity in the region. The latter point would feed into the controversies surrounding the development of the post-D-Day campaign in Normandy as all Allied forces foundered about looking to break free from the beachhead, then out of the *bocage* area that proved eminently suitable for a grueling defensive stand by the Germans. The latter was a medieval landscape of dense hedgerows punctuated with medieval stone farms well suited for quick conversion into forts, a nightmare for advancing Allied infantry and a field of opportunities for retreating German snipers.

The British 50th and 3d Divisions, bracketing the Canadians at Gold and Sword Beaches respectively, also made commendable initial gains, but likewise stopped short of their primary objectives. While Caen and its surrounding area formed the D-Day target for these forces, they did not take the city before German defenders began to arrive in response to the invasion. Due to less than anticipated gains after taking the initial beachheads, the British and Americans failed to unite Omaha and Gold Beaches, leaving a series of isolated landing sites vulnerable to piecemeal destruction by a concerted counterattack. Fortunately, none materialized.[22]

France contributed to the landings with commando units, naval forces, and support from the Resistance. Yet the schizophrenic combination of being, at one and the same time, liberator and liberated, agent and suspect, assured the invasion a distinctive place in national and regional narratives of the war. The liberation that began in Normandy also intensified the ordeal of the French people in the region—something one American historian recently considered. In *The Bitter Road to Freedom*, William Hitchcock argued, "The keynote of this European story of liberation is violence," which made D-Day "both a glorious chapter in military history and a human tragedy of enormous scope." Over 3,000 French citizens died on D-Day, more than the number of American soldiers killed in action on 6 June 1944.[23]

D-Day as a day of destruction also opened a new phase in the European war that led to Germany's ultimate defeat one year later. Yet, during this period, Germany sent a majority of its forces to the Eastern Front, which has attracted public attention to this sector of the country's war. In June 1944, Germany had deployed roughly sixty-two divisions along the Western Front. More than 179 German divisions then confronted the Red Army. June 1944 saw the Second Front open in the West, but it also witnessed the evisceration of Army Group Center on the Eastern Front. The Soviet Operation Bagration destroyed twenty-five German divisions and produced 300,000 casualties in a few weeks.[24]

For the Germans then and since, the horrific experience in the East has assumed the central place in narratives of the war.On the other hand, the stout defense confronting the Allies in Normandy permitted some small measure of self-congratulation for Germans. Friedrich Ruge, Rommel's naval adjutant, argued, "On D-Day, the Allies succeeded in forming beachheads of different sizes and depth in all five attack areas, but did not reach the target line set for that day at any point. The German defense had not been altogether unsuccessful." Ruge cited the "overwhelming strength of the Allies" to explain defeat in Normandy. Despite the odds, the Germans in Normandy had fought doggedly and demonstrated a skillfulness that he averred demanded admiration.[25] Nevertheless, the Allies did land, warded off early German counterattacks, and then settled in for a grinding campaign in Normandy. The Germans, despite some eventual concerted efforts, could neither fragment nor contain the beachhead.

Part of the problem facing the Germans was the dispersal of forces required to hold on to so much real estate—in the West as well as in the East. Soviet commentators maintained that their war effort had enabled the Normandy invasion in the first place. This was a point that delicately sidestepped the fact that many Soviet citizens actually fought for the Germans on D-Day, a product of the extent to which by 1944 German manpower shortages had led the *Wehrmacht* to recruit or impress Russians, Lithuanians, Ukrainians, and even Mongolians captured on the Eastern Front.[26] Although earlier in the war the Soviets clamored for as much Western Allied material and overt military assistance as possible, the world was a changed place by 1944. Stalin, to be sure, still found it amusing to critique his wartime bedfellows for their supposed squeamishness when confronting large-scale German forces in a major contestable region. Then again, by this point in the war the Red Army had not only repulsed the Germans and their allies along the Eastern Front, but they had fundamentally set the course of the war on what was arguably an irreversible path. By 1944, a run down, overspread, worn out *Wehrmacht* faced a zealously angry and increasingly competent opponent in the East—one that soon showed the prescience of interwar military theorists and their "deep battle" operational concepts that would consume entire army groups over the coming year.[27] Thus, as the Red Army obliterated German defenses in the East, and indeed were soon to do so in an even more dramatic fashion on 22 June 1944 (Operation Bagration), Stalin and his military leaders could claim with a great degree of truth that their successes tied down so many Germans that the Western Allies were granted an easier passage through the coming clash in Normandy. While the devil is in the doing, there still was a degree of desire and apathy or outright opposition to the Normandy invasion as something that would detract from the Red Army's successes—and impending victories.[28]

Setbacks and backbiting aside, the main confrontation was decided in favor of the Allies. At the end of D-Day, more than 150,000 men stood on French soil ready to continue the fight. In the face of extreme challenges, Allied Forces had prevailed. Hitler's vaunted Atlantic Wall shattered, quickly in most places, within a few hours in the most staunchly held sectors. With fighting on the Eastern Front soon to be renewed in a major Soviet offensive, the Germans had precious few resources to shift to Normandy. Deception operations continued to tie down significant German forces in other areas, such as Pas-de-Calais, in the advent of another potential invasion.[29] Nevertheless, D-Day was but one day of hard fighting and the Germans were far from capitulating at night's end.

The Normandy campaign that followed exposed a host of problems within the Allied forces as well as the continued fortitude and capability of the *Wehrmacht*. Caen did not fall on D-Day, as pre-invasion plans sought, and was a source of a see-saw battle until 9–10 July.[30] The Canadians halted north of Carpiquet Airfield on 6 June and then faced the onslaught of fanatical opposition by mainly SS armored units. Things went in a relatively better manner for the Americans at Utah Beach, where a less costly landing turned into a slow drive across the Cotentin Peninsula. Yet the confused airborne landings exacted a tremendous toll from the Allies and by the end of the first day Carentan remained in enemy hands, thus leaving Utah and Omaha separated from one another. In fact, the Rangers at Pointe du Hoc were isolated and subjected to intense attacks until 9 June.[31]

Although the Allies would turn to consolidating and joining their beachheads over the next few days, the German defenders did not sit idly by watching these developments. As historian Robert Kershaw suggested, D-Day—though important—was but one day in a crucial several-week period that saw the Allies establish a lodgment, secure the invasion zone, consolidate, and start the grueling task of expanding inland.[32] In the eastern sector, the British, Canadians, and other Allied units under their direction faced the brunt of the German response to the invasion, which centered on the area surrounding Caen. In the western sector, the Americans devoted attention to securing the port city of Cherbourg (26 June), then the rest of the Cotentin Peninsula, and after bogging down in the *bocage* country inland for several weeks of hard fighting next turned to breaking out of the invasion area. Preparatory to the breakout American forces took Saint Lô on 18 July and then launched Operation Cobra, after a fitful start, on 25 July. This latter move unhinged German defenses in the western zone so quickly that the Allies were also caught off guard, as the squabbling over and less-than-stellar performance during the race to Falaise indicated. At that final point, the Allies intended to link British, Canadian, and other forces with the American advance sweeping around from the south and the west. The Allies devoted the first few weeks of August to perform this attempted encirclement of the German Normandy defense force (known as the short envelopment as opposed to another plan for a wider encircling movement). Although Falaise fell on 21 August, trapping upwards of 50,000 Germans and a tremendous amount of materiel, key leadership figures and the core personnel required to rebuild shattered German defenses in the West managed to escape the trap.[33] Overall, the Normandy campaign constituted a mixed experience of stunning successes, problematic reverses, and missed opportunities for the Allies.

Despite major interruptions, such as Operation Market Garden in September and the Battle of the Bulge in December, the Allies continued a slow yet unyielding advance into Germany. Debates over the course and real effects of D-Day emerged on the day of battle, continued through the remainder of the war, and have lingered even to the present day. Though it took almost another year for completion, the Normandy landings ushered in the final stage of the war in Europe. Granted, the Second World War was a global conflict, one that required a wide array of efforts on behalf of all the Allied countries in their quest for victory. Normandy was one vital piece of the puzzle, but it depended upon earlier and near-coterminous successes in Eastern Europe, North Africa, and even the Pacific to make the campaign conceivable in the first place. Yet D-Day formed an obvious turning point, one that saw the Western Allies return to Northern Europe and open a multi-pronged, war-winning drive into the German homeland.

D-Day in History and Memory

The allure of D-Day, its size, scale, and significance, always assured the battle some degree of attention in global public remembrance; after all, writers, photographers, and film-makers all followed the troops ashore eager to interpret and record the proceedings, and many of those involved in Overlord were very aware that they were living history. GEN Eisenhower even singled-out the first anniversary of the landings for somewhat muted ceremonies and celebrations. Nonetheless, if acts of commemoration connected to D-Day were always likely, the precise *forms* of these acts, their shape and structure, place and purpose, would be a product of many variables, among which were the politics, prejudices and, perhaps most importantly, the national identity of those involved. This book, then, examines the origins and nature of D-Day remembrance; it provides a comparative examination of how distinct national cultures have memorialized, remembered, and represented the Normandy landings. To do this, each chapter, in broad terms, takes the same approach: they offer a history of the construction, communication, and contestation of collective memory(s). Here, we outline the recurrent themes, ideas, and terms employed in this volume.

Collective Memory and War

The concept of collective memory originated with the French sociologist Maurice Halbwachs, a pupil of the eminent Emile Durkheim.[34] Working in the 1930s, Halbwachs set out to reassess the nature of human memory, its forms, function, and structure. He asserted that contrary to psychological understandings that situated memory processes solely within the individual mind, memory was in actual fact a product, a construction, of social groups.[35] Halbwachs went on to suggest that not only is it in social groups that we, as individuals, are provided with the "tools" to remember, but that the memory constructed is inextricably tied to the opinions, preoccupations, attitudes, and beliefs prevalent in that group at that particular moment in time.[36]

In many respects, Halbwachs was before his time, and it was not really until the late twentieth century, as the grand narratives of history and identity fractured and fragmented in the West, that scholars began devoting time to the idea that the present constructs the past as much as discovers or uncovers it. Understandably, many of these scholars were drawn to the ways in which different individuals and groups invoked and invented histories of the First World War, the event often considered as marking the beginning of the "modern" world. Studies of collective memory, in short, have often been studies of *war memory*. The late twentieth century duly witnessed the publication of several landmark texts and articles. Jay Winter's highly respected 1995 book, *Sites of Memory, Sites of Mourning: The Great War in European Cultural History*, has been particularly influential, for example, in establishing the idea that war memorials, vast numbers of which were built after 1918, need to be understood not only for their artistic merit, but also for the mourning rites and rituals from which they often emerge, and with which they are thus inextricably connected, rites and rituals which, for Winter at least, have their origins in a Victorian culture of death.[37] In other words, Winter invites historians to recover the grief, fear, and tears that these structures originally called forth, and that these structures were often designed to alleviate. Numerous subsequent scholars accepted this invitation, including Alex King in his work, *Memorials of the Great War in Britain*, and Mark Connelly in his examination of the memorials built in the East End of London during the 1920s and 1930s.[38]

Similarly, Daniel Sherman's award-winning history of post-1918 French memorial building—*The Construction of Memory in Interwar France* (1999)—persuasively contends that the historian should pay close attention to the disagreements, disputes, and arguments that acts of commemoration often provoke. Indeed, for Sherman it was actually from *within* these arguments that a post-1918 discourse of commemoration "emerged." Thus, the interwar period witnessed, for example, frequent disagreements regarding how best to memorialize the French war dead, disagreements which pitted Paris against the provinces, men against women, the old against the young, civilians against veterans, commercial entrepreneurs against bastions of the artistic establishment.[39] Likewise, the contentious nature of post-1918 commemorative activity, particularly that connected to historical events deemed important to the national community, is also explored in many of the chapters in John Gillis's edited collection, *Commemorations: The Politics of National Identity*,[40] while David Lloyd, on the other hand, has also examined some of the tensions present in war commemoration, this time with a focus on the pilgrimages made by British and Commonwealth veterans to the battlefields of Europe in the 1920s and 1930s.[41] Scholarly interest in the cultural and commemorative aftermath of the First World War persists even now. Take, for instance, Lisa Budreau's recent study of post-1918 American war commemoration, as well as Janet Watson's excellent examination of how those Britons who endured the war later made sense of their experiences.[42]

Elsewhere, the events, experiences, and aftermath of the Second World War have also drawn considerable scholarly attention. In 1996, Henri Rousso published his acclaimed *Vichy Syndrome*, a text which explored the complicated and contested place of the Second World War in French memory, while James Young's two influential studies of Holocaust memory emerged in 1993 and 1994.[43] In more recent years, several innovative studies have been published demonstrating the complex interactions between nationally specific commemorations and the transnational nature of the conflict, while other scholars have pursued the emergence of powerful dominant discourses shaping the war's remembrance in particular cultures, such as the "Good War" in the United States and the "People's War" in Britain.[44] Contemporary scholarship in memory studies has also often engaged with specifically American wars. Pulitzer Prize-winner David Blight, for example, has explored the place of the Civil War in American memory, while the controversial legacies of the Vietnam War have been the subject of numerous studies, foremost of which is the recent contribution by Patrick Hagopian.[45]

By the early twenty-first century, this burgeoning literature had produced a backlash, in the form of several insightful and thought-provoking critiques, many of which often returned to two key ideas: first, that scholarly use of the word "memory" represented an unnecessary terminological invasion as the issues it was used to describe were already well-served by other, more established, terms such as myth or ritual; second, that the use of the word "memory" in the humanities and social sciences led to conceptual inaccuracy because, as a term, it originates within psychology. Memory, it was argued, is distinctly individual and personal and hence to talk of "collective memory," or to examine the social "memory" connected to a particular experience, is to deploy an oxymoron.[46] The sting has since been taken out of many these criticisms, particularly once it became apparent that psychologists did not, as some critiques assumed, possess memory as an idea, and nor indeed did the majority of them conceive of memory in such simplistic terms. Indeed, at the very moment in which historians, sociologists, anthropologists, and cultural theorists began examining the collective and constructive dynamics to memory, so too were many psychologists. Indeed there was a rich scholarly tradition already behind them, a tradition which reached back to the British psychologist F. C. Bartlett, a contemporary of Halbwachs.[47] Today, therefore, Memory Studies has emerged as a genuinely interdisciplinary field of scholarly enquiry, a fact which has been consolidated by the establishment of the "H-Memory" discussion network in 2007, and by the founding of the new Journal of *Memory Studies* in the very same year.

Even so, aspects of these early criticisms of memory studies do still remain, particularly as the twenty-first century has witnessed the emergence—or perhaps explosion—of what Jay Winter has referred to as the "memory boom." Further, Winter suggests that "one of the unfortunate features of the memory boom is the tendency of commentators to term any and every narrative of the past events as constituents of national memory or collective memory."[48] Any study of memory today, therefore, still demands a word on the precise ways and means through which it will be defined, and interrogated.

Drawing upon the work of those such as Winter and Sherman, and partly inspired by the ideas of the 1990s Popular Memory Group, this book examines collective memory not as a "thing," but as a productive *process* in which agents of memory—writers, filmmakers, memorial builders, journalists, politicians—embark upon efforts to construct culturally meaningful representations of the past.[49] It is this social dynamic that makes valid use of the prefix "collective," while the noun "memory" is appropriate because the groups and individuals involved are "remembering," that is, they are reflecting on the past from a position in the present, and they are doing so in order to produce a public representation of a past event. As Sherman has suggested:

> Just as individual memories constitute a fund of images and impressions—sensory as well as conceptual, auditory and tactile as well as visual—through which we seek out and recast our pasts, the discourses of collective memory and the practices of commemoration represent a society's past to itself.[50]

In line with this idea, our authors interrogate just those acts of public commemoration through which the D-Day past has been recast, represented, and narrated. These include: the production of memorials, museums, and commemorative souvenirs; the speeches and ceremonies which accompany anniversaries; and commemorative performances such as veterans' pilgrimages, historical re-enactments, and the production of films and other cultural texts.

As such, when discussing the means and mechanisms of this process of memory production, the contributors to this volume often privilege terms such as "commemoration," "memorialization," and "remembrance." The distinctions between these three terms are fluid rather than sharp and the activities associated with them frequently complement each other. Thus, both commemoration and remembrance are defined here as social activities that produce images, ideas, statements, and other *representations* of the past, while memorialization refers to the production of a particular type of representation: a memorial. Use of these terms also grounds this study in time and space, for these social activities are linked to tangible "sites of memory," or, in the words of another scholar, "frames of remembrance."[51] Such sites or frames include: memorials, monuments, museums, commemorative re-enactments, films, memoirs, historical pilgrimages. These things, objects, places, or activities do not themselves constitute collective memory(s). Rather, they are the locations around and within which collective memory(s) are produced, and thus they are locations which the historian or social scientist can study: "A collective memory—as a set of ideas, images, feelings about the past—is best located not in the minds of individuals, but in the resources they share."[52]

Each different type of location, or "resource," provokes specific questions, but there is also much which is similar about the ways and means employed here to interrogate them. With regard to the construction of memorials, for example, our authors consider who is involved. What are their motivations? How do their actions and concerns connect to the historical moment in which they are working? What do they wish their memorial to declare? How have they sought to script and re-script the past according to dominant discourses produced in the present? The conclusions drawn are not intended to define all that a commemorative structure might say; our authors do not seek to identify and outline an entirely hegemonic memory that neatly explains *all* that a person might subsequently think, or remember, as they stand before a particular memorial, or as they watch a particular film. Rather, as Irwin-Zarecka has remarked, by examining the production of collective memory(s), as witnessed in a variety of different representations, the "aim is not to freeze one particular 'reading' as *the* correct one, rather, it is to establish the likely range of meanings."[53] Put differently, by examining a variety of different cultural texts, our authors identify and explore the discursive frameworks established around one event—D-Day; they identify the different meanings attached to this event, and they explore how these meanings have been *produced*.

Finally, employing terms such as commemoration and remembrance also allows our authors to break down the clear-cut opposition often believed to exist between the workings and nature of "memory" and those of "history" and thus link the work of historians to the production of collective memory(s).[54] There are, of course, differences between the form and function of history and that of collective memory; the former is an academic discipline with all the rules, procedures, and traditions that come with it. Yet if there are distinctions, we should also acknowledge the connections, especially in our post-modern age. As Rosenberg writes: "Memory and history are blurred forms of representation whose structure and politics need to be analyzed not as oppositional but as interactive forms."[55] Similarly, Winter once more:

> History and Memory overlap, infuse each other, and create vigorous and occasionally fruitful incompatibilities…In virtually all acts of remembrance, history and memory are braided together in the public domain, jointly informing our shifting and contested understandings of the past.[56]

The chapters in this volume frequently draw attention to this "blurring" and "overlap" as history and memory inform one another in a dynamic relationship.

D-Day as Discourse:
National Memories of a Transnational Event

The story of D-Day that emerges from the chapters that follow is one of, paradoxically, national parochialisms shaped by transnational imperatives. Thus, all of our authors identify the extent to which D-Day—after nearly seventy years of cultural activity—has been surrounded by, and enfolded within, nationally specific discourses, discourses which were themselves framed by nationally (and occasionally regionally) specific experiences of the war and post-war period. The significance of this point should not be under-estimated: the Second World War was, perhaps, the pre-eminent *transnational* event of the twentieth century. In Europe, it was begun by an act of border transgression—the invasion of Poland—and it culminated in a distinctly "new" world, at least in terms of political geography. Germany was truncated; Poland was disappeared; Britain lost an Empire; the Soviet Union created one. Moreover, the Europe that emerged in 1945 would be dominated by the power and politics of two multinational blocs: East and West, NATO and Warsaw Pact. In Asia and Africa, too, the war produced new geographies and new nations: an independent India and, soon after, Pakistan; the birth of Communist China, and a divided Vietnam; and two decades of wars and "emergencies" in the African territories of the old European empires as the dispossessed and disenfranchised embraced anti-colonial nationalism.

Just as importantly, D-Day—as an event—was a microcosm of this transnational war. It involved an unparalleled degree of cooperation between the militaries of the United States *and* the British Empire and Commonwealth, that was itself a polyglot entity. These militaries, in turn, commanded significant numbers of soldiers provided by the governments in exile of occupied Europe. The operation itself was launched from Britain but unfolded on the territory of France. This assault was designed to deal a fatal blow to the military of the Nazi empire at a moment in time specifically intended to help the Soviet ally. The roll call of those nations and peoples involved in the D-Day landings (or affected by them) is thus extensive, and certainly includes: Americans, Britons, Canadians, French, Belgians, Poles, Norwegians, Irish, Australians, South Africans, New Zealanders, Indians, Danes, Dutch, Czechs, Germans, Austrians, and Russians.[57] Yet despite all of this, the essays in this volume—which are themselves indicative of D-Day's international dimensions—make clear that understandings of the Normandy landings remain firmly, indeed stubbornly, national in tone, tenor, and form. There is, in short, an American story of D-Day, a British story, a French story, and so on. That is not to deny, of course, that points of connection exist. The story of D-Day that resonates in American culture, for instance, bears many similarities to that which exists in British culture: a story of selfless sacrifice for Europe, and especially for France. Similarly, the annual commemorations of D-Day on the Norman beaches have always ensured that nationally specific stories of the landings remained able to accommodate alternative readings. After all, when Americans, Britons, and Canadians, as well as many others, gather in France each June to commemorate the D-Day landings, the space for a culturally parochial D-Day is significantly circumscribed. While interrogating a similar issue, the structure of what he terms "collec*ted* memory," James Young suggested that although "individuals cannot share another's memory any more than they can share another's cortex" they can, nonetheless, "share the forms of memory, even the meanings in memory generated by these forms."[58] This book is suggestive of a similar dynamic at the level of competing and contrasting national memories. The six essays in this volume *do* identify shared points of contact with regard to meaning; but so do they also identity at least six different D-Day's. Indeed, within each national cultural there are frequently several variations on a central theme.

In America, as Michael Dolski demonstrates, D-Day has firmly established itself in contemporary culture as a heroic myth of self-affirmation. The origins of this idea can be traced to the hours and days immediately after the landings; it was here that a variety of different agents—politicians, press, the president—began constructing the "mythic framework" that still surrounds D-Day in American culture today. To be sure, local memories of D-Day—especially in places like Bedford, Virginia—did, on occasion, exist in tension with the emerging national "myth"; for some, D-Day would always mean death, rather than victory; and it would always bring tears rather than relief. But the national myth has, nonetheless, tended to crowd out alternative readings. Similarly, in Britain, the post-1945 period witnessed the emergence and consolidation of a particular narrative of the Normandy landings, a narrative ultimately structured by the conjoined ideas that D-Day marked a final demonstration of Imperial power, that it redeemed the humiliation of Dunkirk, and that it was the product of a transatlantic equality of effort and endeavor. For many Britons, as Sam Edwards explains, D-Day was thus a celebration of what the "special relationship" could achieve. Indeed, it was the event in which this relationship proved its reality.

Compared to the Americans and British, representatives of other nations have often had a more difficult relationship to D-Day and a rather more complicated collection of memories. For Canadians, as Terry Copp and Matt Symes make clear, efforts to commemorate D-Day have often been sidelined by the extent to which popular and political interest has tended to focus on Canada's First World War experiences, rather than those of 1939–45. Thus, despite the fact that Canadian troops landed in significant numbers on D-Day, third behind the United States and the British; despite the large casualties suffered on the day; and despite even the fact that many Normans responded far more positively to their liberation at the hands of French Canadians compared to local responses to American and British troops, Canadian culture has, nonetheless, often privileged Vimy Ridge over Juno Beach; 1917 over 1944. This sidelining of the Normandy experience is, of course, also connected to questions beyond Canada's borders. Indeed, Canada's D-Day has often been overwhelmed by the American-authored discourse explored by Dolski, a discourse powerfully articulated and sustained by the artifacts of popular culture. So, too, Canada's D-Day has also often been subsumed within the British-sponsored Imperial discourse identified by Edwards. As a result, Copp and Symes suggest that D-Day remains surprisingly marginalized in Canadian culture.

For the French, as Kate Lemay shows, the situation is even more complicated, a result of the social fractures and fissures that the war produced (and indeed of which the war was itself a product). First of all, there is the matter of terminology. For while D-Day (or, rather jour-j) now has cultural currency in French discourse, the original term employed to describe *and* designate D-Day was "the landings" (*le débarquement*). This is significant. Postwar French culture had no time or space for the idea that D-Day was an invasion. The term suggests something unwanted, something to be repelled. To talk of "landings" is, therefore, to nullify and neutralize an otherwise contentious vocabulary. French understandings of D-Day are also complicated by regional inflections and differences generally absent in the other nations discussed in this volume. After all, for the French, D-Day was, first and foremost, a *regional* experience: it unfolded in Normandy. Thus, Normans sustain a regional commemorative discourse, a discourse that acknowledges—and celebrates—deliverance and liberation, and that is formed in acts of transatlantic commemoration during which local communities establish "kinships of memory" with D-Day veterans.[59] At the same time, Normans also sustain another discourse, a discourse that exists at the margins and between the lines, and that includes space for the problems of the regional experience: the death and devastation that liberation brought with it; the martyrdom of French towns and villages (Caen, Saint Lô); the roles of resistors and collaborators. Meanwhile, French politicians, wary of celebrating national deliverance at the hands of those frustrating Anglo-Saxons, have often sought to sideline or re-script D-Day. Such efforts began with Gen. de Gaulle himself, a man who made concerted efforts to convince the French that they had, in actual fact, liberated themselves. For de Gaulle, then, it was much better to celebrate that other D-Day of August 1944 (Operation Dragoon), an operation which took place in the South of France, and which was dominated by Free French troops (many of whom were from the French Empire). That said, on other occasions, and in the hands of other French presidents, the Normandy landings were also trawled for sentiment suitable to the discourses of diplomacy. Indeed, if Gaullists have often been uncomfortable with invoking the idea of liberation at the hands of the Anglo-Americans, others in France—Atlanticists—have seen in D-Day commemorations a useful means to secure the transatlantic alliance in the present. Today, in fact, the landings are most likely to be appropriated by French politicians in the service of Franco-American relations, much to the annoyance of the British.

For those opposing the landings—the Germans—D-Day has likewise occupied a difficult and contested space in national culture. As Günter Bischof and Michael S. Maier demonstrate, this is, of course, because it was the beginning of a defeat, and a defeat, moreover, of a morally reprehensible and murderous political regime. To be sure, commemorating a military defeat is entirely possible: the Spartans managed it at Thermopylae; Southerners did so following the American Civil War; and the inheritors of Imperial Germany managed it in the 1920s.[60] But, how to commemorate the defeat of Nazism at the hands of Western democracies in the post-1945 period? Especially given that post-Nazi West Germany—controlled by the Anglo-American militaries—was being democratized and de-Nazified? In eastern Germany, occupied by the Red Army, an idea emerged in the immediate postwar period that might have met the commemorative needs of the moment: East Germans were quickly taught by their Soviet-sponsored government to celebrate defeat as national liberation. But there was no scope in the east for connecting this idea to D-Day—liberation was won by Soviet arms, not by the militarily insignificant activities of those late and lazy Anglo-Americans. Far easier in both West Germany and Austria, therefore, to draw a line after 1945, to silence and suppress, rather than acknowledge, confront, or comprehend what began on 6 June 1944. Seen in this light, postwar German and Austrian silence regarding D-Day was just another feature of the postwar culture of silence identified by those such as W. G. Sebald.[61] As Bischof and Maier show, it was only in the 1980s, therefore, that (West) Germans began to acknowledge D-Day more widely in popular and political culture. This interest was animated by contemporary Cold War concerns, and especially the resentment among certain quarters of the German political establishment concerning their exclusion from the large-scale Normandy gatherings of the leaders of the other western, NATO, nations. German politicians discovered the idea of "liberation" after two decades of concerted Franco-German efforts to build a unified Europe and drawing upon ideas popularized by President Reagan during a controversial visit to Bitburg Military Cemetery in 1985. Thus, just as the defeat of Nazism had liberated nations such as France (and others occupied by German forces), so too had Germans themselves been liberated by destroying the Hitler regime. D-Day, therefore, marked the beginning of German liberation; this was the idea that Chancellor Gerhard Schröder took with him to Normandy in 2004, the first occasion on which an official German delegation was invited to attend the annual commemorative ceremonies. Austrian culture, in contrast, remains persistently uninterested in recognizing the immediate effects and aftermath of the D-Day landings.

Also present for the first time during the sixtieth anniversary in 2004 were representatives of the Russian Federation, including Pres. Vladimir Putin. Russian officials had long expressed frustrations with their exclusion from the Normandy events. An unofficial delegation of army officers and veterans had attended in June 1984, but the higher echelons of state and government had not before been invited to attend by the French hosts. For some Russians, as Olga Kucherenko explains, such exclusion was merely a manifestation of the extent to which Anglo-American culture had always overvalued and overemphasized the significance of the Western Front, and especially of D-Day. Already by the 1950s, Russian historiography sought to downplay the military value of American and British campaigns in northwest Europe. The real war against Nazi Germany was, these historians maintained, won on the plains of the Russian Steppe, and among the towns and cities of eastern Germany. Seen from Soviet Moscow, the Allied landings in Normandy—involving a paltry eight divisions—were thus little more than a sideshow, a distraction at best. The German war machine was destroyed by the divisions—and deaths—of the Red Army, not by the daytrip to Normandy that was, anyway, two years too late. As Kucherenko demonstrates, this understanding of D-Day—long-established in Soviet and now Russian culture—shows no sign of disappearing. Indeed, Kucherenko concludes that, with regard to Russian views of D-Day, "[w]hat began as a premeditated manipulation of history and memory has overtime turned into a kind of popular inertia." The continued prevalence of anti-Americanism in Russian popular and political culture, together with the contemporary "rise of the Russian bear," suggests that D-Day will continue to be disparaged, or simply ignored, by many Russians.

Common Themes and Ideas: Sacrifice and Redemption

With regard to the place of D-Day in history and memory, the story that emerges from the chapters in this volume is thus one of national differences and distinctions. Nonetheless, while this volume does demonstrate the continued power exercised over the artifacts of culture by the circumscriptions of the nation state (and language), on occasion continuities of theme, form, and idea *between* the different national stories of D-Day here discussed can still be detected. In large part, this is because the persistent attractiveness of D-Day in different national cultures lies in the extent to which it appeals to a

set of values (and narrative forms) common to all, and which ultimately find their roots in the Classical past.[62] Thus, if we assume that
to talk of such a thing as "Western" culture is not merely to embrace
empty description but, rather, to imply that the nations of the
modern "West" do indeed trace their distinctive national cultures
to a common point of origin, at least in terms of cultural conventions and narrative forms, we *can* identify a set of commonalities in
our multinational and multi-authored D-Day. These commonalities
center on the themes of "sacrifice" and "redemption." Each is present
in at least two of the D-Days herein described. Only the Russian
story of D-Day, a story that is in many respects a counter-narrative
to those emanating from the United States and Western Europe, has
no place for these narrative conventions.

Sacrifice

As a commemorative trope, "sacrifice" is well established in Western
culture. Indeed, if the memorial established to those Spartan
warriors killed at Thermopylae in 480 BC is taken as a start point
for the Western *idea* of war commemoration, then sacrifice—that
is, to give one's life for values or structures external to the individual
(religion, the state)—is contemporary to the Classical birth of war
memory.[63] Medieval culture, meanwhile, later elevated sacrifice to
the level of theology: humanity was redeemed through the selfless
sacrifice of Christ. Little wonder, given this long-running history,
that, as an idea, sacrifice dominated post-1918 commemorative
projects throughout the United States and Western Europe. In fact,
many of these projects actually found sustenance in a contemporary
cult of medievalism, itself a descendent of Victorian Romanticism.[64]
Thus, having recently experienced a century of Victorian secular
nationalism, which replaced the worship of God with the worship of
the state, and having now called on the citizen's body in the service
of that State, Americans and Europeans assimilated the death and
destruction of the First World War into the national experience
through the idea of sacrifice. The death of Tommy Atkins, or of
nameless *Poilou*, or of Yankee doughboys—in their thousands—was

defined as a heroic sacrifice for the nation.

In its basic form, this was the same idea that would be applied to combat deaths in 1939–45. In the war's aftermath, Britons and Americans would add memorial plaques listing the names of another generation of heroes sacrificed at the national altar to the memorials they built after 1918. On both sides of the Atlantic, too, the deaths of the Second World War would be validated in political culture as sacrifices rendered on behalf of Europe, and for noble, righteous goals: Freedom, Liberty, Democracy. American claims to world leadership were justified by these blood sacrifices; British appeals for continued American aid were predicated on the same. It is hardly surprising, then, that the idea of sacrifice emerged in American, British, and Canadian commemorations of D-Day. On the Calvados Coast, as Dolski describes, Americans would establish a vast memorial cemetery declaring that European liberation was won by the blood spilled on the beach below. A few miles to the east, meanwhile, the British Imperial War Graves Commission would declare something very similar with their military cemetery at Bayeux; as all such cemeteries do, it would even include a cross of sacrifice carved from Portland stone. Even the French, lacking "useful" demonstrations of military valor to commemorate, nonetheless put the sacrifice trope to work after 1945. As Lemay shows, it was the cornerstone of a powerful commemorative discourse of martyrdom, a discourse that had a rich tradition in both Catholic and Republican France. Thus, the obliteration of Caen in the summer of 1944—by the Allies—represented "martyrdom." Here was a French sacrifice to equal that of the Allied soldiers on the beaches, and among the *bocage*.

Redemption

A concept firmly connected to that of sacrifice, "redemption" is also present in several of the stories of D-Day identified in this volume. When applied in acts of war commemoration, redemption is often deployed to suggest that one act makes good an earlier act; an early failure is replaced by a later victory. In American culture, for example, some commentators, particularly amidst the celebratory age of the

Good War and the Greatest Generation, saw in D-Day the redemption of the Old World by the sacrifice of the New. Thus, having sailed west in the seventeenth century in order to build their city on a hill, and in so doing redeeming themselves, Americans returned in the twentieth century to redeem those they had left behind.

For many postwar Britons and Canadians, on the other hand, the idea that D-Day was a redemptive act found inspiration in the hard facts of the war experience. For the former, as Edwards explains, D-Day was represented as a return to France after the retreat and humiliation of 1940. D-Day, in short, redeemed Dunkirk. Likewise, in Canadian culture a very similar idea emerged in the postwar period to suggest that D-Day redeemed the debacle of Dieppe (the disastrous landing of 1942). In both national cultures, then, D-Day has carved out a space as a redemptive act that put right an earlier defeat. Even French narratives of D-Day hint at the idea of redemption. In postwar France, for example, the emergence of a commemorative discourse centered on liberation implicitly accommodated the idea that this was, in part, a redemptive act: defeat, occupation, and collaboration were expunged by liberation. In Germany, meanwhile, the adoption in the 1980s of an older French discourse of liberation brought with it the same idea. Indeed, in the German context, the idea of redemption became even more prominent: D-Day did not just begin the liberation of Germany; it initiated a national rebirth that would see Germany (re)-emerge as a modern democratic nation-state.

Common Chronologies

The final commonalities identified by the chapters in this volume concern questions of moment, place, and, more specifically, periodization. First, while the six chapters that follow do indeed identity at least six distinct and comparative D-Days, it must also be highlighted that this in itself represents, paradoxically, a point of connection. Simply put, all the chapters that follow make clear that *D-Day* itself was and remains a common point of reference for all those peoples and nations involved in, or affected by, the landings. To disagree over D-Day's meaning, in short, still demands agreeing that it did indeed have meaning. Few, if any, other events in the European War, let alone the Pacific War, are recognized in this way by members of so many different nations. Second, all the chapters that follow identify two distinct moments of commemorative agency. The first emerged toward the end of the 1940s and lasted until the late 1950s. This was the era in which the war dead were buried, mourned, and memorialized; the era in which national elites initiated efforts to shape and structure the story of the Second World War; the era in which peace quickly gave way to a new, tense, global political climate. Commemorations of D-Day—in all their forms—first took place within this moment. In the United States, Britain, Canada, and France national agencies constructed memorials, museums, and war cemeteries. Here, the story(s) of the Normandy landings, its purpose and worth, were inscribed on the Norman landscape. These years also witnessed the earliest efforts to establish the borders and boundaries of D-Day as *History*. In the victor nations of the West, for instance, D-Day was historicized as the "beginning of the end," the moment in which the armies of democracy launched their final assault on Nazi tyranny, an idea which, with a bit of tinkering, also nicely accommodated the new bipolar global structure of West versus East, Democracy versus Communism. In Germany, meanwhile, the historiography of the Normandy landings was noticeable by its absence; it was too soon, it seemed, to interpret the invasion as initiating domestic liberation. And in the Stalinist Soviet Union, historians were put to work to deny the significance of D-Day; the emerging narrative of the Great Patriotic War had neither time nor space for the Anglo-American amphibian adventure.

The second period of commemorative agency identified by the contributors to this volume emerged in and around the early 1980s. Designating precise dates as a watershed moment is always difficult in history. To be sure, we are often tempted by the attractive precision and clarity offered by such designations. But history is rarely so clear, clean, and accommodating. Nonetheless, when it comes to the place and prominence of D-Day in different national cultures, one date does stand out: June 1984. Orwell, one suspects, would have been delighted. D-Day had, of course, been the subject of commemorative interest for many years preceding this, and we should be wary of overemphasizing the significance of 1984. Indeed, in the domestic French context, the more important year—in terms of French interest in the Allied landings—was perhaps 1978 when Jimmy Carter became the first sitting American president to visit the D-Day beaches, an act much discussed and reported in France. Even so, 1984 was the year that firmly launched D-Day—as myth and symbol—on its path to the elevated status it enjoys today. For this was the first "big" anniversary involving the major Allied Heads of State; this was the first "big" anniversary in terms of the presence of veterans; this was the anniversary in which President Ronald Reagan, always the consummate political actor, stole the show with a feat of impressive theatrics. The anniversary events of 1994, 2004, and 2009, not to mention the commercially successful D-Day products of the late twentieth and early twenty-first centuries—*Saving Private Ryan* (1998), *Band of Brothers* (2001)—all owe part of their success to the media swarm surrounding the fortieth anniversary of 1984. Indeed, one French historian has suggested that the very structure and form of modern D-Day anniversary commemorations was first established during the 1984 events.[65]

The reasons for this "swarm" were complex and multifaceted, and they defy the identification of a single cause. Suffice to say here, then, that post-1984 interest in D-Day—as expressed in both political and popular culture—is connected to the psychology of veterans' life cycles *and* a product of wider cultural, social, and economic trends, trends that have been succinctly summarized elsewhere as the "memory boom" or the "heritage industry."[66] The late twentieth century, in short, offered a warm climate for the cultivation of war memory, particularly that connected to the Second World War: the passage of fifty years called forth an age of nostalgic reflection, especially among the children of the baby-boomers; a spate of anniversaries and large-scale commemorative ceremonies drew media attention; trials of Nazi war criminals turned attention back to the horror of the Holocaust; the end of the Cold War opened up space for a final celebration of the Good War's ultimate victory; and military action in the Gulf suggested that an American-led military alliance could still vanquish evil when the moment demanded. Events and activities in the early twenty-first century only accentuated this interest in the war and in D-Day in particular: 9/11, the War on Terror, the passing of the "Greatest Generation." This was the climate which enabled D-Day to claim the spotlight in memories of the Second World War; this is also the climate in which the seventieth anniversary of June 2014 will take place.

NOTES

1. Flint Whitlock, *The Fighting First: The Untold Story of the Big Red One on D-Day* (Boulder, CO: Westview Press, 2004), xi.

2. Gordon A. Harrison, *Cross Channel Attack, United States Army in World War II* (Washington, DC: United States Army Center of Military History, 1951; New York: BDD, Inc., 1993), remains an authoritative account on the invasion.

3. Robert Kershaw, *D-Day: Piercing the Atlantic Wall* (Annapolis, MD: Naval Institute Press, 1994), 26-28, 37. Kershaw noted that even Rommel's energy was insufficient for the task before him in early 1944 and that much of the effort expended in hurried defensive preparations ultimately enervated the defending units in the region.

4. Intelligence and counter-intelligence operations form largely absent features of earlier treatments of the battle due to the continuing government restrictions on relevant information after the war. A great deal of insightful material on this aspect of the battle has come out in the past few decades. Michael Howard, *Strategic Deception in the Second World War: British Intelligence Operations against the German High Command* (New York: W. W. Norton & Company, 1995), 105-29; Mary Kathryn Barbier, "Deception and the Planning of D-Day," in ed., John Buckley, *The Normandy Campaign 1944: Sixty Years On* (New York: Routledge, 2006), 170–84, and John Ferris, "Intelligence and OVERLORD: A Snapshot from 6 June 1944," 185–200 in the same volume.

5. The Americans secured the supreme command position by dint of the eventual preponderance of power in the West coming from them. The British, as the country contributing the most forces for the invasion, held the deputy

supreme commander position along with the three subordinate commander slots (ground, air, and naval).

6. Rather soon after the war, authors began to focus on the threat of inclement weather potentially wreaking the invasion itself. Eisenhower himself discussed the weather factor in his book, *Crusade in Europe* (New York: Doubleday and Company, 1948), 248-52. See also, Bruce Bliven, Jr., *The Story of D-Day: June 6, 1994*, Fiftieth Anniversary ed. (1956; reprint, New York: Random House, 1994), 40; and David Howarth, *Dawn of D-Day: These Men Were There, 6 June 1944* (London: Collins, 1959; London: Greenhill and Mechanicsburg, PA: Stackpole Books, 2001), 30.

7. Howarth, *Dawn of D-Day*, 201–3.

8. Ronald J. Drez, ed., *Voices of D-Day: The Story of the Allied Invasion Told by Those Who Were There*, fwd. Stephen E. Ambrose (Baton Rouge: Louisiana State University Press, 1994), 63.

9. Ed Ruggero, *The First Men In: US Paratroopers and the Fight to Save D-Day* (New York: HarperCollins, 2006).

10. For a popular account of these events, see Stephen E. Ambrose, *Pegasus Bridge: June 6, 1944* (New York: Simon & Schuster, 1985).

11. G. A. Harrison, 278–300, offered a straightforward account of the American airborne landings. Mark Bando, *Vanguard of the Crusade: The 101st Airborne Division in World War II* (Bedford, PA: Aberjona Press, 2003), 23–98, actually provided a wealth of detail on both American airborne divisions on D-Day.Carlo D'Este, *Decision in Normandy* (Old Saybrook, CT: Konecky & Konecky, 1983; New York: Harper Perennial, 1994), 120–50, covered the British air landings.

12. G. A. Harrison, 300–1.

13. Howard A. Andersen, "D-Day at Normandy with USS *Corry* (DD-463)," unpublished manuscript, quoted in Edward F. Prados and US Navy Memorial Foundation, eds., *Neptunus Rex: Naval Stories of the Normandy Invasion, June 6, 1944* (Novato, CA: Presidio Press, 1998), 53.

14. Omar N. Bradley, *A Soldier's Story* (New York: Henry Holt and Company, 1951), 254.

15. Joseph Balkoski, *Utah Beach, June 6, 1944: The Amphibious Landing and Airborne Operations on D-Day* (Mechanicsburg, PA: Stackpole Books, 2005), 330.

16. John Julius Moglia Questionnaire, n.d., Folder 12, Box 12, "The Longest Day" records, Cornelius Ryan Collection of World War II Papers, Robert E. and Jean R. Mahn Center for Archives and Special Collections, Ohio University Library, Athens, OH. Hereafter referred to as CRC.

17. There is a multitude of works on the Omaha Beach assault. Several of the better books include Flint Whitlock, *The Fighting First*; Adrian Lewis, *Omaha Beach: A Flawed Victory* (Chapel Hill: University of North Carolina Press, 2001); and Joseph Balkoski, *Omaha Beach: D-Day, June 6, 1944* (Mechanicsburg, PA: Stackpole Books, 2004).

18. Steve Twomey, "Soldiers of Germany Return for D-Day, Too," *Philadelphia Inquirer*, 5 June 1984, NewsBank (accessed 5 June 2008). For more on Severloh, see Max Hastings, *Overlord: D-Day and the Battle for Normandy* (New York: Simon & Schuster Inc., 1984), 89–90.

19. For treatment of the Pointe du Hoc action, see Douglas Brinkley, *The Boys of Pointe du Hoc: Ronald Reagan, D-Day, and the US Army 2nd Rangers Battalion* (New York: Harper Perennial, 2005), 63–98.

20. John Keegan pointed out the trepidation stemming from woeful tales of the Dieppe failed landings mixed with a stern sense of duty and desire for vengeance as the Canadian 3d Division men prepared for their own invasion. John Keegan, *Six Armies in Normandy: From D-Day to the Liberation of Paris*, with a new introduction for the fiftieth anniversary of D-Day (New York: Viking Penguin, 1982; New York: Penguin, 1994), 120. The Canadians also provided an airborne unit to attack near the Pegasus Bridge assault. Even more tellingly, Canada, the world's third largest sea power in 1944, played a paramount role in the naval side of the Normandy invasion.

21. Terry Copp, *Fields of Fire: The Canadians in Normandy* (Toronto: University of Toronto Press, 2003), 51–52.

22. One controversy surrounding the landings stemmed from the inability to take Caen on the eastern zone of the invasion area. Initial plans called for the city's capture on D-Day. Despite the general Allied failure to reach ambitious objectives along the entire battlefront, this particular lapse produced a great deal of recrimination at the time and since. Carlo D'Este, in an approach typical of American authors, castigated Montgomery for creating an overly ambitious plan, failing to achieve his objectives, and then finessing official reports and postwar history to promote a more favorable view of his generalship. D'Este, *Decision in Normandy*, 476–80, and passim.

23. William I. Hitchcock, *The Bitter Road to Freedom: A New History of the Liberation of Europe* (New York: The Free Press, 2008), 3. On one German-instigated atrocity from 10 June, see Sarah Farmer, *Martyred Village: Commemorating the 1944 Massacre at Oradour-sur-Glane* (Berkeley: University of California Press, 2000). For a critical treatment of the costs and consequences of the Normandy campaign as a whole, see Olivier Wieviorka, *Normandy: The Landings to the Liberation of Paris*, trans. M. B. DeBevoise (Cambridge, MA: Harvard University Press, 2008).

24. H. P. Willmott, *June 1944: In France, Italy, Eastern Europe, and the Pacific, Allied Armies Fought Momentous Battles which Decided the War and the Future of the World Itself* (London: Grub Street, 1999), 66, 125, 145.

25. Friedrich Ruge, "The Invasion of Normandy," in eds., Hans-Adolf Jacobsen and Jürgen Rohwer, *Decisive Battles of World War II: The German View*, trans. Edward Fitzgerald, introduction by Cyril Falls (Frankfurt am Main: Verlag für Wehrwesen Bernard & Graefe, 1960; New York: G. P. Putnam's Sons, 1965), 317–48.

26. Alexander Werth, *Russia at War, 1941–1945* (New York: E. P. Dutton & Co., Inc., 1964), 852–55.

27. For more on the development of this operational focus in the Red Army, see Richard Harrison, *The Russian Way of War: Operational Art, 1904–1940* (Lawrence: University Press of Kansas, 2001).

28. David Glantz and Jonathan House, *When Titans Clashed: How the Red Army Stopped Hitler* (Lawrence: University Press of Kansas, 1995), covers the Russian approach to the Eastern Front in commendable detail.

29. Even the joyous news releases made by Allied leaders contained the suggestion that other landing sites were potentially forthcoming. See, for instance, President Roosevelt's news conference on 6 June 1944, "38 Excerpts."

30. D'Este, *Decision in Normandy*, 298–320.

31. G. A. Harrison, *Cross Channel Attack*, 353.

32. Robert Kershaw, *D-Day: Piercing the Atlantic Wall* (Annapolis, MD: Naval Institute Press, 1994), 6.

33. For coverage of the Normandy campaign, see Russell F. Weigley, *Eisenhower's Lieutenants: The Campaign of France and Germany, 1944–1945* (Bloomington: Indiana University Press, 1981); Keegan, *Six Armies in Normandy*; D'Este, *Decision in Normandy*; and Russell A. Hart, *Clash of Arms: How the Allies Won in Normandy* (Boulder, CO: Lynne Rienner, 2001).

34. Louis A Coser, ed., *Maurice Halbwachs: On Collective Memory* (London: University of Chicago Press, 1992).

35. Maurice Halbwachs, as quoted in Coser, ed., *On Collective Memory*, 38–39.

36. See Susan Crane, "Writing the Individual Back into Collective Memory," *American Historical Review* 102 (1997), 1376.

37. Jay Winter, *Sites of Memory, Sites of Mourning: The Great War in European Cultural History* (Cambridge: Cambridge University Press, 1995), esp. 78–116.

38. Alex King, *Memorials of the Great War in Britain: The Symbolism and Politics of Remembrance*, (Oxford: Berg, 1998); Mark Connelly, *The Great War, Memory and Ritual: Commemoration in the City and East London, 1916–1939* (London: Royal Historical Society, 2001).

39. Daniel Sherman, *The Construction of Memory in Interwar France* (London: University of Chicago Press, 1999). See also Daniel Sherman, "Bodies and Names: The Emergence of Commemoration in Interwar France," *The American Historical Review* 103 (1998): 443–66; Daniel Sherman, "Objects of Memory: History and Narrative in French War Museums," *French Historical Studies* 19 (1995): 49–74.

40. John R. Gillis, ed., *Commemorations: The Politics of National Identity* (Princeton: Princeton University Press, 1993).

41. D. W. Lloyd, *Battlefield Tourism: Pilgrimage and the Commemoration of the Great War in Britain, Australia, and Canada, 1919–1939* (Oxford: Berg, 1998).

42. See Lisa M. Budreau, *Bodies of War: World War I and the Politics of Commemoration in America, 1919–1933* (London: New York University Press, 2010). See also, Janet S.K. Watson, *Fighting Different Wars: Experience, Memory and the First World War in Britain* (Cambridge: Cambridge University Press, 2007).

43. Henri Rousso, *The Vichy Syndrome: History and Memory in France since 1944*, trans. A. Goldhammer (Cambridge: Harvard University Press, 1996); James Young, *The Texture of Memory: Holocaust Memorials and Meaning* (London: Yale University Press, 1993); James Young, ed., *The Art of Memory: Holocaust Memorials in History* (New York: Prestel, 1994).

44. See, for example, Jay Winter and Emmanuel Sivan, eds., *War and Remembrance in the Twentieth Century* (Cambridge: Cambridge University Press, 1999); Nancy Wood, *Vectors of Memory: Legacies of Trauma in*

Postwar Europe (New York: Berg Publishers, 1999); Francesca Cappelletto, ed., *Memory and World War II: An Ethnographic Approach* (New York: Berg Publishers, 2005); Richard N. Lebow, Wulf Kansteiner, and Claudio Fogu, eds., *The Politics of Memory in Postwar Europe* (Durham, NC: Duke University Press, 2006); Susan R. Suleiman, *Crises of Memory and the Second World War* (Cambridge, MA: Harvard University Press, 2006); Sophie Wahnich, Barbara Lášticová, and Andrej Findor, eds., *Politics of Collective Memory: Cultural Patterns of Commemorative Practices in Post-war Europe* (London: Lit Verlag, 2009); Michael Keren and Holger H. Herwig, eds., *War Memory and Popular Culture: Essays on Modes of Remembrance and Commemoration* (Jefferson, NC: McFarland and Company, 2009); John Bodnar *The "Good War" in American Memory* (Baltimore: Johns Hopkins University Press, 2010); Philip D. Beidler, *The Good War's Greatest Hits: World War II and American Remembering* (Athens: University of Georgia Press, 1998); Mark Connelly, *We Can Take It! Britain and the Memory of the Second World War* (London: Pearson, 2004). Although not yet published when this book went to press, judging from the names of the editors and the list of contributors involved, another new publication about British war memory looks set to be a valuable addition to this field of study: see Lucy Noakes and Juliette Pattison, *British Cultural Memory and the Second World War* (London: Continuum, 2013).

45. David W. Blight, *Race and Reunion: The Civil War in American Memory* (Cambridge, MA: Harvard University Press, 2001); Patrick Hagopian, *The Vietnam War in American Memory: Veterans, Memorials, and the Politics of Healing* (Amherst: University of Massachusetts Press, 2009). See also G. Kurt Piehler, *Remembering War the American Way* (1995; reprint, Washington, DC: Smithsonian Books, 2004).

46. For examples of these critiques, see Alon Confino, "Collective Memory and Cultural History: Problems of Method," *American Historical Review* 102 (1997): 1386–1403; Crane; N. Gedi and Y. Elam, "Collective Memory— What is It?," *History and Memory* 8 (1996): 30–50; Patrick Hutton, "Recent Scholarship on History and Memory," *The History Teacher* 33 (2000): 533–48; Wulf Kansteiner, "Finding Meaning in Memory: A Methodological Critique of Collective Memory Studies," *History and Theory* 4 (2002): 179–97; Jeffrey Olick, "Collective Memory: the Two Cultures," *Sociological Theory* 17 (1989): 333–48.

47. For a few examples of this psychological literature, see M. Conway and
M. Ross, "Getting What You Want by Revising What You Had," *Journal
of Personality and Social Psychology* 47 (1984), 738–48; J. L. McClelland,
"Connectionist Models of Memory," in *The Oxford Handbook of Memory*,
ed. E. Tulving (Oxford: Oxford University Press, 2000), 583–95; U.
Neisser, and L. K. Libby, "Remembering Life Experiences," *The Oxford
Handbook of Memory*, ed. E. Tulving, 315–32; Ulrich Neisser and Ira
Hyman, "Snapshots or Benchmarks," *Memory Observed: Remembering in
Natural Contexts* (San Francisco: W. H. Freeman and Company, 1982),
43–49; K. Nelson, and R. Fivush, "Socialization of Memory," in *The Oxford
Handbook of Memory*, ed. E. Tulving, 283–95; H. L. Roediger, "Memory
Metaphors in Cognitive Psychology," *Memory and Cognition* 8 (1980),
231–46.

48. Jay Winter, *Remembering War: The Great War Between Memory and History
in the Twentieth Century* (London: Yale University Press, 2006), 183.

49. Popular Memory Group, "Popular Memory: Theory, Politics, Method," in
Making Histories: Studies in History-Writing and Politics, eds., R. Johnson,
G. McLennan, B. Schwarz, and D. Sutton, (London: Hutchinson, 1982),
205–52.

50. Sherman, 2.

51. I. Irwin-Zarecka, *Frames of Remembrance: The Dynamics of Collective
Memory* (New Brunswick, NJ: Transaction Publishers, 1994), esp. 3–21.

52. Ibid., 4.

53. Ibid.

54. Understandably, the connections and distinctions between History and
Memory have occupied numerous historians. See, for example, Rousso, 3–4.
Rousso essentially understands Memory and History to be oppositional,
with the former being the subject matter of the latter. However, he later
qualifies this distinction by suggesting that historians are always situated
within collective memory and are themselves thus a "vector" of memory.
For a rather nostalgic critical lament of the historian's role in the destruction of memory see P. Nora, "General Introduction: Between Memory
and History," in *Realms of Memory: Rethinking the French Past*, eds. Pierre
Nora and L. Krtizman,vol. 1 (New York: Columbia University Press, 1996),
1–20. For a more nuanced take on the relationship between History and
Memory, see Marita Sturken, *Tangled Memories: The Vietnam War, the*

AIDS Epidemic, and the Politics of Remembering (Berkeley: University of California Press,1997), 3–7; Winter, *Remembering War*, 5–7; and Hutton, "Recent Scholarship."

55. Emily Rosenberg, *A Date Which Will Live: Pearl Harbor in American Memory* (London: Duke University Press, 2003), 5–7.

56. Winter, *Remembering War*, 5–6.

57. There are just a handful of existing works discussing D-Day in memory, none of which pursue the comparative dimension central to this volume. See, for example, Bodnar, *The "Good War"*; Marianna Torgovnik, *The War Complex: World War II in Our Time* (London: University of Chicago Press, 1998). For some details about of D-Day commemorations see Serge Barcellini, "Diplomatie et commémoration: Les commémorations du 6 juin 1984: Une bataille de mémoire," *Guerres mondiales et conflits contemporains*, 47, no. 186 (1997), 121–146. And for an engaging discussion of the commemorative connections between the Republic of Ireland and France, specifically with regard to D-Day and the liberation of Europe, see Gerald Morgan and Gavin Hughes, *Southern Ireland and the Liberation of France* (Bern: Peter Lang AG, 2011).

58. Young, *The Texture of Memory*, xi.

59. Jay Winter, "Forms of Kinship and Remembrance in the Aftermath of the Great War", in *War and Remembrance in the Twentieth Century*, eds., Jay Winter and Emmanuel Sivan, 40–60.

60. For an excellent discussion of the ways in which specific societies have responded to the challenge of military defeat, see Wolfgang Schivelbusch, *The Culture of Defeat: On National Trauma, Mourning, and Recovery*, trans. J. S. Chase (London: Granta Books, 2004). See also Bruce Rosenberg, *Custer and the Epic of Defeat* (State College: Pennsylvania State University Press, 1974). And for a discussion of the 'Lost Cause' in the South, see Charles Reagan Wilson's *Baptized in Blood: the Religion of the Lost Cause, 1865–1920* (Athens: University of Georgia Press, 1982).

61. W. G. Sebald, *On the Natural History of Destruction* (London: Hamish Hamilton, 2003).

62. For a discussion of the extent to which D-Day—as event—conforms to the idea of Classical "unities," see Torgovnik.

63. For an excellent discussion of continuities in war memory between the Classical age and the twentieth century, see James Tatum, *The Mourner's*

Song: War and Remembrance from the Iliad to Vietnam (London: University of Chicago Press, 2003).

64. Stefan Goebel, *The Great War and Medieval Memory: War, Remembrance and Medievalism in Britain and Germany, 1914–1940* (Cambridge: Cambridge University Press, 2007).

65. Barcellini, "Diplomatie et commémoration."

66. See, for example, Winter, *Remembering War*; David Lowenthal, *The Past Is a Foreign Country* (Cambridge: Cambridge University Press, 1990). See also David Lowenthal, *The Heritage Crusade and the Spoils of History* (Cambridge: Cambridge University Press, 1998).

CHAPTER ONE

"PORTAL OF LIBERATION": D-DAY MYTH AS AMERICAN SELF-AFFIRMATION[1]

MICHAEL R. DOLSKI

If there has sometimes been a messianic note in American foreign policy in postwar years, it derives in part from the Normandy configuration. America gave its begotten sons for the redemption of a fallen Europe, a Europe in the grip of a real Satan with a small mustache.

–Lance Murrow, 1984

A VIRTUAL REALITY

The early morning gloom pulls back to reveal a foreboding shoreline dominated by stark bluffs. Looking to the right and left, you notice an armada of ships advancing toward shore. Geysers in the water announce nearby explosions, accompanied by the high-pitched whine of bullets ricocheting off the sides of water craft. You hear shouted instructions: note the obstacles, beware of the fortifications, target some return fire, watch out! Suddenly, a large explosion rocks your ship, dazing you and provoking cries from shipmates to jump overboard. This is 6 June 1944, the invasion by Allied forces of northwestern France on the Normandy Beaches, D-Day. You are an American, one of the thousands of Allied soldiers taking part in the early landings on this German-held coast.

The above details describe the 2005 video game, *Call of Duty 2: Big Red One*.[2] This entry into the franchise focuses, as with other titles in that series, on heroic soldiers fighting grand battles for noble purposes.[3] The D-Day landing scene that takes place midway through the experience constitutes one of the most exciting and challenging stages in the game. The player/soldier accompanies his squad of fellow named American soldiers as they defeat waves of nameless German enemies. Screams of pain or terror usually accompany deaths, though the player/soldier seems nearly indestructible as he can receive repeated hits while still moving to the ultimate goal. Borrowing from a cinematic "verité" style, shocking explosions daze, unbalance, and nearly drown out the sounds of the played world in several-second bursts.[4] Despite a series of challenging encounters from the coastal waters, over the beaches, and inland, the player's squad secures its D-Day objective. The sergeant commends his soldiers for "kicking down Hitler's front door" and surviving the most difficult fight he had ever known.[5]

First Person Shooters (FPS) are games of violence that employ a first-person perspective to navigate the game world. Prior to the late 1990s, most FPS games had borrowed heavily from science fiction tropes. Game developers recognized the allure of the Second World War with the commercial success of the 1998 blockbuster film *Saving Private Ryan* (more below). That film's director, Steven Spielberg, assisted in the development of historically themed video games, particularly those centering on the Second World War. The *Medal of Honor* suite of games that explored this direction and led to imitators like *Call of Duty* has often included D-Day as a major component of played activity.[6]

These games are more than mere entertainment pieces. The vicarious experience imparted by playing, by inserting oneself into a virtual reality, constitutes an instructive immersion. These war games have constructed an engaging world for players too young to have participated in this real world past. This world is one of danger (albeit muted), action, individualism, heroics, initiative, killing without question, and saving the world for freedom. Yet worth pondering at some length is the selection of this particular past, presented in this manner. Over the past seventy years in America, the Second World War and its shining moments like D-Day have transformed into a celebratory story of national sacrifice for liberty and freedom. Although D-Day-related video games present this story in a rather innovative manner, they represent merely the culmination of decades' worth of memory work centered on this battle.

Building the Mythic Framework

From the day the Allies stormed the Normandy beaches, efforts to ascribe meaning to D-Day arose in a number of forms. The high-toned war era rhetoric coincided with other American efforts to emphasize the moral correctness of their position in this conflict, often espoused as one of freedom versus tyranny (such as in President Franklin D. Roosevelt's "Four Freedoms" speech). Collectively, these propagandistic activities began setting the temper in American collective memory regarding this battle, the larger war, and indeed, the entire direction of the American Century.[7] Often the emphasis of these messages resided on the moral authority of Allied, particularly American, forces and their fight for liberation.

President Roosevelt addressed his nation on 6 June 1944 over the radio at 10:00 p.m. Eastern War Time. Beseeching "Almighty God," Roosevelt focused attention on the difficult battle raging on French soil in June 1944. He presented a morality lesson regarding this phase of the Second World War. Roosevelt explained that the American peace-loving forces "fight not for the lust of conquest. They fight to end conquest. They fight to liberate."[8] Not only did Roosevelt have to acknowledge the sacrifices of American combatants in this "mighty endeavor," but he also had to soothe their loved ones on the home front. This prayer also presented another chance to indicate what the Allies fought for and how they differed from their opponents. Stressing the Allies' intent "to set free a suffering humanity" lauded the soldiers, inspired civilians, reassured those in Nazi-occupied lands, and vilified the enemy.[9] When families throughout the United States, such as in the small town of Bedford,

Virginia, gathered around the radio to listen to Roosevelt's benediction, this message struck home.[10] The president assured all that American soldiers fought in Normandy to save the world in a righteous cause.

Invasion jitters abounded in the United States well before D-Day. As a result, the American public was primed to react to the earliest indication that fighting had erupted in Normandy. The abrupt disclosure of this much-anticipated event triggered a cathartic release of pent-up tension. Residents of New York City halted for observances, including a moment of silence before the opening of the Stock Exchange, before it went on to a new high for the year. Work absences were low, while bond purchases and blood donations hit tremendous highs. Returning to work, buying a bond, or giving blood all served as ways to feel connected to the war. Movie theaters throughout the land continued playing films, but usually in conjunction with prayer services, bond sales, or group singing of the national anthem.[11] Most of these activities came before Roosevelt's prayer that evening. The president lent his authority, his insight, and his eloquence to the process of shaping D-Day in the wider public understanding. His interpretation, however, hardly arose in isolation.

GEN Eisenhower's order of the day, issued before the landings, attempted to impress soldiers soon to engage in battle with the importance of their mission. Eisenhower's words also received wide distribution. In this order, Eisenhower expressed a paradigm that would characterize D-Day, the American role in the Second World War, and the man himself for a long time. He called the invasion the "great crusade," a resonant phrase that he would tap for the title of his 1948 book on the war. Eisenhower used such high-minded adjectives as "liberty-loving," "free," and "noble" to describe the Allied peoples or their wartime purpose.[12]

A barrage of laudatory commentary on D-Day—such as that offered by Roosevelt or Eisenhower—blanketed the home front, crowding out other considerations.[13] Within a week of D-Day, newsreels of the landings honored the American forces in France. The *News of the Day* clip that began playing on Thursday, 15 June, opened with a dedication to those men fighting and dying for liberty in northwest

Europe.[14] The newsreel's focus on common soldiers from across the country emphasized the democratic ethos of the fighting forces.

War correspondents also imparted a basic understanding of the events that comprised D-Day. Don Whitehead accompanied the troops who stormed Omaha Beach.[15] In dispatches that Whitehead dated 5-9 June, he cast the invasion as a major turning point and recounted tales of heroism on the beaches.[16] War correspondent Ernie Pyle landed on 7 June to find "bodies, uncollected, still sprawling grotesquely in the sand or half-hidden by the high grass beyond the beach." He stood there, the carnage filling his eyes, and wondered how the American troops had overcome such fierce resistance. Pyle wanted to tell people at home "what the opening of the second front in this one sector entailed, so that you can know and appreciate and forever be humbly grateful to those both dead and alive who did it for you."[17]

The impressions journalists conveyed helped people at home understand at least some aspects of the battle. The still photographs of the invasion comprise, perhaps, one of the more resounding early influences on the wider understanding of D-Day. By far the most powerful photos come from the few surviving images taken by famed war photographer Robert Capa. Capa felt that in order to capture war with the camera, he had to plunge into the midst of danger and excitement. Upon landing on Omaha Beach, he snapped a series of photos before boarding a craft full of wounded men returning to the Channel. Due to a processing mishap, the photographs came out somewhat blurred. Yet the hazy images of men huddled behind beach obstacles seemed to encapsulate the dramatic intensity of the day.[18]

Combined, all this reporting began setting the framework for D-Day in the public consciousness. President Roosevelt's main points reinforced the messages conveyed across the media. Stressing the collective achievements of common men, bonded together in the face of enormous difficulties, presented a way to laud supposed American values. This celebration stood out even more clearly when contrasted against the authoritarian system of the Nazi regime. These early depictions of the battle cast Americans, and their allies, as the heroes in a divinely sanctioned quest to liberate the oppressed.[19]

Local Remembrance: Framed by Grief

Following the Second World War, there were small-scale, local community efforts to memorialize D-Day in the United States. Staged in locations affected by the battle because of the sacrifices borne by hometown combatants, such as Bedford, Virginia, these early commemorations did not resonate with much force in American society. In a period that witnessed the return of soldiers' bodies from overseas, public attention fixed on the losses of war. The resultant somber mood dampened feelings of success as individuals coped with the pain of lives torn apart by the Second World War. Nevertheless, the hesitant embrace of victory in mainstream society during these early postwar years proffered some sense of meaning for these losses.

Great Depression-related penury and a local martial tradition motivated Bedford residents, such as brothers Ray and Roy Stevens, to join the National Guard before the war. With the outbreak of hostilities came mobilization and unit reconfigurations. The 29th Infantry Division consisted mainly of National Guard units mobilized from Virginia and Maryland. A significant number of Bedford men—including Ray and Roy—had ended up in A Company, 116th Infantry, one of the groups that assaulted Omaha Beach in the initial waves on D-Day.[20] The company landed on the far western end of the beach. Isolated from other units due to general confusion, Alpha Company faced a formidable German strong point, which had no other American targets in view. Nearly 100 of the company's 155 men who struggled ashore died in mere minutes, nineteen of them from Bedford County. Roy Stevens survived most likely because his landing craft hit a mine leaving the waterlogged men stranded until picked up and returned to England by a passing naval craft. Ray was not so fortunate; he died on the beaches that day.[21]

Bedford residents did not immediately commemorate the battle that claimed so many local men. People instead dwelt on their own private grief, which began hitting home one day in July 1944 with a flood of War Department telegrams notifying families of the dead. As journalist Alex Kershaw poignantly noted, "All across Bedford County, joy died that summer."[22]

Eventually, locals like D-Day veteran LT Elisha "Ray" Nance pushed for a commemorative display. The impetus to mark the community's link to D-Day gained strength as the bodies of those killed returned home for burial. Due to the violent chaos that had defined the Normandy campaign, it took graves registrations personnel several years after the war to locate, identify, and then dispose of American remains. Official US policy permitted next of kin to decide on final resting grounds for their loved ones. Either the body remained in American cemeteries abroad or returned for burial in the United States.[23] Brief ceremonies accompanied these returns in Bedford, but left some like Nance dissatisfied. By the end of the decade, Bedford township officials opted to install a plaque at the courthouse that listed the names of all local residents killed in either World War.[24] On 30 May 1949, Memorial Day, approximately 200 citizens of Bedford dedicated a $500 plaque bearing 174 names of men killed in both wars.[25]

In Bedford, where so many losses hammered a small community, commemorative activity centered on D-Day remained muted. Instead of highlighting the local connection to D-Day, residents at first focused on private mourning, often leaning on religion for support. Some people censured Eisenhower or Roosevelt, blaming them for the deaths. Only later did the community turn to public commemorations to deal with the hole left by those killed in France.[26] Still, in comparison to the far greater losses experienced by others, such as the French communities where the landings took place, the particular form of the Bedford commemorations proves revealing.[27] Although Bedford suffered far less than did these French communities, the eventual turn to D-Day commemoration served as a means to transform the story of the battle from just loss to one that assuaged grief by providing a meaning for that loss. This memory work, however, took time to develop.

For one Bedford veteran, a couple of early ephemeral commemorative works seemed insufficient tributes to the sacrifices made on D-Day. Ray Nance lobbied hard for years to push Bedford County toward a more fitting marker of just D-Day. Initially, Nance's proposal attracted limited enthusiasm. His constant lobbying eventually won the support of a few key people, like the editor of the local newspaper.

Bedford decided to erect a monument to its D-Day dead. This new marker consisted of a slab of rock cut from the bluffs in Normandy that overlooked the assault beaches. The French provided the rock, the funds, and a suitable escort for the official dedication ceremony held on 6 June 1954. A crowd of over 5,000 people gathered to hear of the gallant sacrifice of men sent to save France from despotism. GEN Charles Gerhardt, major general when he had led the 29th Infantry Division on 6 June 1944, helped dedicate the new monument in 1954. Summarizing Gerhardt's speech, Kershaw wrote, "The Bedford boys had been engaged in a great crusade, an ultimately glorious battle to preserve the very foundations of Western civilization of Christendom itself."[28] Ten years after D-Day enough people supported Nance to ensure the creation of a monument acknowledging Bedford's contribution to a vital battle.

NATIONAL REMEMBRANCE: ODES TO LIBERATING VICTORY

The postwar period saw the rise of concerted efforts by the federal government to shape public memories of the past.[29] Bedford residents understandably focused on their personal experiences or losses due to D-Day. Their local take on the battle did not shape national perceptions of D-Day—yet. Instead, federal agencies like the American Battle Monuments Commission (ABMC) sought to influence national views by overseeing the commemorative interpretation of Second World War battle sites.[30] The ABMC shaped remembrance activities on grounds ceded to American oversight by European governments. Once France granted control over parts of the Normandy battle zone, the commission's interpretations of artistic merit and its desire to avoid cluttering sacred space influenced commemorative activities there.

A process of honoring the dead took place in Normandy. It began with the erection of temporary cemeteries by the US Army's Graves Registration units, followed by the acquisition of permanent resting places for the dead.[31] Identifying those buried in the area consumed much time, as did disinterring and repatriating those whose next of kin desired the bodies to be returned home. Consolidation, dedication, construction, and opening ceremonies for the Normandy American Cemetery spanned more than a decade. The US government pushed families to leave the bodies of their loved ones abroad. Historian Kurt Piehler explained why: "The overseas cemeteries served to symbolize US global military commitments undertaken after 1945. The Army, by placing most of the cemeteries in Europe, indicated that it wished to have even greater ties with the Continent."[32] Choosing where to deposit American war dead, and where to honor their sacrifice, acquired political significance. Americans alive and dead remained in Europe to show a continued commitment to defend freedom.[33]

The Normandy American Cemetery site quickly became a center of symbolic activity. On Memorial Day in 1946, ceremonies held at the still-forming cemetery drew some Americans and up to 32,000 French people. Speeches honored the liberation of France and stressed the glory earned by Americans fighting for others in a civilization-saving effort.[34] By the following year, regular tours came by the busload.[35] The year 1947 also saw a Benediction Ceremony on 14 September that marked the final interment. This ceremony brought in an estimated crowd of 5,000 French and American people. Clarence Huebner, a major general in command of the 1st Infantry Division when it assaulted Omaha Beach on D-Day, gave one of the day's speeches. Speaking at the very spot where his men had fought, he suggested, "There is only one way in which we the living can even partially repay these dead for their sacrifices. That is, we shall not forget the purpose for which they died," which was to preserve freedom.[36]

The American Graves Registration Command eventually handed over responsibility for the cemeteries to the ABMC.[37] The ABMC oversaw the creation of monuments, the selection of inscriptions, and the conduct of ceremonies held on sites in the Normandy region. Honoring the soldiers, extolling their liberating intent, and mourning their sacrifice formed repeated themes. The liberation paradigm stressed in the commission's Normandy works gave meaning to the losses while burnishing American credentials as a beneficent world power.

The ABMC sought to provide ready answers as to what D-Day meant. The commissioners, such as the organization's secretary BG Thomas North, began setting the scope of official and public memories connected to this battle and the overall war. One of the inscriptions displayed at the Normandy American Cemetery set the tone for remembering D-Day: "This embattled shore, portal of liberation, is forever hallowed by the ideals, the valor, and the sacrifice of our fellow countrymen." Highlighting the "hallowed" grounds, "valor" of the soldiers, and honoring their "sacrifice" echoed the language enshrined at other ABMC sites in Europe. The difference here, however, related to the unique function of the Normandy area as the "portal of liberation." D-Day often gained traction in American public conversations as the start of the end in a just war. The ABMC, as North wrote, sought not only to instill reverence in Americans but also to impress "upon alien people . . . the sacrifices made by Americans."[38] The inscriptions and activities held at the cemetery reminded all that here common Americans died as heroes. These men died so that others could live in freedom.[39]

The cemetery's dedication ceremony, held on 18 July 1956, attracted up to 2,000 people. Starting at 3:30 p.m., the event lasted just over an hour. The observances included a military escort and salute, a wreath-laying, and several speeches. The French President, René Coty, pointed out in a statement read on his behalf, "Twelve years have passed since that spring daybreak when the soldiers of the young and free America landed on our shores to deliver our old Europe from oppression." Coty asserted, "We do not forget, we shall never forget, the infinite debt of gratitude that we owe to those who have given all for our freedom."[40] Coty's dedication stressed the liberating role of Americans.

The liberation paradigm presented in these observances both demonstrated and reinforced popular understandings of the battle. Then-President Dwight D. Eisenhower sent his American delegation off to Europe for the ceremonies claiming "the American soldiers who rest forever near the beach-head they won, and in the land they helped free, will never be forgotten." He added, "Their memory will always help strengthen the bonds of friendship between our countries, historic allies for the cause of human freedom."[41] As these words suggest, by the late 1950s, American D-Day stories had narrowed to a few central themes that emphasized America's moral rectitude in past and present.

Figure 2: "The Spirit of American Youth" by Donald de Lue stands at the eastern end of the Normandy American Cemetery. Riding atop a cresting wave, a young American looks skyward in an allegorical depiction of those lost in the quest for liberty ascending to heaven. This photo appeared in 1956 in conjunction with the cemetery's 18 July dedication. It looks eastward at the statue. Image courtesy of the US National Archives and Records Administration.

In addition, the Normandy American Cemetery provided a site for considering American losses. The large sculpture situated in the center of the memorial area, *The Spirit of American Youth*, honored the young men killed in battle. The bronze statue of a male figure, standing on a cresting wave with hands raised to the sky, conveyed an uplifting impression for visitors. Sculptor Donald De Lue surrounded his statue with an inscription bearing multivalent significance for Americans. Borrowing from the "Battle Hymn of the Republic," the famous Civil War rallying song, De Lue chiseled "Mine Eyes Have Seen the Glory of the Coming of the Lord" on the stone base surrounding his construction. Historian John Bodnar claimed this sculpture "transformed the legacy of the slaughter at Omaha Beach . . . transcending the idea of tragedy completely."[42] Yet pamphlets, books, speeches, and ceremonies focusing on the cemetery have often borne witness to the specific number of deceased buried in its grounds. The final number of graves at the cemetery amounted to 9,386. The backdrop to the eastern section of the cemetery listed the names of an additional 1,557 missing persons. The cemetery has served as a commemorative site for 10,943 killed or missing Americans from the Normandy campaign.[43] The cemetery's creators intended to focus attention on the scale of American sacrifice for freedom. Admittedly, the sheer numbers alone risk effacing the tragedy behind each individual loss. Nevertheless, the presentation of the past at this site served to transmit the official interpretation of D-Day's meaning to countless individuals over the years.

Heroic Mold Set

For a brief period up to the early 1950s, as America faced a new Cold War, the significance of conventional military experiences seemed less acute in light of terrible new realities. Therefore, D-Day discussions receded into more generalized coverage of the war as a whole thus coming to be seen as less of a guide to future action. D-Day stories fit comfortably into a self-affirmative worldview by extolling the themes of honorable service for world civilization carried out by gallant yet non-militaristic men. Still, the battle tended to fade away from mainstream consideration—despite periodic flare-ups such as with the cemetery's dedication—as the war and its key events appeared less instructive in light of the new-found atomic fears of the early Cold War era.

The first decade following the Second World War witnessed certain fluctuations in the coverage of D-Day. At times, especially on anniversary dates, newspapers would carry an article on some aspect of the invasion.[44] Aside from a ceremony or the occasional movie, however, there was no constant hammering home of D-Day's importance in American public conversations. Despite its oscillating presence, the themes attributed to the day were solidifying in this period, laying the foundation for later remembrances of the battle. There were disputes over the authority to depict the battle. Yet these quarrels did not encompass the interpretation of the battle so much as they sorted out who had the authority to shape commemorative processes.[45]

D-Day served as one way to extol America's democratic ethos. Unavoidably, this message was rather militant in nature. American fighting men got the job done, even in the most adverse of circumstances. These soldiers were not lifelong militarists, but citizen-soldiers, as Gerhardt reassured audiences at the 1954 Bedford memorial dedication.[46] They left their normal lives and banded together for a necessary, though unpleasant, task. With the job done, and civilization saved, they returned home, married, pursued civilian careers, raised families, and made America great. Americans served as the liberators, the guarantors of freedom and democracy, the preservers of justice and fair play. The D-Day battlefields constituted the "portal of liberation," the beginning of this quest to restore freedom, as the ABMC reminded visitors to the Normandy American Cemetery. Divine sanctioning for this role stood assured, and often mentioned, as God's chosen people beat back the darker impulses of savage humanity. The crusade paradigm first evoked by Eisenhower implicitly cast the invasion as an act in accordance with divine will. That a new enemy, albeit a former ally, fit so well into the old mold prepared for the Germans only served to perpetuate and strengthen such claims. D-Day's role as exemplar of all that was right about America, therefore, assured it growing popular attention as the Cold War confrontation with the Soviet Union intensified during and after the Korean War.[47]

With D-Day signifying American probity, it seems that by the mid-1950s the battle had assumed a firm place in the country's public consciousness. Speeches, books, films, ceremonies, and monuments attesting to the importance of this day proliferated.[48] For years, the public on both sides of the Atlantic had traveled to Normandy to visit the battlefields and the still-forming cemetery. The inscriptions along the southern doors of the chapel there proudly reminded visitors of America's "sons who gave their lives in the landings on the Normandy Beaches and in the liberation of Northern France."[49] The pilgrimage of American visitors to Normandy proved revealing. People came out of a reverent sense of devotion, hailing the grounds as sacred due to the selfless sacrifices commemorated there.[50]

Printed homage to D-Day also appeared during this period.[51] Cornelius Ryan published his honorific account of the battle, *The Longest Day*, on 6 June 1959. Ryan characterized D-Day as "the day the battle began that ended Hitler's insane gamble to dominate the world."[52] He focused on this single moment as the key turning point in the war, and indeed in Western civilization. Ryan's work grabbed attention because of his superlative ability to convey the drama of battle in accordance with popular perceptions of D-Day. He perpetuated the moral assessment of the fighting forces that resonated with Americans.[53]

Ryan assured, "The great crusade's unalterable purpose was not only to win the war, but to destroy Nazism and bring to an end an era of savagery which had never been surpassed in the world's history." His story highlighted the gallantry of soldiers in hazardous situations. Ryan suggested that the Allies "had history on their side" by linking this battle to the American tradition of fighting for freedom.[54] *The Longest Day* became an immediate best-seller.[55]

By 1959, publishers, authors, veterans, and some political leaders felt that more Americans should pay attention to D-Day. Several authors, like Ryan, sought to capitalize on the anniversary.[56] The

116th Regiment Association used the occasion to erect a monument in the Omaha Beach area of Normandy.[57] Reenacted airborne landings, dedication ceremonies for new monuments, and celebrations at liberated French towns also marked the anniversary in France.[58] D-Day had come into its own in American society. The battle served as an indicator of past alliance strength and as a potential precedent for any Cold War military venture. The shibboleth of liberation fit contemporary concerns in the US.[59]

Taking heed of the cultural mood, major Hollywood film projects covering the Second World War and this battle in particular began to take shape. Producer Darryl F. Zanuck read Ryan's book late in 1960 and saw it as the basis for a successful movie. Zanuck secured the movie rights and launched a comeback effort for his flagging career.[60] As an advanced promotional sheet proclaimed, Zanuck "fully expect[ed] it to be the most important war film ever made."[61] The effects of this film were so immediate, and turned out to be so long lasting, that it became the main historical primer on D-Day for millions of people.

Zanuck assembled an international cast and production team, which lent an air of authenticity to the film. Yet the product unmistakably bore the stamp of Zanuck himself. Even with factual inaccuracies, Ryan admitted that this film was a brilliant piece of work.[62] Zanuck's interpretation of D-Day gives some hint of the movie's appeal. He asserted, "[W]e can only come to the conclusion that God was on our side."[63] Audiences viewed an epic movie that depicted a grand event. Historian Stephen Ambrose indicated the "film reinforces one patriotic theme: the triumph of democracy over dictatorship."[64]

Zanuck went to extreme lengths to ensure a "realistic" depiction of the events, even if some of the plot elements were distortions.[65] Before the title, the movie opened with rousing drums while displaying an upended helmet resting alone on the beach. The camera shifted to German occupiers pursuing and gunning down in cold blood a French resistance agent. With the moral stakes established, the plot developed as German leadership prepared for battle and Allied troops fretted over the impending action. The difference here was instructive: the film perpetuated the Prussian militarist image while humanizing the Allies. The story began on 5 June, just one day before the "longest day." This abrupt introduction to the war afforded no chance for strategic discussion or historical grounding. Although seeking a realistic depiction of warfare, a jaunty musical score and stirring combat scenes carried a glamorized tint.[66]

Audiences flocked to see *The Longest Day*. The film earned over $17 million in its first year, or about $127 million in inflation-adjusted 2012 dollars. The overall reception proved favorable.[67] Further, in letters, memoranda, publicity releases, and interviews, Darryl Zanuck insisted that his was a patriotic film that inspired love for America.[68]

D-Day had provided a means for politicians, writers, and filmmakers to tell a palatable story: America had triumphed over evil on the beaches of Normandy. D-Day, in these stories, constituted a world-saving battle of Allied forces with America at the helm. These themes echoed throughout commemorative activity centered on D-Day such as a filmed return to the beaches by Eisenhower in 1963, the anniversary celebrations in 1964, and the by-then muted celebrations in 1969.[69] The testament to combined strength, under America's beneficent leadership, spoke to Cold War concerns in the confrontation with communist oppression. By the end of the decade, however, the complacent rendering of the nation's history common in D-Day tales of glory became less sustainable in the midst of the divisions of the Sixties.[70]

Mythos Revived

Due to Vietnam-induced war weariness in America, from the late 1960s to the outset of the 1980s, D-Day subsided somewhat in American public remembrance. D-Day never disappeared entirely from the public sphere, as news stories, books, speeches, and ceremonies covered the battle. Yet it did not occupy a central position in national conversations.[71]

Nevertheless, a major turn in public appreciation of the battle, the larger war, and even of America itself would appear by the mid-1980s. In the process, D-Day commemoration would take the national stage. That re-emergence reflected a prevalent American desire to see redeeming value in the country's military actions. This inclination required some memory work to overcome the less inspiring Vietnam War experience. President Ronald Reagan struggled to place that conflict within a celebratory metanarrative of the American past. Reagan proclaimed in his 1980 election campaign that the Vietnam War represented a "noble cause."[72] He faced an uphill battle when attempting to spin Vietnam as a positive interlude of American history. The Second World War offered a more convincing sell.

A commemorative resurgence formed in the early 1980s that included increased visitation at the Normandy American Cemetery and the release of several popular histories on the campaign.[73] During this period, Reagan famously denounced the Soviet Union as an "evil empire" in an 8 March 1983 speech.[74] The Soviet Union typified evil whereas America championed good in the world.[75] The salability of Reagan's moralistic conception of America would help push D-Day to the forefront of national consciousness in the next year.

Oral historian Studs Terkel correctly claimed that Americans thought of the Second World War as a "good war."[76] Romantic nostalgia defined America's approach to D-Day by 1984, the year of the fortieth anniversary of the invasion. A younger generation coming of age honored its elders while envying the supposed clear morality and sense of purpose of the earlier war period. After experiencing the ultimately unsuccessful Vietnam War, public actors in the 1980s sought to restore a veneer of morality, perhaps even righteousness, to the national mission in past and present. The heroism of grand events like D-Day helped cast America as a virtuous, powerful, and benevolent country—all themes that stand in almost inverse relationship with critiques of the Vietnam morass.

In a build-up to the fortieth anniversary, D-Day dominated *Time's* 28 May 1984, issue. The cover article, "D-Day: Every Man Was a Hero," began with the Shakespearian paean to the band of brothers from *Henry V*.[77] Another article in this issue of *Time* mourned the lost morality of the Second World War era. Journalist Lance Murrow claimed, "The invasion of Normandy was a thunderously heroic blow dealt to the evil empire." "Never again," he continued, "would war seem so unimpeachably right, so necessary and just. Never again, perhaps, would American power and morality so perfectly coincide." Murrow Americanized the battle by arguing, "Normandy was, of course, a joint Allied operation. But the Americans, from Eisenhower down, dominated the drama." "There was an aspect of redemption in the drama," Murrow explained, "redemption in the Christian sense. The Old World, in centuries before, had tided westward to populate the New. Now the New World came back, out of the tide, literally, to redeem the Old." As he expounded, "If there has sometimes been a messianic note in American foreign policy in postwar years, it derives in part from the Normandy configuration. America gave its begotten sons for the redemption of a fallen Europe, a Europe in the grip of a real Satan with a small mustache."[78] This issue epitomized the self-satisfied tone of American D-Day celebrations.

The uncharacteristically mild 1984 anniversary date in France seemed tailor made for a younger American generation to honor and thank the fading wartime heroes. Also benefitting the Reagan administration's looming nostalgia trip down D-Day's memory lane was the fact that for the first time in quite some while the French government seemed intent upon celebrating the battle in grandiose and grandiloquent terms.[79] Historian Douglas Brinkley estimated that anywhere from 10,000 to 15,000 American D-Day veterans traveled to France that June.[80] People flocked to honor the living historical relics on hand.

Reagan adroitly conveyed multiple messages in his Pointe du Hoc speech, timed to occur at 1:30 p.m. in France just as the morning news programs aired in America.[81] After noting the vile Nazi enemy, Reagan proclaimed, "Europe was enslaved, and the world prayed for its rescue. Here in Normandy the rescue began." In Reagan's version, D-Day formed the turning point in the American-dominated attempt to restore moral order to the world. D-Day's enormity combined here with a sentimental depiction of its participants. Reagan called them "the boys of Pointe du Hoc." "These are the men who took the cliffs," he announced, indicating the surviving US Army Rangers in his audience. "These are the champions who helped free a continent. These are the heroes who helped end a war." These boys did not fight alone either. As Reagan asserted, they benefited from a "rock hard belief that Providence would have a great hand in the events that would unfold here; that God was an ally in this great cause." For Reagan, the Second World War exemplified a just war due to the aggression and brutality of the Nazi foe. He opined that there is a "moral difference between the use of force for liberation and the use of force for conquest." Reagan noted that the Soviet forces remained in Eastern Europe, "uninvited, unwanted, unyielding, almost forty years after the war." Due to that occupation, Americans had to remain in Europe. "Today, as forty years ago, our armies are here for only one purpose—to protect and defend democracy." Righteous Americans fought a trying battle to free a continent and that dedication to liberty persisted in the present.[82]

Echoing Eisenhower in the Omaha Beach address a few hours later, Reagan expounded, the Allies "came not to take, but to return what had been wrongly seized. When our forces marched into Germany, they came not to prey on a brave and defeated people, but to nurture the seeds of democracy among those who yearned to be free again." American soldiers spread the blessings of liberty even to the defeated. Reagan intoned, "Today . . . we celebrate the triumph of democracy." At the end of this speech, Reagan avowed, "We will always remember. We will always be proud. We will always be prepared, so we may always be free."[83] Reagan called upon Americans to sacrifice for his new noble cause—defeating Soviet tyranny—and used the heroism of D-Day to elicit acceptance of these demands.

Running on a presidential campaign slogan of "It's Morning in America" in 1984, Reagan used D-Day to tell the American people why they should be proud of their country as well as of his invigorating leadership. He mimicked Lincoln's Gettysburg Address and Roosevelt's D-Day prayer by alluding to a sanctification of the world through bloodshed. Reagan cited the heroism of ordinary men to burnish America's credentials as a benevolent power at home and abroad. These messages reappeared over the following weeks on radio, television, and in newspapers.[84]

After this anniversary, mainstream society would no longer depict D-Day as just one battle among many. Following Reagan's lead, D-Day became shorthand for sacrifice, liberation, or the commitment of democratic countries to ensure freedom. Reagan celebrated the democratic heroism of a nation's youth that supposedly went off willingly to restore morality to a world beset by evil. An array of tourists, ceremonies, news stories, books, and other commemorative activities also trumpeted D-Day's moral dimensions.[85] When Reagan argued that ordinary Americans fought evil in the past, he aimed at inspiring his people to battle the evils of the present. Such messages combined with the sentimentalized honor paid to a passing generation.

Enshrinement of the Celebratory Narrative

Cold War politics and social divisions exacerbated by Vietnam had influenced D-Day commemorations in the 1980s. The end of the Cold War and the rebirth of American confidence, due in part to the Persian Gulf War, betokened a new period of cautious optimism in the 1990s. President George H. W. Bush exclaimed, "By God, we've kicked the Vietnam syndrome once and for all," upon the successful conclusion of the Gulf War in 1991.[86] President Bush recognized that mainstream America sought to move on from Vietnam Era divisions. As his predecessor shrewdly sensed, however, the likely way to make this happen was through a selective and celebratory focus on the more successful Second World War experience. Remembrance activities, as a result, promulgated familiar themes ascribed to D-Day.

Several historians have provided useful suggestions about the cultural climate during the 1990s and its fixation on the past.[87] A passing generation, current social divisions, veteran determination to transmit their experiences, growing news media interest, and the expansion of historical consumption pushed this reverence of things past. D-Day remembrance fed off and contributed to this nostalgic turn in the late 1990s.

Adding to the frenzy of interest in D-Day, Stephen Ambrose released another installment on the battle, aptly titling it *D-Day, June 6, 1944*. Ambrose called this popular book, with 320,000 copies printed in a few years, his "love song to democracy." Allied success on D-Day rested largely on the cooperative, selfless spirit that democratic systems had allegedly inspired in their citizens. Ambrose discussed all the Allies, but he focused mostly on the Americans in this nostalgia trip. As Ambrose would have it, America was unblemished morally, its people great, and the world's fate turned on the actions of a few heroes. He described the carnage of battle, but acknowledging the soldiers' sacrifices made them seem nobler. Ambrose linked deity and democracy to the Americans he saw engaged in a "trial of systems" on the sands of Normandy.[88] By conjuring up tales of heroism that vindicated America's democratic ethos, Ambrose touched a nerve that led to skyrocketing sales and personal media appearances.

Ambrose's popularity evinced the public fixation on D-Day, reaffirmed by the attention devoted to the 1994 Normandy ceremonies. In April 1994, one journalist noted that officials expected 25,000 American veterans to attend the celebrations.[89] President William J. Clinton, as a primary speaker at the events, sought to sell a mythic image of America to the public akin to President Reagan's performance in 1984.[90]

At 7:00 a.m. on 6 June, speaking to the sailors aboard the USS *George Washington*, Clinton tapped divine assistance to explain Allied success on D-Day. "It was faith in their Maker's mercy and their own ability that helped to carry the day," he claimed. "It was also raw courage and love of freedom and country." Clinton exhorted, "As we begin this new day of remembrance, let us also ask God's blessing for all those who died for freedom fifty years ago and for the Americans who carry on their noble work today."[91]

An hour later, Clinton rose to speak in the official ceremonies at Pointe du Hoc. Addressing the theme of the day, Clinton argued, "Most of them [US Army Rangers] were new to war, but all were armed with the ingenuity of free citizens and the confidence that they fought for a good cause under the gaze of a loving God." God's democracy had bested an evil enemy. Clinton drew out the thought by arguing, "[T]he mission of freedom goes on; the battle continues. The 'longest day' is not yet over."[92] Americans should celebrate and even emulate the world-saving conduct of the D-Day soldiers.

President Clinton echoed Reagan in his 6:00 p.m. speech at the cemetery. Clinton stressed the youth of American soldiers who stepped reluctantly into the role of liberators, a role they nonetheless brilliantly filled. He made the standard references to the horrors of the battle and the individual heroism that had surmounted fierce German opposition. Clinton characterized D-Day's outcome as an example of democratic power. American soldiers sacrificed and acted together "to free a continent," not for national aggrandizement. "[T]hey had all come to stop one of the greatest forces of evil the world has ever known," the president intoned. "At that exact moment on these beaches, the forces of freedom turned the tide of the twentieth century." Clinton impelled Americans to guarantee freedom across the world in the present as well.[93] Strikingly, however, rhetoric failed to match reality as liberation and salvation proved nice buzzwords even as Clinton shied away from halting genocidal rampages in the Balkans or sub-Saharan Africa during the early 1990s.[94]

Clinton's remarks demonstrated the continuities in American conceptions of D-Day that had settled in by the last quarter of the twentieth century. D-Day, not the Eastern Front, had started the end of Nazi tyranny. The heroism of American soldiers had saved the day and deserved veneration. The example of this battle should embolden Americans to continue the fight against other tyrannies deemed a threat to America. D-Day served as a guide that centered the narrative of American international leadership in the pursuit of freedom. The 1994 observances also presented an opportunity to praise a fading generation while symbolically passing responsibility for world leadership to younger Americans.

Journalist Tom Brokaw, caught up by this romantic nostalgia, claimed that he had a "life-changing experience" while reporting the 1984 D-Day anniversary. The 1994 ceremonies further impressed upon him the heroic nature of America's people. Brokaw's hagiographic and reductionist interpretation of America's wartime populace suffused his best-selling 1998 book, *The Greatest Generation.* The entire generation, he averred, had united to confront evil, defeated it, and then made America great in the years that followed the Second World War.[95]

Brokaw was not alone in celebrating the war generation and one major Hollywood film would disseminate a similar romantic message to enormous audiences. Film historian Janine Basinger argued that the 1998 blockbuster movie, *Saving Private Ryan*, had rejuvenated the war film genre.[96] Most discussions of the film in contemporary press and media concerned the graphic twenty-five-minute long portrayal of D-Day that sets the tone for the rest of the production. The director, Steven Spielberg, the main star, Tom Hanks, and their consultant historian, Stephen Ambrose, touted the film's gruesome realism. Ambrose asserted, "There's no other World War II movie like this. The only things missing are the smell of battle and the smoke of battle." Spielberg claimed, "I wanted the audience to realize what it was like to be in a real war rather than a Hollywood war."[97]

Spielberg employed a cast of thousands to convey the enormity of the Allied military effort in Europe. The grainy footage used to elicit an air of authenticity evoked film stock taken during the war in striking contrast to the polished imagery audiences expected in blockbuster movies. The loving attention to detail devoted to the Omaha Beach scenes had demanded twenty-four days of shooting out of the fifty-nine days expended on the entire movie.[98]

Spielberg claimed that he made *Saving Private Ryan* in order to honor his father and the "greatest generation." That declared intention resonated with audiences, as demonstrated by its haul of nearly $500 million in domestic and international markets. The shocking violence of the film's opening and closing scenes was not, as in many Vietnam movies, senseless or devoid of purpose. The nobility of soldiers engaging in deadly work for the clear, justifiable goal of securing a fellow citizen appealed to American audiences. Moreover, the rescue of one man seemed to counter the Vietnam story, at least the version of that war that focused on those left unaccounted for by a corrupt government and fickle society that was, in turn, the latest installment on the "captivity" narratives that have enraptured

American audiences for centuries.[99] *Saving Private Ryan* told a story about America that Americans wanted to hear. The older generation had come together in a time of intense danger and succeeded. The film, in a sense, redeemed the country from its Vietnam nightmare scenario by lauding the venerated Second World War generation as its members faded from the scene. Spielberg, Hanks, Ambrose, and Brokaw all sang the same tune in 1998, one that the American public absorbed in rapt awe.[100]

Although the movie was cloaked in sentimentality, the D-Day scene was gory. An ominously overcast sky hovered over the American forces making their way toward Omaha Beach. The over-burdened landing craft advanced with loads of nervous men, many vomiting, praying, or both. The landing craft approached the beaches as small arms fire and thunderous explosions confirmed the enemy stood ready. When the ramps on the Higgins boats went down, the debarking American troops met a hail of withering fire. Chaos ensued in the midst of a technologically induced frenzy of destruction. Agonizing deaths eroded cohesion as well as collective morale. A few dazed survivors gathered for cover behind the German anti-landing obstacles. They rallied under the direction of junior leaders. A mad dash led to relative safety along a seawall. Limited cover in the lee of the Germans' own structures afforded the chance to prepare for a determined assault. The Americans forced a break in the defenses due to sheer tenacity and the heroic action of several individuals. CPT John Miller (Tom Hanks), one source of inspiration, led the remnants of his Ranger company through such a breach. The local front then dissolved as the youthful sacrifices enabled victory.[101] In many ways, the video game experiences that followed *Saving Private Ryan*'s release sought to recreate its iconic D-Day scene, as if it were the new reference for the kinetic carnage of modern battle.

People flocked to see *Saving Private Ryan* and then enthused over its depiction of war.[102] *Saving Private Ryan* offered a story about a "good war" with American heroes defeating German foes. Watching the movie implicitly offered a way to pay homage to the "greatest generation." Spielberg asserted, "This isn't the kind of movie you see and then go to a bistro and break bread talking about it—you have to go home and deal with it privately."[103] Some veterans publicly lent *Saving Private Ryan* their approval by acknowledging its bloody "realism."[104]

Certain themes recurred in public discussions of the movie. One Second World War veteran contended that *Saving Private Ryan* "is a movie that every American should see. It depicts better than any words ever could, the *Price of Freedom*." "It is a story of sacrifice, duty, honor and country," he argued. "It is a story of courage, bravery and heroism. It is a story about soldiers. It is a story about America."[105] Discussions of *Saving Private Ryan* have often asserted that civic duty demanded viewing a movie that reminded Americans "freedom isn't free."

This thought coexisted along with claims, as succinctly expressed by Tom Hanks, that in *Saving Private Ryan* "[t]here's no overt sort of patriotic statement or even curve."[106] The assertion of American honor and morality in the Second World War, of militant civic duty in restoring moral order to the world, seemed so obvious by the late 1990s that these arguments transcended "politics." Journalist Neal Gable, however, identified the cultural and generational politics that had suffused the film and the public reaction to its portrayal of warfare. "In effect, *Saving Private Ryan* has become the bloody, heartfelt cultural salve to the divisions and tumult that have riven this country throughout the postwar period." Gable insightfully argued, "In short, it is not Private Ryan who gets saved; it is the lost vision of America." That vision stressed unity in trying times had enabled America to defeat evil and rise to global prominence.[107]

Following *Saving Private Ryan*'s success, a new framing point appeared with the carnage of the D-Day scene standing as a ready reference for war's gruesome nature. The film's popularity had long coattails. It boosted fundraising efforts for D-Day and Second World War commemorative projects. Hanks became a national spokesman for American Second World War veterans. He and Spielberg agreed to team up on another Ambrose-generated Second World War story— *Band of Brothers*. The director also turned his attention to producing the first *Medal of Honor* video game title mentioned above.

Books, speeches, Hollywood movies, games, these presented just some of the many venues for an outburst of D-Day fascination in the late 1990s. One other commemorative project included Ambrose's D-Day museum in New Orleans.[108] Opening on 6 June 2000, as the National D-Day Museum, its presentation celebrated honorable service by primarily American troops in a glorious battle. The moral stakes remained unquestionably clear: the democratic ethos of the American forces had contributed to battlefield success and ensured a just peace.[109]

Over the past decades D-Day has served as a glorified moment in the last war that most Americans regarded as "good." People enjoyed these stories because they cast America as the powerful country preserving morality in a benighted world. These tropes tapped popular twentieth- and twenty-first-century components of America's self-perception as the city on a hill holding evil at bay.[110] That the Korean and Vietnam Wars had failed to fit into such a mold helped to explain why the Second World War, and D-Day in particular, returned with such force.

Conclusion: National Myth Trumps Local Mourning

American society remained devoted to the Second World War at the turn of the millennium. D-Day endured as a prominent point in the public appreciation of that conflict. A new monument specifically devoted to D-Day memorialization took center stage in 2001. Following the 1994 anniversary and the success of *Saving Private Ryan*, veterans in southwestern Virginia received wider support for a regional D-Day commemoration project. This undertaking would lead to the creation of the National D-Day Memorial in Bedford.[111]

Stressing themes of "valor, fidelity, and sacrifice," the 88-acre memorial site in Bedford contained many symbolic, figurative, and educational components. The memorial is divided into four sections representing the preparations for the Normandy invasion, D-Day combat, the end of the war, and the postwar development of the free world. The preparation section consisted of a replica English garden with statuary busts of the major Allied commanders. A life-

Figure 3: The Bedford, Virginia, National D-Day Memorial symbolically recreated the Omaha Beach landing with bronze figures struggling to the shore. The towering Overlord Arch captured the epic nature of the invasion. President George W. Bush dedicated the memorial on 6 June 2001, to an estimated crowd of 20,000. Photo from the author's personal collection.

size statue of Eisenhower dominated this area. A large adjacent plaza evoked the Channel crossing. At one end, a symbolic recreation of a Higgins boat opened onto a pool containing several bronze figures of American soldiers struggling through the surf and onto the beach. Off to a side, several recreated pieces symbolized the role of airborne forces on D-Day. The names of nearly 4,500 Allied soldiers killed on D-Day appeared around the plaza. Bronze plaques informed visitors on Allied units. Only the plaques covering American forces went to the regimental level. Throughout the site, deference to the coalitional nature of the invasion clashed with the emphasis on American soldiers and their D-Day exploits. After navigating the amphibious assault area, visitors beheld the *pièce de résistance*, the Overlord Arch. Impressively emblazoned with "OVERLORD," the arch towered an emblematic forty-four and a half feet (June 1944 representing the *half*way point of the year). The enormity of this memorial risked overwhelming visitors, in all likelihood the intended effect, to elicit awe over the scope of the operation and the size of the sacrifice it had demanded. Once they have marveled over this impressive construction, visitors ended the peregrination in a small plaza with the flags of twelve Allied nations acknowledging wartime unity and postwar amity.[112]

The National D-Day Memorial Foundation also pursued an educational mission. Foundation employees sought to instill a respect for the American citizen-soldier tradition that has preserved freedom at home and abroad.[113] This memorial has helped to connect the trials of Bedford, Virginia, to a key event in national history. By the turn of the century, this small community's D-Day-related suffering captured the attention of national audiences already in a mood to commemorate the heroism of American soldiers and the stoicism of the wartime home front.[114]

President George W. Bush dedicated the memorial in person on 6 June 2001. He honored the fallen soldiers and hailed their efforts to protect global freedom. On D-Day the New World liberated the Old, and, as Bush suggested, "Free societies in Europe can be traced to the first footprints on the first beach on June 6, 1944." He dutifully acknowledged the painful losses that this liberating quest exacted. Nevertheless, Bush assured the 20,000 people joining him that day in Bedford that these sacrifices had established lasting peace and promoted the spread of democracy. After noting that American interests demanded vigilance abroad, Bush concluded his speech by praying "that our country will always be worthy of the courage that delivered us from evil and saved the free world."[115] While Bush's words echoed former commemorations, his claims took on an added resonance in a period soon to be shaped by the terrorist attacks of September 11.

The memorial ultimately presented the standard view of D-Day as an event dominated by American heroes that selflessly fought to liberate others. Public treatments of D-Day admitted the gruesome nature of combat. Yet, in the end, the horrors of industrialized warfare added to the claims of American nobility in a quest to free the world from evil.

Such a narrowing of narrative focus reflected the currents of an America undergoing vast changes first in the uncertain postwar moment, then in the Cold War confrontation that followed, and finally in the post-Cold War and post-9/11 periods. Powerful politicians and ordinary citizens advanced similar characterizations of D-Day. The commemorative approach to a distant battle, conducted often at sites in the US such as Bedford, Virginia, and New Orleans, Louisiana, helped to Americanize what was after all an international experience. Certain themes gained ground in different periods, reacting to prior versions, and served as guideposts at key moments of need. These D-Day stories drew on select mythic images embraced by popular American culture and reaffirmed them at the same time. According to this narrative, D-Day demonstrated the military competence of a free republic that put its faith in citizen-soldiers. Through violent action, America had redeemed the world, reshaping it into a new, improved, quasi-American version of its old self. The redemptive power of D-Day violence enjoyed divine blessing, and even, as sometimes claimed, outright assistance. The notion of a city on a hill fending off darkness in the world, lighting the path for mankind's salvation, helped to shape America's D-Day story. This cultural imperative, likewise, drew strength from America's Second World War experience. America fought on D-Day to achieve benevolent goals—defeat an evil foe and restore moral order to the world—not for territorial aggrandizement. Mythic reinterpretation does not imply fable or fantastical yarn.[116] As used here, mythic collective memories represent socially derived renderings of the past, influenced by present conditions, employed to satisfy a variety of personal and group needs. These views assume mythic nature when they embed in a culture, bear frequent repetition, and acquire a veneer of authority that tends to resist investigation or challenge of their claims.

The D-Day paradigm emerged on 6 June 1944, from many directions all at once and did not represent solely the political leadership's point of view. Without widespread support for such a positive slant, it seems highly unlikely that these instant moralizations would have gained such a powerful presence in American society. Admittedly, D-Day celebrationism receded to the background in certain periods of national confusion or strife, such as during the postwar moment or the Vietnam imbroglio. Furthermore, as the Bedford example indicates, there were contrasting stories that emphasized the many personal miseries stemming from the battle. Yet it is also important to remember that throughout seven decades, from D-Day to the present, approving depictions of the battle have remained intact even during the relative dark days of neglect. D-Day memories have exerted a powerful influence on American conceptions of patriotism, civic duty, martial action, and the efficacious use of warfare. These collective constructions shaped national and individual identity.[117]In the most commonly circulated stories, D-Day attested to positive aspects of American character. Ultimately, tales concerning America's actions at the "portal of liberation" proved liberating in themselves as they freed people to fixate on militaristic romance while avoiding less palatable aspects of their own country's past.

Notes

1. The author would like to thank Sam Edwards, Sarah Wagner, and the two external reviewers for reading earlier versions of this chapter or discussing the concepts presented herein.

2. *Call of Duty 2: Big Red One*, directed by Christian Busic, Activision and Konami, video game, 2005.

3. See, for instance, *Call of Duty 2*, directed by Keith Arem, Jason West, and and Vince Zampella, Activision, 2005. This title permitted gamers to play as a Soviet, British, or American soldier. The first American episode was the D-Day assault of Pointe du Hoc by the 2d Ranger Battalion.

4. Jerome de Groot, *Consuming History: Historians and Heritage in Contemporary Popular Culture* (New York: Routledge, 2009), 133–41.

5. *Call of Duty 2: Big Red One.*

6. Spielberg directed and DreamWorks developed the first game in the series: *Medal of Honor*, directed by Peter Hirschmann and Steven Spielberg, Electronic Arts, 1999.That title released on 11 November 1999, which was Veterans' Day in the United States. See, "Medal of Honor," 2012, accessed 1 May 2012, http://www.medalofhonor.com/game/medal-honor-1999. This series includes more than fourteen titles.

7. For more on American attitudes toward the American Century, see Frank Ninkovich, *The Wilsonian Century: US Foreign Policy since 1900* (Chicago: University of Chicago Press, 1999); Michael Hogan, ed., *The Ambiguous Legacy: US Foreign Relations in the "American Century"* (New York: Cambridge University Press, 1999).

8. Franklin D. Roosevelt, "D-Day Prayer," 6 June 1944, accessed 19 Nov. 2009, http://www.historyplace.com/speeches/fdr-prayer.htm.

9. "Draft of the D-Day Prayer, June 6, 1944," n.d., Franklin D. Roosevelt Presidential Library and Museum, accessed 28 Sept. 2010, http://docs.fdrlibrary.marist.edu/04DD010.HTML.

10. Alex Kershaw, *The Bedford Boys: One American Town's Ultimate D-Day Sacrifice* (Cambridge, MA: Da Capo Press, 2003), 172; *New York Times*, 7 June 1944.

11. A. Kershaw, 166;*New York Times*,7 June 1944; Thomas Doherty, *Projections of War: Hollywood, American Culture, and World War II*, rev. ed. (New York: Columbia University Press, 1999), 84, 242; Stephen E. Ambrose, *D-Day June 6, 1944: The Climactic Battle of World War II* (New York: Simon & Schuster, 1994), 499.

12. Text from the order is widely available. See, Dwight D. Eisenhower, Order of the Day, n. d. (6 June 1944), Folder 335.18, Supreme Headquarters Allied Expeditionary Forces (SHAEF) Special Staff Adjutant General's Division Executive Section, Record Group 331 (RG 331), National Archives and Records Administration in College Park, Maryland. Hereafter referred to as NACP. See also, Dwight D. Eisenhower, *Crusade in Europe* (New York: Doubleday and Company, 1948).

13. Years later, one disgruntled veteran of the Italian campaign contacted Cornelius Ryan, the author of the 1959 book on D-Day, *The Longest Day*. The letter pushed Ryan to consider writing about "the longest four months" of the Anzio landing, which deserved equal, if not greater, recognition than

D-Day in this veteran's opinion. Letter, W. H. Ellis to Cornelius Ryan, n. d. (1963?), Folder Ryan, Cornelius Letters and Correspondence—Fan MailA-J1959–63 #2, Miscellaneous Supplementary Material records, Cornelius Ryan Collection of World War II Papers, Robert E. and Jean R. Mahn Center for Archives and Special Collections, Ohio University Library, Athens, OH. Hereafter referred to as CRC.

14. *News of the Day, Invasion Extra!*(15, no. 280), 10 min., Metro-Goldwyn-Mayer, 1944, VHS, accessed at the UCLA Film and Television Archive, Los Angeles, California. Cf., Doherty, 243–44.

15. Don Whitehead for the Combined Press, "No News of Americans for 18-Hours with American Troops in France," 9 June 1944, Folder #2, Office of War Information, Record Group 208 (RG 208), NACP.

16. John B. Romeiser, "Introduction," in *"Beachhead Don": Reporting the War from the European Theater, 1942–1945*, ed., John B. Romeiser (New York: Fordham University Press, 2004), xxi.

17. James Tobin, *Ernie Pyle's War: America's Eyewitnesses to World War II* (New York: The New Press, 1984), 173–78, 265–68. Tobin's book featured an excellent analysis of Pyle and his wartime experience as well as reprints of some of his major articles. Pyle wrote three columns on this initial experience, which newspapers throughout the US reprinted and one member of Congress read into the *Congressional Record*.

18. Robert Capa, *Slightly Out of Focus* (New York: Henry Holt and Company, 1947), 145–51; Richard Whelan, *Robert Capa* (New York: Alfred A. Knopf, 1985), 209–14. Unfortunately, Capa's darkroom assistant in London exposed the film to excessive heat and destroyed most shots. The eleven salvageable shots came out blurred.

19. *New York Times*, 6 June 1944; *New York Times*,7 June 1944.

20. A. Kershaw, 7.

21. Joseph Balkoski, *Omaha Beach: D-Day, June 6, 1944* (Mechanicsburg, PA: Stackpole Books, 2004), 121; Roger H. Hill, "Memorializing Community Grief: Bedford, Virginia, and the National D-Day Memorial" (DA diss., George Mason University, 2006), 90–91. On the 29th Infantry Division's D-Day performance, see Joseph Balkoski, *Beyond the Beachhead: The 29th Infantry Division in Normandy*, foreword by Stephen E. Ambrose (1989; reprint, Mechanicsburg, PA: Stackpole Books, 1999).

22. A. Kershaw, 207, 214. The telegrams flooded the local area beginning on 17 July 1944. See also, R. H. Hill,84.

23. "Presentation of the Plans and Problems of the American Graves Registration Command to C/S of TSFET and Chiefs of his General Staff," 27 Dec. 1945, Folder—AGRC Organizational & Operations History June–Dec. 1945, Records of US Army Operational, Tactical, and Support Organizations (World War II and Thereafter), Unit Histories, 1940–1967, Quartermaster Commands, Record Group (RG) 338, NACP; John Bodnar, The "Good War" in American Memory (Baltimore: Johns Hopkins University Press, 2010), 98.

24. G. Kurt Piehler, Remembering War the American Way (1995; reprint, Washington, DC: Smithsonian Books, 2004), 129–33.

25. R. H. Hill, 85–88.

26. A. Kershaw, 222–24.

27. For the French commemorative response to D-Day, see Kate LeMay's chapter in this volume

28. As quoted in A. Kershaw, 225–29; R. H. Hill, 92–96.

29. Michael G. Kammen, Mystic Chords of Memory: The Transformation of Tradition in American Culture (New York: Vintage Books, 1991), 531–33. Kammen, as well as Piehler, saw the Civil War as the beginning of the federal government's increased participation in memory-history work. In the twentieth century, as both scholars noted, that activity increased greatly even as local or group memories sometimes came into conflict with the official versions pushed by the federal government. For more, see Piehler, 2–6.

30. For treatment of the ABMC's activities in Normandy, France, see Sam Edwards, "War and Collective Memory: American Military Commemoration in Britain and France, 1943 to the Present" (Ph.D. diss., Lancaster University, 2007), esp. 73–74, 137–59.

31. "Presentation of the Plans and Problems of the American Graves Registration Command to C/S of TSFET and Chiefs of his General Staff," 27 December 1945, Folder—AGRC Organizational & Operations History June–Dec. 1945, Records of US Army Operational, Tactical, and Support Organizations (World War II and Thereafter), Unit Histories, 1940–1967, Quartermaster Commands, RG 338, NACP.

32. Piehler, 132. Ten of the fourteen overseas Second World War cemeteries are in Europe.

33. Edwards, 128–50; Ron Robin, *Enclaves of America: The Rhetoric of American Political Architecture Abroad, 1900–1965* (Princeton: Princeton University Press, 1992), 109–35.

34. LT K. W. Lange (HQ AGRC), "Memorial Day Ceremonies at St. Laurent," n. d., Folder—97-AGRC-0.3.0 US Military Cemetery Reports (N-St. M)—Hq. AGRC, European Theater Area—1946–48, Records of the Adjutant General's Office, WWII Operations Reports, 1940–48, European Theater, RG 407, NACP.

35. Memorandum, COL George C. Traver to Commander AGRC Eur, "Narrative Report of Activities, Second Zone, AGRC, Camp John B. Franks, Week Ending 9 April," 10 April 1947, Folder 7856 AGRC, Second Zone Narrative Reports Sept. 1946–Dec. 1947 (II), Records of US Army Operational, Tactical, and Support Organizations (World War II and Thereafter), Unit Histories, 1940–1967, Quartermaster Commands, RG 338, NACP.

36. Memorandum, Headquarters Army Graves Registration Command, Europe, "Five Thousand Attend 'Benediction Ceremony' Closing St. Laurent US Military Cemetery at Omaha Beach, Normandy, France", 14 Sept. 1947, Folder 97-AGRC-0.3.0 US Military Cemetery Reports (N-St. M)—Hq. AGRC, European Theater Area—1946–48, Records of the Adjutant General's Office WWII Operations Reports, 1940–48, European Theater, RG 407, NACP.

37. The transfer was a drawn-out process. The AGRC was the primary authority for constructing the cemeteries and handling the bodies. The ABMC oversaw the selection and erection of monuments. The two worked together in the years following the war with the final hand-over from AGRC to ABMC in Normandy taking place in 1949.

38. As quoted in Robin, 122.

39. For a compelling discussion on the democratization of war memory and the focus on losses, see George Mosse, *Fallen Soldiers: Reshaping the Memory of the World Wars* (New York: Oxford University Press, 1990); Kammen, 420–22, 700; Piehler, 5–6, 187.

40. The quoted text comes from the translated memorandum, René Coty, "Message from the President of the Republic at the Dedication of the American Military Cemeteries in France," 18 July 1956, binder titled "American Battle Monuments Commission Dedication Ceremonies 1956," n. d., Records of the American Battle Monuments Commission, Record Group (RG) 117, NACP.

41. Dwight D. Eisenhower, "To Those Who Participate In The Dedication At St. Laurent," 7 July 1956, binder titled "American Battle Monuments Commission Dedication Ceremonies 1956."

42. Bodnar, *The "Good War,"* 86.

43. The numbers involved, however, must give us pause. Any count of D-Day losses remains an estimate. The best estimate for the day is that the American forces suffered approximately 2,500 *casualties*, including wounded, killed, captured, and missing. No sources used in this research ever claimed that the numbers represented by this memorial site stood for D-Day alone. Nevertheless, over time the commemorative activities connected to the cemetery did risk a conflation. The cemetery acquired an aura as a place for *D-Day* commemoration rather than as a site marking those lost in the Normandy *campaign* that had resulted in many of those graves. For death estimates see, Gordon A. Harrison, *Cross Channel Attack, United States Army in World War II* (Washington, DC: United States Army Center of Military History, 1951; New York: BDD, Inc., 1993), 329–30; Williamson Murray and Allan R. Millett, *A War to Be Won: Fighting the Second World War* (Cambridge, MA: Belknap Press of Harvard University Press, 2000), 422.

44. For several examples, see, *New York Times*, 5 June 1949; *Daily Boston Globe*, 6 June 1949; *Chicago Daily Tribune*, 7 June 1950; and *New York Times*, 7 June 1953.

45. See, for one example of such a dispute, Michael R. Dolski, "'To Set Free a Suffering Humanity': D-Day in American Remembrance" (Ph.D. diss., Temple University, 2012), 94–96.

46. A. Kershaw, 228.

47. Dolski, 103–6.

48. Monuments at this time included pieces installed at the Normandy American Cemetery and the Bedford, Virginia, D-Day Memorial. Speeches that touched upon D-Day's lessons were numerous, but the most telling instances appeared with President Eisenhower's campaigning efforts in 1952 and 1956. Other notable speeches referring to D-Day occurred at the dedication ceremonies for the Normandy American Cemetery in July 1956. See, binder titled "American Battle Monuments Commission Dedication Ceremonies 1956," n. d., Records of the American Battle Monuments Commission, Record Group (RG) 117, NACP. For movies, consider the 1950 film *Breakthrough*, dir. Lewis

Seiler, 91 min., Warner Bros. Pictures, 1950; 1994, VHS; or the 1956 film *D-Day, the Sixth of June*, dir. Henry Koster, 106 min., Twentieth Century-Fox, 1956; Twentieth Century-Fox Home Entertainment, 2002, DVD. The latter was based on the 1955 book by Lionel Shapiro, *The Sixth of June: A Novel of World War II* (New York: Doubleday, 1955). One other noteworthy D-Day book coming from this period was the US Army's official history of the Normandy Campaign by G. A. Harrison. An extended treatment of the 1956 film, *D-Day, the Sixth of June*, appears in Sam Edwards' chapter on British memory of D-Day in this volume.

49. The ABMC has published pamphlets on the cemeteries with photos, histories, and interpretive guidance on the monuments since at least 1957. Pamphlet, "Normandy American Cemetery and Memorial," American Battle Monuments Commission, 1957, accessed at US Army Heritage and Education Center, Carlisle, Pennsylvania.

50. Edwards, "War and Collective Memory," 170; Kammen, *Mystic Chords of Memory*, 547. Examples of "pilgrimages" to Normandy appeared in US news stories (1952) and *Bridgehead Sentinel* articles (1953). The Robert R. McCormick Research Center, Cantigny First Division Museum, in Wheaton, IL (hereafter referred to as CFDM), holds copies of the *Bridgehead Sentinel*, the newsletter for the Society of the First Division.

51. For other printed works treating D-Day in this period, see Dolski, "To Set Free," 96, 106–8, 132–36.

52. Cornelius Ryan, *The Longest Day* (New York: Simon & Schuster, 1959), foreword, n. p. (9).

53. Letter, Cornelius Ryan to Miss Frances Ward (his research assistant in Europe), 1 July 1958, Folder Readers Digest Correspondence between Ryan and Ward (Europe) & Lang, "The Longest Day" records, CRC.

54. Ryan, *The Longest Day*, 54, 177, 191, 196, 253, 266.

55. Gordon A. Craig, review of *The Longest Day*, by Cornelius Ryan, *New York Herald Tribune*, 22 Nov. 1959; Hanson Baldwin, "D-Day—This Is the Way It Was," *NY Times Magazine*, 31 May 1959; Letter, BG John P. Cooper, Jr., to Cornelius Ryan, 10 November 1959, Folder Ryan, Cornelius Letters and Correspondence—Fan Mail A-J 1959–63, Miscellaneous Supplementary Material records, CRC.

56. Letter, Cornelius Ryan to William Buckley (Henry Holt & Co.), 19 Nov. 1957, Folder—Original idea letter—Buckley, "The Longest Day" records, CRC.

57. Edwards, 175–78.

58. Kenneth E. Crouch, "Memorial to 116th Regiment Being Built on Omaha Beach," *The Bedford Democrat*, 23 Oct. 1958, Folder Publicity—D-Day Book, "The Longest Day" records, CRC; "D-Day Landing Re-Enacted by Paratroopers," *Chicago Daily Tribune*, 7 June 1959, ProQuest, accessed 28 Nov. 2010.

59. For instance, the Senate Judiciary Committee held hearings in 1959 on the creation of a "Freedom Academy." See Folder Orlando Group (1), C. D. Jackson Papers, Dwight D. Eisenhower Presidential Library, Abilene, KS.

60. Mel Gussow, *Don't Say Yes Until I Finish Talking: A Biography of Darryl F. Zanuck* (New York: Doubleday, 1971; Reprint, New York: Pocket Books, 1972), 198–201.

61. Advanced Fact Sheet on "The Longest Day," n. d., Folder Ryan, Cornelius Printed Matter The Last Battle #3, Miscellaneous Supplementary Material records, CRC.

62. Letter, Cornelius Ryan to Kenneth E. Crouch (*Bedford Bulletin-Democrat*), 20 Aug. 1963, Folder Ryan, Cornelius Correspondence Zanuck, Darryl F., Miscellaneous Supplementary Material records, CRC.

63. Darryl F. Zanuck, "The Longest Day Second Revised Story Outline," 13 Jan. 1961, "The Longest Day" records, CRC.

64. Stephen Ambrose, "*The Longest Day* (US, 1962): 'Blockbuster' History," in *World War II, Film, and History*, eds. John Whiteclay Chambers II and David Culbert (New York: Oxford University Press, 1996), 98.

65. Harry Brand (Director of Publicity, Twentieth Century-Fox), "'The Longest Day' (Fact Sheet)," n. d., Folder The Longest Day 20th Century-Fox 1962, Core Collection, Margaret Herrick Library, The Academy of Motion Picture Arts and Sciences, Beverly Hills, California. Hereafter referred to as MHL.

66. *The Longest Day*, dir. Ken Annakin, Andrew Marton, Bernhard Wicki, and Darryl F. Zanuck, (Darryl F. Zanuck Productions, Inc. and Twentieth Century Fox Film Corporation, 1962; Twentieth Century Fox Home Entertainment, 2006), DVD, 178 min.

67. Gussow, 232; Lawrence Suid, *Guts and Glory: The Making of the American Military Image in Film*, rev. ed. (Lexington: University Press of Kentucky, 2002), 185.

68. *Los Angeles Times*, 1 Apr. 1962.

69. *D-Day Plus 20 Years: Eisenhower Returns to Normandy*(CBS Reports, Columbia Broadcasting Systems, Inc., 1964 (filmed August 1963); Ambrose Video Publishing, Inc., 1990), VHS, CFDM, 123 min.

70. Tom Engelhardt, *The End of Victory Culture: Cold War America and the Disillusioning of a Generation* (New York: Basic Books, 1995), 10.

71. For multiple examples of D-Day commemoration in this period, see Dolski, 167–208.

72. Patrick Hagopian, *The Vietnam War in American Memory: Veterans, Memorials, and the Politics of Healing* (Amherst: University of Massachusetts Press, 2009), 11.

73. On visitation rates, see: ABMC's Annual Report for Fiscal Year 1979, 14 Aug. 1980, 103; Annual Report for Fiscal Year 1980, 30 Sept. 1980, 92; Annual Report for Fiscal Year 1981, 30 Sept. 1981, 60; and Annual Report for Fiscal Year 1983, 30 Sept. 1983. Each of these reports remains in a separate folder with that report's title, Records of the American Battle Monuments, RG 117, NACP. Two of the more popular books of this period include: John Keegan, *Six Armies in Normandy: From D-Day to the Liberation of Paris* (New York: Viking Penguin, 1982); and Carlo D'Este, *Decision in Normandy* (Old Saybrook, CT: Konecky and Konecky, 1983).

74. Ronald Reagan, "Remarks at the Annual Convention of the National Association of Evangelicals in Orlando, Florida," 8 Mar. 1983, accessed 7 Jan. 2011, Ronald Reagan Library http://www.reagan.utexas.edu/archives/speeches/1983/30883b.htm.

75. Richard H. Immerman, *Empire for Liberty: A History of American Imperialism from Benjamin Franklin to Paul Wolfowitz* (Princeton: Princeton University Press, 2010), 204.

76. Studs Terkel, *"The Good War": An Oral History of World War II* (New York: The New Press, 1984), 3. Years later, Terkel explained that his wife insisted on the title to emphasize the dissonance between the words good and war. Studs Terkel with Sydney Lewis, *Touch and Go: A Memoir* (New York: The New Press, 2007), 110.

77. *Time*, 28 May 1984, accessed 23 Dec. 2009, http://www.time.com/magazine/article/0,9171,951086,00.html.

78. *Time*, 28 May 1984, accessed 23 Dec. 2009, http://www.time.com/magazine/article/0,9171,95108,00.html.

79. For more on the shifts in French commemorative politics, see Kate LeMay's chapter in this volume.

80. Douglas Brinkley, *The Boys of Pointe du Hoc: Ronald Reagan, D-Day, and the US Army 2nd Rangers Battalion* (New York: HarperPerennial, 2005), 8.

81. Ibid., 137–38; John Ehrman, *The Eighties: America in the Age of Reagan* (New Haven, CT: Yale University Press, 2005), 84.

82. Brinkley provided a full copy of Reagan's speech in *The Boys of Pointe du Hoc*, 225–32. For an audio recording of this speech, see "Ronald Reagan on the 40th Anniversary of D-Day," *The History Place*, n. d., accessed 9 Mar. 2007, http://www.historyplace.com/speeches/reagan-d-day.htm.

83. "Remarks of the President at US-French Ceremony Commemorating D-Day," 6 June 1984, Box D-Day Anniversary VOF Dawson Gen. Smith/Gen. Allen & Gen. Huebner, CFDM.

84. For instance, the *New York Times* reprinted the majority of Reagan's Omaha Beach speech the next day. *New York Times*, 7 June 1984.

85. D'Este; Charles Cawthon, "On Omaha Beach," *American Heritage* (Oct./ Nov. 1983), 49, Folder Robert A. Rowe—Published Material—On Omaha Beach—Cawthon, Charles, Robert A. Rowe papers, U.S. Army Heritage and Education Center, Carlisle, Pennsylvania; "D-Day…The Normandy Invasion," *World War II: The War Chronicles*, dir. Don Horan, 25 min., A&E Television Networks, 1983; A&E Home Video, 2000, DVD.

86. As quoted in George C. Herring, "America and Vietnam: The Unending War," *Foreign Affairs* (Winter 1991/92), accessed 28 July 2010), http://www.foreignaffairs.com/articles/47440/george-c-herring/america-and-vietnam-the-unending-war.

87. Kammen, 533, 625–28, 655–58; Jay Winter, *Remembering War: The Great War Between Memory and History in the Twentieth Century* (New Haven: Yale University Press, 2006), 1. See also, Emily S. Rosenberg, *A Date Which Will Live: Pearl Harbor in American Memory* (Durham, NC: Duke University Press, 2003), 116–38.

88. Stephen E. Ambrose, *D-Day*, 10, 25–26, 167, 195, 238, 256–57, 344, 579. *Publishers Weekly*, 17 Aug. 1998, accessed 24 Mar. 2011, http://www.publishersweekly.com/pw/print/19980817/21721-pw-ambrose-backlist-soars-.html.

89. *Philadelphia Inquirer*, 26 Apr. 1994.

90. The festivities of 1984 had created new standards. Some journalists explicitly forecast a less-inspiring performance by President William Clinton than

Reagan's superb oratory in 1984. For one such example, see *New York Times*, 26 May 1994.

91. William J. Clinton, "Remarks Honoring the Role of the United States Navy in the Normandy," 6 June 1994, Folder MG Albert Smith, Jr., D-Day Anniversary, Box Rare Books—Research Historian Normandy, CFDM.

92. William J. Clinton, "Remarks on the 50th Anniversary of D-Day at Pointe du Hoc in Normandy," 6 June 1994, Folder MG Albert Smith, Jr., D-Day Anniversary, Box Rare Books—Research Historian Normandy, CFDM.

93. William J. Clinton, "Remarks on the 50th Anniversary of D-Day at the United States Cemetery in Colleville-sur-mer, France," 6 June 1994, Folder MG Albert Smith, Jr., D-Day Anniversary, Box Rare Books—Research Historian Normandy, CFDM.

94. For a critical discussion of the failure by US officials and the international community at large to halt genocide in the Balkans, see Sarah E. Wagner, *To Know Where He Lies: DNA Technology and the Search for Srebernica's Missing* (Berkeley: University of California Press, 2008), 21–57.

95. Tom Brokaw, *The Greatest Generation* (New York: Random House, 1998), xviii–xix, xxx, 17–18.

96. Jeanine Basinger, *The World War II Combat Film: Anatomy of a Genre*, with an updated filmography by Jeremy Arnold (New York: Columbia University Press, 1986; Middletown, CT: Wesleyan University Press, 2003), xii–xiii.

97. *Philadelphia Inquirer*, 19 July 1998.

98. "Saving Private Ryan Nomination Sheet for the 1998 Academy Awards," Core Collections, MHL.

99. Michael J. Allen, *Until the Last Man Comes Home: POWs, MIAs, and the Unending Vietnam War* (Chapel Hill: University of North Carolina Press, 2009), 302–3. Regarding captivity narratives, see Richard Slotkin, *Regeneration through Violence: The Mythology of the American Frontier, 1600–1860* (Middletown, CT: Wesleyan University Press, 1973), 94–115.

100. Basinger, 262.

101. *Saving Private Ryan*, dir. Steven Spielberg (DreamWorks Pictures and Paramount Pictures, 1998; DreamWorks Home Entertainment, 1999), DVD, 169 min.

102. Andrew Hindes, "'Private Ryan's' Saving Grace," *Variety*, 20 July 1998, Folder SAVING PRIVATE RYAN DreamWorks 1998 (1–23 July 1998), Core Collections, MHL.

103. As quoted in Bill Higgins, "*Ryan* Leaves Them Speechless" *Los Angeles Times*, 23 July 1998, http://articles.latimes.com/1998/jul/23/news/ls-6210.

104. See, for instance, *Philadelphia Inquirer*, 26 July 1998.

105. "Freedom Isn't Free," *Dagwood Dispatches*, October 1998, Box Dagwood Dispatches 18th [*sic*] Infantry Regiment Assoc. Jan 1991-, CFDM. Emphasis in original.

106. As quoted in Jon Meacham, "Caught in the Line of Fire," *Newsweek*, 13 July 1998, 50.

107. *Los Angeles Times*, 9 Aug. 1998.

108. For one publicity effort, see "The Making of the National D-Day Museum," *Save Our History*, (A&E Television, 1996), VHS, CFDM, 50 min.

109. *Philadelphia Inquirer*, 7 June 2000. The institution has since changed its name to the National World War II Museum.

110. Walter A. McDougall, "American Exceptionalism . . . *Exposed*," Foreign Policy Research Institute E-Notes, October 2012.

111. R. H. Hill, "Memorializing Community Grief," 90–91, 126–65. Cf., A. Kershaw, 231–32. On Charles Schulz's role, see David Michaelis, *Schulz and Peanuts: A Biography* (New York: HarperCollins, 2007), xii–xiii, 143, 151.

112. Details come from a personal visit to the site; Pamphlet, "The National D-Day Memorial," The National D-Day Memorial Foundation, n. d. (2002?); R. H. Hill, 150–53, 165–68.

113. "Sol Education Packet," The National D-Day Memorial Foundation, 2002.

114. James W. Morrison, *Bedford Goes to War: The Heroic Story of a Small Virginia Community in World War II*, 2d ed. (Lynchburg, VA: Warwick House Publishing, 2006), 232.

115. George W. Bush, "Remarks at the Dedication of the National D-Day Memorial in Bedford, Virginia," 6 June 2001, *The American Presidency Project*, accessed 23 Apr. 2010, http://www.presidency.ucsb.edu/ws/index.php?pid=45818.

116. Mark Connelly, *We Can Take It!: Britain and the Memory of the Second World War* (New York: Pearson, 2004), 49; Slotkin, 294; Joseph Campbell, *The Hero with a Thousand Faces*, 3d ed. (New York: Pantheon Books, 1949; Novato, CA: New World Library, 2008); and Roland Barthes, *Mythologies*, ed. and trans. Annette Lavers (Paris: Editions du Seuil, 1957; New York: Noonday Press, 1972); John Shelton Lawrence and Robert Jewett, *The Myth of the American Superhero* (Grand Rapids, MI: William B. Eerdmans Publishing Company, 2002), 111.

117. Here, I draw on Benedict Anderson's path-breaking work covering the fictional bonds, or "mystic chords of memory," that tie large groups together into an "imagined community." Benedict Anderson, *Imagined Communities: Reflections on the Origin and Spread of Nationalism*, rev. ed. (New York: Verso, 1991).

Chapter Two

The Beginning of the End: D-Day in British Memory[1]

Sam Edwards

It has been said that the Battle of Alamein was the end of the beginning. The invasion of Normandy was the beginning of the end.

–Field Marshal Lord Montgomery, 7 June 1948

"D-day. Always D-day," said Ragno. "It made a sideshow of us, of Italy. They forgot about us after Normandy."

–Robert Ryan, *After Midnight*, 2005

In November 2003 Prime Minister Tony Blair was widely criticized in the tabloid press for comments questioning the British "fixation" with World War II. For Blair, this fixation hindered full participation in a forward-looking European Union. One newspaper even quoted the Prime Minister as remarking that:

> The Germans were defeated in the war and have managed to come to terms with it, the French were humiliated in the war and have come to terms with it. Britain won the war and has never got over it.[2]

Blair's suggestion that the British have a long-running obsession with the 1939–45 war was certainly apt. In recent years, considerable scholarly attention has been directed toward understanding the shape and structure of this obsession. The results of this attention have been illuminating, shedding light on the ways in which particular events from Britain's war experience—especially Dunkirk, the Battle of Britain, and the Blitz—have been the subject of recurrent memorializing, and mythologizing.[3] Yet while these largely Home Front events of 1940–41 have often seemed to dominate British war memory, a few other episodes do stand out on the nation's cultural landscape. In recent years, the Holocaust has been the subject of increasing attention, while the battle of El Alamein has long been remembered in Britain as the war's turning point.[4] Elsewhere, the heroics of British paratroopers at Arnhem in September 1944 have been the subject of several popular feature films, most notably *A Bridge Too Far* (1977), and the war fought by RAF Bomber Command—the "black sheep" of British war memory—has recently been acknowledged with the dedication of a new national memorial in London.[5] Even so, and just as novelist Robert Ryan suggests in *After Midnight* (2005),the only overseas event to receive the same kind of attention in British culture as the "little ships" or the "Few," the only military moment appearing to offer the attractive qualities of scale, significance and success, has been D-Day; the Allied invasion of Normandy in June 1944.[6]

As early as 1954, a British-funded D-Day museum had already been established at the small Norman fishing port of Arromanches-les-Bains, and the British government was also well-represented at the large-scale anniversary commemorations of June 1964 and June 1984. These anniversary events also saw thousands of British veterans return to France to revisit the past, and remember lost friends. Such was contemporary interest in D-Day that by June 1994 local councils on the south coast of England—the area from whence so many Allied troops had departed on their journey to France—even decided to replicate elements of the commemorative events in Normandy. That summer witnessed, for example, a huge rally of allied military vehicles and Second World War re-enactor groups in Portsmouth and Southampton, together with parades and street parties. Similar activities recurred during the sixtieth anniversary of the landings in June 2004. Little wonder that one student of British war memory—Geoff Eley—has suggested that the late twentieth century was an era of "commemorative excess."[7]

Nonetheless, contrary to the opinion expressed by Blair, such "excess" was not simply an expression of a problematic and unhealthy national psychosis; nor was it merely demonstrative of a persistent and peculiarly British Euroscepticism. Rather, British interest in the Second World War—as expressed in a variety of different commemorative activities and cultural media—should be understood as a product of the experience of that event *and* of the way it has been assimilated within British culture. This chapter examines this process of assimilation, exploring how D-Day—as moment and myth—has been represented in British culture over the last seventy years.

First, I show how the historical details of the Allied invasion framed the construction in postwar Britain of four key commemorative themes, themes that have come to form the basis of Britain's Normandy story: that D-Day was an expression of Britain's commitment to France; that D-Day vindicated the retreat from Dunkirk; that D-Day was a final demonstration of Imperial unity and of national power; and that D-Day marked the last moment of transatlantic military and political parity. Second, this chapter shows how subsequent commemorative activities and cultural media—involving writers, historians, politicians, film-makers, and veterans—have re-emphasized and reshaped these ideas in accordance with the fluctuating imperatives of the ever-changing present. At its broadest, therefore, this chapter explores how evolving historical realties—foreign and domestic—have shaped the mythologization of D-Day in British culture.

The British Role in D-Day

During World War II, the idea of launching some kind of "D-Day"— that is, an amphibious operation intended to land significant military forces on the mainland of Continental Europe—ultimately lay with the British, and specifically with the decision by Prime Minister Winston Churchill to initiate plans for a return to France following the evacuation of Dunkirk in the summer of 1940. To be sure, at this stage any such return was a distant ambition, rather than a realistic objective, and the plans produced represented an effort to inject some Churchillian resolution into a British military command then worried about a German invasion. Nonetheless, for the British, the origins of D-Day lie here, in the aftermath of the defeat and despair of Dunkirk: having been evicted from the French coast, British military planners were tasked with finding ways to return. The man with initial responsibility for formulating such plans was Cdre. Louis Mountbatten, designated by Churchill his Chief Advisor for Combined Operations in 1941.[8]

Two years later, and drawing upon some of the ideas previously explored by Mountbatten, an Anglo-American planning committee headed by another British officer—Lt. Gen. Frederick Morgan—put together the outline plan for a direct amphibious assault on occupied Europe.[9] Morgan's plan—codenamed Overlord—envisaged landing three Allied divisions on three invasion beaches, all of which would be located on the Norman coast between the Cherbourg Peninsula and the port of Le Havre, an area of land that had a long-established military connection to England, from William the Conqueror to Henry V. General (later Gen. Fd. Mar.) Bernard Law Montgomery then revised this plan in early 1944.[10] The victor of El Alamein elected to increase the number of divisions and landing beaches from three to five, and he also recommended the use of a relatively new type of light infantry formation to secure the western and eastern flanks of the invasion sector: paratroopers. Crucially, in terms of troops on the ground, Montgomery's plan also envisaged an Anglo-American parity of effort: two of the amphibious infantry divisions would be American (landing at beaches codenamed Utah and Omaha), two would be British (landing at Gold and Sword), and one Canadian (landing at Juno). Similarly, of the airborne divisions involved, two would be American and one British.[11]

The details briefly discussed above are well known, and have been rehearsed in much more detail many times elsewhere. Of interest here, though, are two key issues connected to these details. First, for the British, the origins of D-Day lay in the aftermath of Dunkirk.

Landing on the Norman coast, in short, represented vengeance for an earlier eviction from the Pas-de-Calais. Second, the D-Day plan, authored at different stages by three senior British officers—Mountbatten, Morgan, and Montgomery—was a collaborative venture that demanded an equality of effort and energy from the Great Republic *and* from the Great Empire. Indeed, if anything, the US Navy's commitment to the Pacific War ensured that the British military—not the American—would be preponderant on the day itself: 79 percent of the Allied vessels involved in the D-Day landings flew the White Ensign of the Royal Navy, and just 16 percent flew the Stars and Stripes.[12]

The command structure tasked with implementing the operation confirmed this idea of a collaborative undertaking and of relative Anglo-American parity. In recognition of the fact that, in time, American men and materiel in Western Europe would vastly outnumber the available resources of the British Empire, the man in overall charge of the landings was an American—GEN Dwight D. Eisenhower. Yet in recognition of the fact that the initial plans had been British, and that British and Commonwealth troops would land in equal numbers to those of the United States, all the command positions immediately subordinate to Ike—including that of overall land forces commander—were filled by Britons. As historian Max Hastings has explained, "this was the final occasion of the war on which British officers achieved such a measure of authority over Americans, and Americans bowed to British experience and allegedly greater military wisdom."[13] In planning and organization therefore, D-Day was an impressive demonstration of Anglo-American co-operation.[14]

Crucially too, the execution of the operation followed suit. As such, by midnight of 6 June there were approximately 130,000 Allied troops on the sand and soil of Normandy, and of these, 75,215 were British or Canadian (troops of the Commonwealth under overall British command) and 57,500 were American.[15] In the days and weeks that followed, this degree of relative Anglo-American parity would fade and then disappear, and by September 1944 the balance of power—in terms of divisions on the ground—had firmly shifted to the United States. Indeed, the British army had already reached its manpower limits by May 1944; once contact was made with the enemy in Normandy, British military strength would only diminish.[16] But this subsequent American preponderance in Europe is of secondary importance here. When understanding the place of *D-Day* in British memory, the more arresting fact is that on the day itself, on 6 June 1944, the British Lion was able to match—for one last time—the strength of the American Eagle. In fact, efforts to consolidate this very idea would quickly consume all those Britons involved in the production of the allied documentary film intended to record the campaign to liberate occupied Europe, a film that took D-Day as its start point: *The True Glory* (1945). As James Chapman has demonstrated, this film—following an earlier transatlantic collaborative venture, *Desert Victory* (1943)—was an Anglo-American co-production, but, at the same time, it was shaped by a persistent rivalry. Thus, the British production team members, conscious of the contemporary shift in the transatlantic balance of power, were keen that the film "present their part in the liberation in as favourable light as possible." Meanwhile, their American counterparts were similarly intent that "their part in the campaign...be foregrounded."[17] The result was a production that worked hard to ensure that both Allies were equally represented, even going so far as to parallel scenes of American soldiers battling on bloody Omaha with similar scenes of British Tommies fighting through the rubble of Caen.[18]

In the days immediately after the Allied landings, a similar attention to the British role in a great transatlantic endeavor to liberate and redeem France was present in the national press. In Parliament, Prime Minister Churchill was reported as announcing that "Anglo-American" armies had launched a "liberating assault" on France, while the London *Times* took care to make it clear that British, Canadian, and American troops, in that order, were involved in this assault, and that all were under the command of Gen. Sir Bernard Law Montgomery.[19] Much of the press in Britain also assimilated the landings into the nation's war experience by emphasizing that they represented a distinctly British return to the continent. Thus, *British Movietone News* showed images of British troops landing in

Normandy with the caption, "[t]hey tell their own story, I think. The story of how four years after Dunkirk; four years after Hitler thought it was all over bar the shouting, Britain came back."[20] Similarly, the popular *Daily Mirror* counseled its readers that while there remained a long fight ahead, and although, just like after Dunkirk, this fight would again require the "sublime obstinacy which is the British character," this time at least the mood was different: "Then the skies were grey. Now they are ablaze with the light of triumphs achieved, and victory to come."[21] Across the page was a cartoon of a British Tommy, gun in hand, kicking down a door in Hitler's Atlantic Wall; just below, an American soldier stands ready to follow him through the breach.[22] In the same vein, an article in the *Times* noted that "[f]our years ago... the tide of war had flooded from the east into the French channel ports," but now "the tide has turned, and in this suspended moment of history the first mighty wave is gathered before it crashes down on the enemies' beaches."[23] Elsewhere, the same issue of Britain's pre-eminent national paper included a poem simply titled "D-Day": it began with the lines—written in the voice of a British soldier lamenting the lot of France—"[f]our years ago I bade you my farewell."[24]

While reflecting on childhood memories of the D-Day landings the British military historian, John Keegan, suggested that at the time such an Anglo-centric vision of the invasion "accorded with national feeling about the fitness of things." After all, as Keegan continued, that the "Americans might in time come to supply the larger number of men in the battle and liberation of Europe" was offset in 1944 by the fact that D-Day was, nonetheless, "a British conception, an endeavour long promised, by Churchill to the country, by the British to themselves, an act of historical vindication, a paying back five-, ten-, and twenty-fold for the nation's expulsion from the continent four years before and for all it had subsequently suffered."[25] Similarly, while commenting on British responses to the landings in June 1944, Hastings has noted that

> for the British people far more than the Americans, the invasion
> represented a rebirth, a return, a reversal of all the humiliations

and defeats that they had endured since 1939. Here, at last, the British army could resume that which it had so disastrously abandoned at Dunkirk: the battle to defeat a major German army in north-west Europe."[26]

To be sure, the historical record makes more than apparent that the British high command frequently had to be pushed, prompted and persuaded into this battle by their American allies; Churchill in particular was often consumed by fears of disaster and defeat.[27] Yet such American pressure and patience attracts little attention outside of specialist D-Day historiography; in British culture D-Day is a British story.

Constructing Britain's D-Day Story: Normans, Saxons, and the End of Empire, c. 1945–62

The size, scale, and significance of D-Day ensured that it had already begun to receive commemorative attention by the end of the 1940s. In June 1945, GEN Eisenhower proclaimed the first anniversary of the landings a holiday for all Allied troops not on active duty, and by the early 1950s the French organization in charge of commemorating "the landings"—the Comité du Débarquement—had already begun to establish several "signal" monuments along the Norman coast in order to mark the key moments in the invasion.[28] Similar interest in the Allied landings was also apparent in postwar Britain. In 1948, the dedication of a D-Day memorial at Portsmouth—from whence the Allied armada departed—drew a crowd of 25,000, while the same year also saw at least two groups of British veterans make pilgrimages to Normandy in order to erect a memorial to their fallen comrades.[29]

Yet, despite such activities, these early postwar commemorative endeavors were still rather muted. One French scholar of D-Day commemorations notes, for example, that the solemn ceremonies of remembrance witnessed in Normandy in the late 1940s were generally "discreet" occasions.[30] Thus, it was not until the 1950s, as the war drifted further into the past, as the Empire dissolved, and as contemporary Cold War tensions—such as the conflict in Korea—drew attention to the continued significance of a transatlantic military alliance, that the events of 6 June began to receive more dedicated attention in British culture.

In 1951, for example, British attempts to appropriate the story of D-Day were more than apparent in a rather unusual memorial to the Allied landings unveiled to the public for the first time, an embroidered tapestry (although still only half complete). Commissioned and funded by Lord Dulverton of Batsford, and developed with the approval of senior military officers, this tapestry represented an attempt to assimilate D-Day into British history by establishing it as a counterpoint to an earlier, medieval, invasion joining the south-coast of England and Normandy, an invasion that had been likewise memorialized with cloth and thread: the Battle of Hastings, recorded for posterity by the Bayeux Tapestry. As such, this D-Day Tapestry represented the Normandy landings as a return; the liberation and redemption of an ancestral Norman homeland. One of the embroiderers even explicitly remarked that it depicted the "Norman invasion in reverse."[31] Similar sentiment also animated contemporary efforts to ensure that Britain's D-Day sacrifices were marked on the Norman landscape. Indeed, the largest British war cemetery in Normandy was completed at Bayeux in 1952, and the nearby memorial carries the legend: "We who were conquered by William have liberated the fatherland of the Conqueror."

Comparable efforts to secure a distinctly Anglo-French reading of the Allied landings were evident just a few years later when the first official D-Day museum was established in Normandy. Built at the small fishing village of Arromanches-les-bains, and thus in the British invasion sector, the origins and design of this museum were firmly French, but much of the material it displayed had been donated by the British, and so too was much of the funding.[32] Hence the choice of Arromanches-les-bains for location: ruined and wrecked on the sands next to the village lay the remains of a man-made harbor dragged across the Channel to ensure the logistical demands of the D-Day operation could be met without having to secure a heavily defended port. Code-named Mulberry, this harbor was, to many, a symbol of British technical ingenuity and industrial know-how. Little wonder that Queen Elizabeth II led the museum's unveiling ceremony in 1954, while the British ambassador to France delivered a message from Winston Churchill—recently returned to power—expressing the British government's "keen pleasure in contributing to the creation of the museum" and his hope that it would "symbolize the lasting friendship which unites, in peacetime as in time of war, the French and British peoples."[33] Tellingly, a year later, the presence of the first professional British cycling team in the Tour de France was reported in the Norman press as just such an expression of cross-Channel friendship; a *débarquement* not dissimilar in symbol and significance to that witnessed on the coast of Calvados in the summer of 1944.[34]

These attempts to establish the place of D-Day in a long history of Anglo-French relations demanded a rather imaginative take on history. After almost fifty years of Entente Cordiale, and after two Anglo-French military alliances in response to a German threat, a much older history of cross-Channel tensions was pushed into the background; there was no space here for Agincourt or Waterloo. No doubt to the delight of Fd. Mar. Montgomery—a long-time admirer of the Norman contribution to England, an aristocrat whose very name was Norman in origins, and a man who, after the war, actually gave this name to a Calvados coastal village (Colleville-Montgomery)— even the Norman Conquest becomes, via a new commemorative tapestry, just a prelude to Anglo-French co-operation.

Nonetheless, if this Anglo-French reading of D-Day was central to the story told by the tapestry and by the Arromanches-les-bains museum, the more pervasive commemorative theme emerging in postwar Britain centered on the idea that the invasion was the result of *Anglo-Saxon* unity and, just as importantly, of transatlantic parity in power and resources. Reassuringly grounded in the operational details of Overlord and celebrated by the postwar production *The True Glory* (1945), the ceremonies that took place in Normandy each June refined and developed this idea. In 1947, for example, the June commemorations in Normandy were evenly divided between the

American and British invasion sectors, while by the tenth anniversary in 1954 the *Times* could openly state that the commemorative events had begun with a "British" day before then moving the "emphasis" to the American landings (an arrangement that remains the framework for the annual commemorations today).[35] In fact, those Britons involved in planning for the tenth anniversary were determined to ensure that the British presence matched that of the United States. As one official at the British Embassy in Paris explained: "It seems to us that our contribution should as far as possible be comparable to that of the Americans."[36]

Significantly, this attempt to emphasize Anglo-American parity ensured that some of the complexities of the D-Day operation, in terms of the nations and peoples involved, soon fell by the wayside. Thus, by the 1950s, the British role on D-Day increasingly included *all* those fighting under British command, wearing British uniforms, or landing on British beaches. There was little space here for specific acknowledgement of Canadians, Fighting French, or Free Poles; all were a part of the military force deployed by the British Empire and Commonwealth.[37] This was a truth of sorts: the troops of the Commonwealth and of exiled European governments *did* use British supplied equipment, and many *did* serve under British command.[38] Yet there were also hints here of that reductionist Victorian mentality—endemic in the British elite for at least a century—that equated England with Britain, and Britain with the British Empire. Indeed, when announcing the news of the invasion to Parliament on 6 June 1944, Churchill was happy to declare that British and American troops were in the vanguard of the attack and that so too were "Allied" soldiers, although he felt it unnecessary to "give lists of all the different nationalities."[39] A similar omission even became apparent on the postwar Norman landscape. For the name of the organization tasked with building Britain's overseas memorials—including the cemetery at Bayeux noted above—was the *Imperial* War Graves Commission, and following policy established after 1918 its task was to commemorate all British, Empire, and Commonwealth troops killed on active service in the two World Wars. Work on the post-1945 memorial landscapes began quickly, and by the end of the

1950s all twenty-five of the Commission's cemeteries in Calvados had been finished.[40] To be sure, the IWGC took great care to ensure that the contributions of specific nations were recognized; the dead of each country, for example, had distinct headstones. Nonetheless, its activities still imparted an impression of British-led Imperial unity. As such, among the fields and lanes of the Norman *bocage*, the wartime sacrifices of a united British Empire, rather than of distinct and different nations, were apparent for all too see.

Contemporary historiography of the Allied landings validated the significance of the British contribution to the "Great Crusade." Chester Wilmot's *Struggle for Europe* (1952), for example, is unapologetic in the equality of emphasis it gives to the forces of both Western allies, even to the extent that he downplays American preponderance in the later stages of the war. Wilmot, an Australian journalist, had been attached to Montgomery's command during the fighting and so such a reading of the conflict is perhaps understandable.[41] Montgomery's history of the European war, published in 1947, likewise emphasized the collaborative nature of the Allied campaign in Western Europe although, unsurprisingly, the emphasis frequently lay with the British and his personal role, again at the expense of recognizing the increasing American preponderance as the war continued.[42] Elsewhere, Eisenhower's *Crusade in Europe* (1948) painted a more sensitive picture of Anglo-American unity in the cause of European freedom, an impression that Ike, ever the diplomat, had painstakingly maintained while Supreme Commander, even in the face of numerous provocations from the likes of Monty.[43]

By 1956, this vision of Operation Overlord as the result of a combined effort by the "English-speaking peoples" had even secured the attentions of the motion picture industry in a feature film titled *D-Day: Sixth of June*.[44] Financed with American money, based on a novel by the Canadian author Lionel Shapiro, and featuring a deliberately Anglo-American cast, this film explored the events of June 1944 as an expression of transatlantic comradeship.[45] Indeed, at times, it almost reduces the Allied invasion of occupied Europe—the largest amphibious operation in military history—to what is, in effect, an Anglo-American daytrip to France.

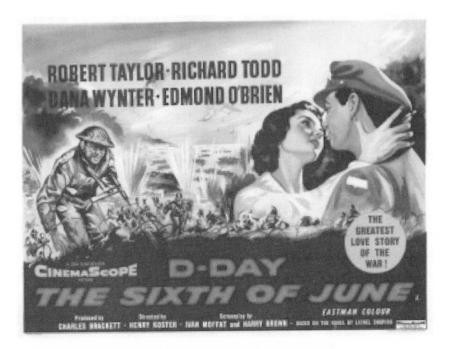

Figure 4: D-Day: The Sixth of June (1956) Promotional Poster.

The opening scenes, set in pre-D-Day wartime Britain, explore the kind of Anglo-American tensions and disagreements that had already become clichés during the war itself: American soldiers are brash and arrogant, British civilians are rude and ungrateful. But as the film develops, these tensions begin to be resolved through a love story involving a British woman (Valerie Russell, played by Dana Wynter) and an American soldier (Brad Parker, played by Robert Taylor): Yanks and Limeys learn to understand each other as they ready themselves for the Great Crusade. There is, however, a twist in the story: Dana Wynter's character is also in love with a British soldier (Capt. John Wynter), played by actor and real-life D-Day veteran Richard Todd. Todd, however, departs Britain for the fighting in North Africa toward the beginning of the film and soon after declaring his love for Wynter. He then returns, wounded, shortly before D-Day, and once recovered quickly assumes command of the Anglo-American commando force—Special Force Six—which has been created to attack and destroy a German defensive position

97

dangerously located between the British and American beaches, thus poised to tear apart the Anglo-American alliance. And of course Wynter's American love interest is a member of just this force, and duly becomes Todd's subordinate. Both men also know of the other's interest in Wynter. Cue arguments, disputes, anger, outrage, perhaps even a bit of fighting between Yank and Limey for the heart and hand of Wynter. Or so one might expect; but there is, in actual fact, nothing of the sort. The Anglo-American alliance does not implode, and the success of the invasion is not compromised by jealousy or distrust. Instead, Todd quietly accepts Wynter's unfaithfulness, and Taylor acknowledges the qualities and character of his love rival. The two men shake hands, and invade Normandy. In *D-Day: Sixth of June*, therefore, success in the Normandy landings is entirely dependent on Anglo-American unity and understanding. Note too, this unity is the product of *British* leadership.

To a degree, this plot referred back to the experience of the war and, just as importantly, to the terms on which British culture had previously explored that experience. For instance, several notable films of the 1940s had already celebrated the closeness of the wartime Anglo-American alliance, and many of these had also sought to ensure that their plot and characters conformed to the idea—long popular on both sides of the Atlantic—of British age and experience, and of American youth or innocence. Take, for instance, *A Yank in the RAF* (1941), *A Canterbury Tale* (1944), *The Way to the Stars* (1945) and *A Matter of Life and Death* (1946): all feature wise Britons harnessing or embracing youthful American energy.

Nonetheless, if the plot and structure of *D-Day: Sixth of June* is suggestive of these wartime precedents, it also bears the imprint of postwar concerns and, in particular, the changing balance of power between the United States and United Kingdom. This shift in power—actual and potential—had first become apparent in the autumn of 1944 as the British military failed to match American troop numbers in France, and it was increasingly obvious in the final stages of the campaign to liberate Western Europe in the spring of 1945. Severe postwar economic difficulties, Prime Minister Clement Atlee's decision to withdraw British troops from Greece, and Indian independence then confirmed the image of British decline in 1946–47.[46]

At exactly the same time, the transatlantic shift in power was also implicit in the emergence of a new discursive short-hand through which to describe the contemporary Anglo-American alliance. For it was precisely this moment that former Prime Minister Churchill, fearful of Soviet intentions in Europe, made his famous plea for a postwar Anglo-American "special relationship," a relationship that he hoped might ensure a future for the "British Empire and Commonwealth."[47] As phrase and idea, therefore, the "special relationship" sought to negotiate contemporary British decline relative to the United States by harking back to—and perpetuating—the Anglo-American comradeship of the wartime Grand Alliance. It sought to fix a moment of relative Anglo-American parity for all time in an attempt to ensure that the United States did not treat the British Empire and Commonwealth like just another Western allied nation. This phrase was quickly grasped by many other British politicians and diplomats likewise seeking to manage growing American strength, while at the same time trying to arrest their decline from Great Power status. As a result, by the early 1950s, the "special relationship" had already become something of a cliché in diplomatic circles, a fact aided by the considerable attention that Churchill in particular continued to devote to its cultivation. It often featured, for example, in his popular postwar writings, most notably *The Second World War* (1954) and *A History of the English-Speaking Peoples* (1958).[48]

The extent to which the assumptions behind this postwar transatlantic discourse shaped the narrative of *D-Day: Sixth of June* is apparent not just in the Anglo-American casting, nor just in Taylor and Todd's "special relationship." Rather, these assumptions are also apparent in the fact that a central thread to the film's story concerns the idea that the war marked an end for the British, and a beginning for the United States. This idea appears quite early in the film. A key moment is the initial meeting between Dana Wynter and Robert Taylor, a meeting occasioned by the assault her aging Dunkirk-veteran father has perpetrated upon an American air force sergeant whom the former accosts for being rude and "unsoldierly." Attempting to explain her father's unfriendly demeanor, Wynter remarks that he fears change and the loss of "his" England. And Americans, she continues, "mean change."

This idea that D-Day marked an end for the British recurs throughout the film. At the film's conclusion, Taylor lies wounded from battle and Todd—his British commanding officer—comforts him on the beach. It is this moment at which Taylor finally decides that he will notstand between Todd and Wynter, a decision he struggles to make earlier in the film; he is then carried from the beach and returned to a hospital in England. Todd, meanwhile, goes for a contemplative wander along the beach, steps on a mine, and is instantly killed. Moreover, Todd's character is not the only Briton to die in the film; a few scenes earlier we learn that Wynter's father—Brigadier General Russell—has committed suicide because the War Office has refused to give him a combat command in the invasion. Thus, the old England of rural, soldierly squirearchy, of stoic and noble gentlemen, of tradition and deference and Empire, dies. The film celebrates a special Anglo-American relationship, and desperately seeks to acknowledge an equality of effort and endeavor, but there can be no mistaking to whom the future belongs. Todd, a British officer, hero of North Africa, strides resolutely toward obliteration after having blooded his previously inexperienced American commandos. Brigadier Russell, rural gentry and warrior for Empire, puts a bullet through his brain rather than continue to live in his changed world.

The suggestion that, for the British, D-Day marked the end of something even offers a framework with which to explore one other important cultural representation of the allied landings: Darryl Zanuck's *The Longest Day* (1962), based on the popular history of the same name by Cornelius Ryan.[49] To be sure, in terms of production costs and screen writing, this was most certainly an American project that tried very hard to offer a reassuring vision of Western unity amidst the tensions of the Cold War. But once again the film leaves no doubt as to whom the future belongs: the United States. Nowhere is this more apparent than at the film's end. Thus, following lengthy scenes of British heroics at a bridge over the River Orne, French perseverance in a commando attack on the sea-port of Ouistreham, and American fortitude on Bloody Omaha, the film draws to a close with two characters—one American and the other British—discussing the cause and costs of the day, and the cause and costs of the war. The American is lost, confused and inexperienced, yet he is also young, energetic and keen. The Briton—played by Richard Burton—is older, wounded and crippled. Nearby is a dead German with his boots on the wrong feet. To the sounds of war in the distance, Burton offers his views on the meaning of all war. "Maybe it's always like this," he ponders, "he's dead, I'm crippled, you're lost." But this moment of melancholy is then displaced by the final scene: Robert Mitchum, as General Norman Cota, looks out over the battlefield of Omaha Beach, now firmly in American control, before joining the long procession of troops winding their way up the bluffs; in the background begins the title music, a jaunty, cheery, whistle.[50]

Figure 5: Richard Burton and Richard Beymer, *The Longest Day* (1962).

We should be wary of pushing this analysis too far, and *The Longest Day* in particular is too vast and multi-authored to reduce it to just one reading. Nonetheless, like *D-Day: Sixth of June*, Zanuck's popular historical epic marks the Allied landings, for the British, not as the start of a bright new future, but as an end. The former concludes with a Briton blown to pieces on the Normandy beach and the latter draws to a close with a grizzled veteran of the Battle of Britain crippled—from "knee to crotch"—in a field not far from the French shore. Here, in short, are cinematic visions of a transfer of power; the "torch" has been passed from "failing hands" to the energetic cousins across the Atlantic.

For contemporaries, this idea of a transfer of power was not simply a Hollywood plot contrivance. Indeed, evidence for its reality was more than apparent in the Suez Crisis of 1956, the event that marked the low point in postwar Anglo-American relations, and an event that only consolidated the premises behind the British-sponsored narrative of D-Day. Briefly, an anti-Western government in Egypt led by General Nasser initiated the nationalization of the Suez Canal, then under joint Anglo-French control. In response, the British and French governments issued an ultimatum demanding withdrawal, threatening military intervention if there was no response. When the ultimatum deadline passed, an Anglo-French invasion force was dispatched to retake the canal, but without first securing American support. In fact, the American government was not even consulted, despite, or perhaps because of, their concerns that interventions of this sort might taint the Western Allies with the brush of old style imperialism. As a result, when President Eisenhower did finally learn of the operation, he quickly demanded an Anglo-French withdrawal, on pain of economic sanctions. Fearing the consequences to their "special relationship," and still very much dependent on American economic aid, the British government soon agreed to a humiliating capitulation, and the troops came home.[51]

This is, of course, a familiar and rather basic description of the Suez Crisis. But of special interest here are two key issues which emerged during this Crisis. First, following President Nasser's decision to nationalize the Canal Zone the British and French, with Israeli support, decided to launch an amphibious and airborne invasion to reclaim the territory. Second, in response to concerted American pressure led by an outraged President Eisenhower this invasion was halted, and British and French troops ultimately withdrawn. An Anglo-French attempt to organize and execute a large-scale military operation independent of the United States ended, therefore, in response to a protest from the man who had commanded Overlord in

1944. Put differently, invading Suez only twelve years after invading Normandy showed just how far British power, in both political and military terms, had declined. Thus, in the very same year that *D-Day: Sixth of June* elegized an Anglo-American operation in which the forces of the British Empire possessed a position and role equivalent to the United States, British troops were *forced* to withdraw from an outpost of the Empire at American insistence. In doing so, the real and "reel" events of 1956 exposed the issues that made the British so attached to their narrative of D-Day: as British political and economic influence declined, as the Empire dissolved, and as British military capabilities ebbed, D-Day became a symbol of the last moment in which Britain had been "Great." As historian Jeffrey Walsh has succinctly explained: "If the ending of the Second World War is taken to signal the End of Empire, then D-Day, redolent with images of heroism and redemptive action, was its apotheosis."[52]

D-DAY, DUNKIRK AND THE "PEOPLE'S WAR": ADAPTING THE STORY IN THE 1960S AND 1970S

It was this idea of a great and glorious finale, together with the widespread publicity that accompanied the release of *The Longest Day* (1962), which ensured that D-Day continued to draw public and press interest in Britain in the 1960s. The visit to southern England by President Eisenhower in late 1963 (for the purposes of a D-Day documentary) received considerable comment in British newspapers, while a year later the anniversary commemorations in Normandy witnessed the return of hundreds of British veterans for memorial ceremonies and battlefield pilgrimages.[53] The British government was also well-represented that summer, seizing the moment to once again emphasize the theme of Anglo-American unity in the cause of Europe freedom. In fact, this British-sponsored narrative—which tended to accentuate the Anglo-American dimension at the expense of a more inclusive sense of Western unity—was bolstered by the return of cross-Channel tensions, as seen in President Charles de Gaulle's repeated use of the veto to prevent Britain from joining the Common Market. Tensions with a resurgent Gaullist France were also apparent in Washington, and relations were hardly then improved by de Gaulle's refusal to attend the 1964 proceedings in Normandy.[54] In this context, it was increasingly difficult to invoke D-Day as either an expression of Anglo-French or Franco-American solidarity. But an *Anglo-American* reading of the invasion still had real traction, particularly as de Gaulle persistently chose to lump together the British and Americans as simply the "Anglo-Saxons."[55] Little wonder that George Jellicoe, the 2d Earl Jellicoe and the official British representative at the ceremonies, was more than happy to play the role of devoted American ally. At one point, for example, he remarked that "there were enemies, the challenges of...tyranny, still at the gate, and they [America and Britain] must confront them as allies and comrades."[56] Similar expressions of faith in the Atlantic alliance followed five years later, during the twenty-fifth anniversary of the landings, and the British presence in Normandy was once again very prominent. A columnist in *The Times*, for instance, suggested that 6 June 1969, marked the "peak" of "another British Invasion of Normandy," this time by 1,000 active service personnel and many thousands more British D-Day veterans.[57] Significantly, de Gaulle's decision to withdraw the French military from NATO in 1966, and the subsequent eviction of all American troops from French soil, once again ensured that an Anglo-American narrative of the landings came to the fore.

The prominence of D-Day in 1960s British culture was also part and parcel of a growing popular interest in the wider experience of the war years, interest which now consolidated into a particular reading of the conflict: the People's War. Drawing upon images and ideas already present in the 1940s, and partly driven by a similar contemporary interest in the events and veterans of the Great War, just then drifting into history, this myth centered on key moments identified as expressive of British national character.[58] The evacuation of the British army from Dunkirk by an armada of "little ships" and the resilience of the ordinary folk when faced with German terror bombing during the Blitz were singled out for special attention; here were clear demonstrations of British resilience and fortitude in action.[59] The Battle of Britain, meanwhile, was the moment in which the people of the British Empire—led by the Few—stood alone and held the line against Nazi aggression. By the 1960s, this idea of a "People's War"—constructed, commemorated and celebrated in British popular culture—had emerged as the dominant framework within which many Briton's understood their war.

D-Day was not a natural fit within this framework: it was a purely military operation conducted without direct civilian input, and as a victorious offensive action it lacked the romantic qualities the British find so attractive in defense and defeats. Nonetheless, D-Day still found its place in the myth of the People's War. Some, for instance, were certainly content to see D-Day as an expression of national unity. Viscount Montgomery of Alamein once described the invasion of Nazi-occupied Normandy as a result of "the work and fortitude of the whole British nation."[60] But these efforts to find the Blitz spirit in Normandy were always rather strained. More successful were those attempts to mark D-Day's position in the chronology of Britain's war and, in particular, to establish it as the symbolic counterpoint to Dunkirk.[61] D-Day, in short, was the return that redeemed the retreat. Indeed, without D-Day, Dunkirk was *only* a defeat rather than a setback on the road to victory. This idea had a long-running history. As we know, Churchill had first initiated planning for D-Day in the immediate aftermath of the Dunkirk evacuation, and British newspapers frequently drew attention to the connection between these two events in their coverage of the Normandy landings. We recall also that the relationship between the evacuation of 1940 and the invasion of 1944 was implicit in the plot and structure of *D-Day: Sixth of June* (1956): both the British male leads—BG Russell and CAPT John Wynter—fight at Dunkirk, while the latter then returns to France on D-Day. Elsewhere, this very British reading of the Normandy landings was also apparent in several editions of the popular *War Picture Library* (1958) and *Commando* (1961) · series of children's comics. These comics often reveled in descriptions of Dunkirk heroes visiting vengeance on the German enemy in Normandy. Two editions from the *War Picture Library* are suggestive of this narrative approach. In *Up the Marines!*, for example, a lantern-jawed commando is seen storming a German pill-box on a Calvados cliff-top, while in *Close Range* Dunkirk veterans in the "Dartshires" charge across a Normandy beach in the "greatest military operation the world had ever known."[62] In the *Commando* series, meanwhile, among the many comics that took the Allied invasion as the subject matter the most arresting is surely *Operation Bulldog*, which centers on the deployment on D-Day of a rather ingenious form of secret weapon: the formidable partnership of PVT Knuckles MacNeil and his buddy, a British Bulldog.

By the 1960s, therefore, Britons had established a firm narrative of D-Day, albeit one which was fluid in the details of structure and shape. This narrative celebrated the Allied invasion of Normandy as, to varying degrees, an expression of Anglo-American and/or Anglo-French comradeship *and* a final demonstration of British Imperial might that redeemed the earlier evacuation from Dunkirk. Grounded in the history of the landings, constructed by press and politicians during the 1950s, and then deployed in various cultural media and commemorative ceremonies, this narrative was a sop to contemporary decline and imperial retreat. Little wonder that the first high-point of this narrative—in the1960s—occurred at the very moment that the Empire completed its dissolution.

Yet after this high-point, the 1970s then witnessed an apparent decline in British interest in D-Day. In 1971, efforts to establish the incomplete cathedral in Portsmouth as a memorial to the Allied landings were abandoned due to local opposition and a lack of funds: after six years of fundraising, only £65,000 of a target of £400,000 had been raised.[63] Even the thirtieth anniversary of D-Day in 1974 drew very little attention, to the extent that the BBC decided not to bother sending cameras to the ceremonies.[64] At least one correspondent to the *Times* actually complained about this lack of media interest in the D-Day events, while another correspondent suggested that it was due to "an attitude—sincere but determined—among younger people in the media that any publicity of any kind for such a thing as the thirtieth anniversary of D-Day acts as an advertisement *for* war."[65] Elsewhere, while pondering the reasons why the British media seemed to have lost interest in the anniversary, one columnist explained that it betokened "a feeling throughout broadcasting that the history of the war has had sufficient of an airing to be going on with—a feeling strengthened, possibly, by the experiences of the past few years."[66] As he continued:

> We look back to the war as a time of unity, of common objectives, of many rather cheering things which since have not been much in evidence, but which—or so it's tempting to believe—will come to our rescue as soon as we are again hard-pressed. And here we are again, hard-pressed, but differently, and finding ourselves at anything but one. Apparently the old formula will not do.[67]

The apparent failings of the "old formula" did not, however, prevent D-Day from being enlisted by contemporary Europhiles in the service of British membership in the European Community. Nor did it prevent the television series, *World at War*, being aired to popular acclaim in 1973-74.[68] In fact, after a successful 1975 vote in favor of Britain's continued membership in the EC, Home Secretary Roy Jenkins, chairman of the Campaign for Britain in Europe, declared that the positive response from the electorate represented "a second D-Day for British resurgence in Europe based not on sulky acquiescence but on enthusiastic co-operation."[69] Here was an echo of that other, older, reading of D-Day, a reading that marked it as an expression of Britain's commitment to Europe, and especially to France.

Even so, by the 1970s, such efforts to re-invigorate a Euro-centric understanding of Britain's D-Day remained on the margins, while in a more general sense D-Day had similarly faded from view. As in previous years, the reasons for D-Day's change in fortune lay in the contemporary context. Thus, while the 1950s was a good time to celebrate D-Day as an expression of Britain's commitment to the Anglo-French alliance, and while the political and cultural climate of the 1960s was remarkably conducive to the commemoration of Britain's Imperial role in a distinctly Anglo-American D-Day, the climate of 1970s was hostile to both ideas. In Britain, these were tough times: an oil crisis, economic depression, rising anti-European sentiment, social unrest, even race riots. It was in the 1970s, moreover, that the now widespread image of the First World War as a pointless conflict mired in mud, blood, and slaughter became increasingly prevalent.[70] Such ideas also affected contemporary understandings of the century's subsequent global catastrophe. These years also witnessed a growing peace movement in Britain, bolstered by recent anti-Vietnam war protests as well as increasing concerns regarding the presence of American nuclear weapons on British soil.[71] Toward the end of the 1970s, even the myth of a People's War was foundering in the face of Thatcherite attacks on the idea of "society." [72]

The extent to which these circumstances affected D-Day as myth and memory is most apparent in the film about the Normandy landings produced by the Imperial War Museum in 1975. Titled *Overlord*, this film is a moving mixture of wartime documentary footage, a haunting score, and dramatized depictions of key stages in the training of a British soldier destined to land in Normandy.[73] In many respects, it is rather enigmatic and defies easy description or summary. It is not just a documentary, but nor is it only a conventional feature film. It might best be understood as a memorial on celluloid. The story *Overlord* tells centers upon the enlistment and training of Pvt. Thomas Beddows, a young, lower middle-class Englishman conscripted into the army sometime in 1943-44. We see Pvt. Beddows' introduction to military life, his training for war, his mistakes and minor misdemeanors, his yearning for female companionship. But we do not see a hero convinced of the righteousness of his cause, nor do we see a traditional martial male ready and willing to die on the beaches of Normandy. Indeed, throughout Pvt. Beddows seems rather fatalistic, innocent, confused, and uncertain. The somber tone of the film is also accentuated by a musical score that remains decidedly melancholic throughout, especially when it is used to accompany frequent documentary images of the death and destruction wrought by the war. And the film does not follow Beddows from the beaches of Normandy to the *bocage* of the interior. Instead, our protagonist is killed in a landing craft just as he is nearing the Norman coast. He never even sets foot on the beach. With his death, the film ends. As such, *Overlord* finishes before the invasion has even properly begun. Moreover, the very final scene is not of liberated Paris, nor of conquered Berlin, nor is it of Beddow's sacrifice redeemed by the worthiness of the cause; the final scene is of a ruined, crumbling, derelict castle somewhere in the British uplands. In the background, orchestral strings play a mournful musical eulogy.

Such a somber view of the Allied invasion of Normandy and the British role in this operation makes sense when understood within the context of the 1970s. Yet in its essentials, this view of the Normandy landings also conforms to the one of the key commemorative themes already established in the immediate post-war period: that the 6 June marked the beginning of the end for British power, prestige and vitality. Thus, although very different in terms of plot and overall structure, and while indicative of the historical specifics within which they were produced, *D-Day: Sixth of June* (1956), *The Longest Day* (1962), and *Overlord* (1975) are all united in their vision of what the Normandy landings represented for Britain: an end.

THE EMPIRE STRIKES BACK:
D-DAY, THE FALKLANDS, AND THE GULF, C. 1982–2009

Just a few years after the release of *Overlord*, however, changed circumstances would once again return an Imperial and Anglo-American reading of D-Day to the fore. The catalyst for this shift was the Falklands War, an event that challenged the idea of British military decline so visible at Suez in 1956, and an event that returned the Anglo-American special relationship to prominence. Indeed, for the government of Prime Minister Margaret Thatcher the conflict with Argentina over the sovereignty of the Falklands represented a test of American commitment to the "special relationship": would the United States stand with its "special" friend across the Atlantic? Or would they support their New World compatriots, the Argentineans? Ultimately, of course, the Reagan administration sided with their ideological fellow travelers in Thatcher's Conservative government, even to the extent that the US Air Force secretly supplied the latest sidewinder air-to-air missiles to the Sea Harriers of the Royal Navy's Fleet Air Arm.

Thus, whereas in 1956 American pressure had forced Britain to withdraw its troops from an outpost of the old Empire, in 1982 the British government, through skillful diplomacy, managed to secure American support for Imperial intervention, even despite the fact that the Falklands lay within the domain traditionally claimed by the Monroe Doctrine. And with this demonstration of Anglo-American unity secured, the prism through which the rest of the conflict was refracted in Britain was, of course, World War II. After all, the key components were in place: an attack on the Empire; the repatriation of a defeated Royal Marines garrison; a declaration of resolution and commitment to the liberation of the islands; a Royal Navy fleet transporting troops; a departure from the south coast of England; a Prime Minister all too keen to appropriate the mantle of Churchill; an enemy governed by a fascist military dictatorship suppressing the democratic right to self-determination of the freedom-loving British Falkland Islanders. Even the landscape seemed willing to meet the expectations of a very British script. For despite being located deep in the South Atlantic, 8,000 miles from London, the windswept and rocky Falklands Islands looked reassuringly British and thus could readily accommodate the rhetoric and propaganda originally deployed in the defense of Blighty in the 1940s.[74]

As a result, "almost every aspect of the conflict over the islands was compared with that earlier struggle [the Second World War]."[75] Historian Mark Connelly notes, for example, that contemporary press reports identified the Royal Navy's outnumbered Harrier pilots as the "new few," while the battle at Goose Green—where a battalion of British paratroopers defeated a numerically superior Argentinean enemy—"was the new Dunkirk and Battle of Britain rolled into one."[76] And once this victory was won, as John Ramsden has explained, "the British people enjoyed street parties arranged in deliberate imitation of those held by their parents and grandparents in 1945." The official celebrations even concluded with "the return from retirement of one of the leading Second World War singers, Dame Vera Lynn," leading a rendition of "We'll Meet Again."[77] Hardly surprising, then, that the amphibious deployment of British troops at San Carlos Bay was explicitly "framed by references to 6 June 1944."[78] The BBC's Robert Fox went so far as to report that the British landing craft went in "exactly according to the D-Day model," while a couple of weeks after the landings the *Daily Mirror* happily conflated 1940 and 1944 by declaring that the British Task Force had commemorated the thirty-eighth anniversary of the Normandy invasion by subjecting the Argentinean army to a "D-Day Blitz."[79]

This reciprocal relationship between the Falklands and World War II secured still firmer footings just two years later, during the fortieth anniversary of D-Day. The London *Times*, for instance, editorialized that the Normandy landings marked the "zenith of achievement for the Anglo-American wartime partnership"; a partnership which American assistance during the recent Falklands campaign—abundant and informal—demonstrated was still alive and well.[80] Similarly, for those Britons who watched a flotilla of ships depart Portsmouth to attend the proceedings in Normandy the point of reference was likewise the Falklands Task Force of 1982. The official British delegation—headed by the Queen—even lingered at Portsmouth in order to visit a special Royal Navy exhibition all about the "1982 San Carlos landings in the Falklands campaign."[81] The details of British attendance at the commemorative ceremonies only reinforced this past-present connection. At Ranville, British paratroopers—most of whom the daily press identified as veterans of the battle at Goose Green—performed a re-enactment drop of the 1944 airborne operation.[82] At Arromanches-les-bains, meanwhile, Royal Marines veterans of the San Carlos landings stormed ashore through the Normandy surf. And throughout it all, Prime Minister Thatcher, fresh from assuming the mantle of Churchill, reveled in the photo opportunities provided by massed ranks of Normandy *and* Falklands veterans.

This past-present connection even duly worked its way into British military historiography. John Keegan's acclaimed history of D-Day and the Normandy campaign—*Six Armies in Normandy* (1982)—was published in the very same year that British television screens were dominated by the fighting in the cold, grey South

Atlantic. Similarly, Max Hastings, perhaps the most commercially successful British historian of the Allied landings, published his history—*Overlord*—in 1984. This was shortly after he had attended the commemorative events in Normandy, and just two years after he had yomped through the peat bogs of the Falklands as a war correspondent with the *London Evening Standard*.[83] Hastings' foreword to the 1984 edition of *Overlord* even acknowledged the debt of understanding he owed to the Falklands conflict. As he explained:

> One morning early in April 1982, I was sitting at my desk in Northamptonshire seeking to make the leap of imagination that is essential to books of this kind, to conceive what it was like to crouch in a landing craft approaching a hostile shore at dawn on 6 June 1944. By an extraordinary fluke of history, less than two months later I found myself crouched in a British landing craft 8,000 miles away. In the weeks that followed, I had an opportunity to witness an amphibious campaign whose flavor any veteran of June 1944 would immediately have recognized...[84]

To be sure, despite this preface, Hastings' history then proceeded to pay little heed to the demonstration of British military professionalism he had just witnessed in the South Atlantic; *Overlord*, in fact, is rather in awe of German military prowess, frequently finding the Anglo-American soldier to be lacking in energy, ability and initiative.[85] Nonetheless, it was in this post-Falklands twilight that a British narrative of D-Day that reveled in the themes of Imperial power and Anglo-American comradeship became a secure feature of the nation's commemorative landscape. Indeed, such was the extent to which the fortieth anniversary events pivoted around celebrations of that comradeship, that one resident of Devon—Ken Small—was even inspired to re-double his commemorative efforts on behalf of the 946 American servicemen killed during Exercise Tiger, a D-Day training exercise, in April 1944. Three years later, in 1987, his long-running campaign to have the American dead marked with a suitable memorial finally came to fruition on the beach near Slapton Sands: the memorial took the form of a Sherman Tank, itself a victim of the Exercise, raised from the seabed. Ronald Reagan, no less, wrote a letter of thanks to Small on behalf of the people of the United States.[86]

Two other factors further aided the consolidation of D-Day's position in British culture in the 1980s: the aging of the World War II generation, and the emergence, during the Reaganite New Cold War, of a resurgent American interest in the landings. Like the passing of the Great War generation in the 1960s, the former issue prompted renewed commemorative attention directed toward the events of the war as veterans, now retired and reflecting on their youth, returned to the past. Seen in this context, the efforts by one old soldier to establish a nationwide Normandy Veterans Association in 1985 make perfect sense.[87] So, too, do the energetic commemorative activities of organizations like the Suffolk Regiment Association, whose members made several pilgrimages to Normandy in the 1980s and 1990s in order to revisit old friends and build new memorials.[88] Meanwhile, growing American interest in the events of 6 June—partly the product of post-Vietnam soul-searching, and partly an aspect of Reagan's Cold War mission—ensured that D-Day now had global media exposure while also providing the stimulus for a British response for fear that the D-Day story would be overly Americanized.[89]

The opening of Britain's purpose-built D-Day museum at Portsmouth in 1984 amply demonstrates this response; it explicitly connects the origins of D-Day to the "dark days" of Dunkirk, and special space is even devoted to housing the commemorative tapestry of the landings originally produced in the 1950s.[90] Significantly, too, plans for the museum were developed *during* the 1982 conflict in the South Atlantic. In late May 1982—just days after British troops landed in San Carlos—it was publicly announced that part of the museum's role would be to tell the story of Portsmouth's military and naval history, "from 1860....to the Falklands conflict."[91] Just a few years later, British determination to prevent the story of the Normandy landings being overly Americanized was again apparent in veterans' efforts to ensure that a new museum established in Caen provided a suitably "Allied" take on D-Day. According to one reporter, there had been concern among the British veterans' community that "the

Americans, with strong financial backing, were trying to re-write history and eclipse the British role in the invasion." But skillful lobbying, together with the donation of numerous British exhibits, had ensured that visitors to the new museum would be "left in no doubt about the success of a hard-fought British campaign."[92] Indeed, while the 1980s witnessed a resurgence of an Anglo-American D-Day in the pronouncements of politicians, British veterans—concerned about being overshadowed by their American counter-parts—have frequently sustained an Anglo-French reading of the landings, a reading which emphasizes the ties joining England and France, and the ties joining veterans and Normans. This is certainly the idea implicit to many of the memorials veterans have erected with local support in Normandy.[93] Thus, the human life-cycle and the cultural politics of Anglo-American relations worked in concert with post-Falklands national optimism to secure D-Day's place in British culture.

By the 1990s, moreover, contemporary international politics provided further succor to this British narrative of D-Day. In 1989-90, the collapse of the Berlin Wall and the end of the Cold War ensured that Anglo-American culture could finally embrace the victory of World War II without restraint. Here, in short, was a firm conclusion to a narrative left dangling in 1945. Even better, just a year later this conclusion was successfully re-enacted during the eviction of the Iraqi military from Kuwait. Indeed, for President George H.W. Bush one of the most attractive results of the Gulf War was that it enabled Americans—so he claimed—to rid themselves of the infectious and debilitating Vietnam Syndrome by providing a reassuring military victory more akin to those won during World War II.[94] Memories of an unpopular and unilateralist war in Southeast Asia were thus to be replaced with far more attractive images of an American-led *alliance* visiting destruction upon the armed might of a mustachioed military dictator. In Britain, meanwhile, the national press delighted in the military significance of the British contribution to this alliance, the largest after the United States, finding particular pride in the fact that the American general in overall command—Norman Schwarzkopf—seemed to value the opinion of his British subordinate,

Gen. Sir Peter de la Billiere, above that of any other allied officer.[95] As if in tune with Britain's D-Day story, Schwarzkopf even placed some of his American troops under British operational command, the first time this had happened since 1945.[96]

It was in this post-Falklands, post-Cold War, and post-Gulf War context that Britons celebrated the fiftieth anniversary of D-Day in 1994. Just like in 1984, the Prime Minister, now John Major, and Queen Elizabeth II were both in attendance at the Normandy ceremonies, and this time there was also considerable commemorative activity in Britain itself. New D-Day memorials were unveiled in Southsea and Southwick, trees were planted to mark Eisenhower's headquarters at Bushy Park, a Dunkirk-like flotilla of ships escorted the Royal Yacht across the Channel, and thousands of military re-enactors descended on the towns and villages of the south coast.[97] BBC news even took to reporting on D-Day as though it were a contemporary event. Special bulletins, for example, featured present-day journalists and newscasters reporting on the progress on the beaches. (A similar idea shaped efforts to mark the sixty-ninth anniversary of the landings in 2013: Channel Four produced a live twenty-four hour docudrama of the landings, using original D-Day footage and fronted by Peter Snow with the help of historians and military experts; it was aired in "real time" between 5 and 6 June.)[98] Meanwhile, British newspapers published detailed guides regarding the various ceremonies and events, and some even included special commemorative reprints of their editions from 7 June 1944.[99] A month later, therefore, when the caravan of the Tour de France crossed the Channel through the recently completed Tunnel for its first visit to Britain in twenty years, everything was in place to ensure that it could be celebrated as a re-enactment of the allied landings. Indeed, once the English stages of the race were complete, the Tour director—Jean-Marie Leblanc—deliberately returned the teams to France by ferry "as a tribute to the *débarquements* of 1944."[100] Hardly surprising, given all this interest and activity, that in the aftermath of the anniversary English Heritage initiated efforts to identify, assess, and protect all those sites in Britain connected to the landings.[101] Nor should we be surprised to learn that by the early twenty-first century a trip to the Normandy beaches had become almost de rigueur for many British schoolchildren, and indeed for many British tourists. The guide to the Normandy battlefields written by the redoubtable Major and Mrs. Holt has now gone through six editions since it was first published in 1999.[102]

The sixtieth and sixty-fifth anniversaries witnessed similar popular interest in D-Day, particularly as the era of war tourism and commercial commemoration had now firmly come of age.[103] In June 2004, British newspapers again carried numerous reports about the anniversary events, the Imperial War Museum (Duxford) hosted a themed "D-Day week," and the BBC screened a well-received docu-drama titled *D-Day: 6.6.44* (with a hint at the renewed viability—in the age of a Labour government—of the People's War myth, it was subtitled "The Dramatic Story of Ordinary People.")[104] Meanwhile, several media commentators pondered the continuing signifi-cance the British attached to D-Day. Writing in the *Observer*, the historian Tristram Hunt confidently remarked that for the British "D-Day stands for many things—the proud history of British mili-tarism and ingenuity, our sea-faring culture...The Atlanticist spirit [...]."[105] Among the British political establishment, of course, this "Atlanticist spirit" had once again found a new resonance amidst the American-led war on terror and the invasion of Iraq, again, essen-tially an Anglo-American affair.

But if this was all rather familiar, there was also something new emerging. For by 2004, aspects of Britain's D-Day story had also taken a strange post-modern twist, with attendance at the sixtieth anniver-sary led by a Prime Minister—Tony Blair—intent on appropriating a Thatcherite appropriation of Churchill. For where victory in the South Atlantic had given Thatcher her D-Day and her Churchillian moment, Blair hoped to find his Falklands and, by implication, his D-Day, in the Anglo-American invasion of Iraq. For Blair, then, the 2004 commemorations of D-Day were attractive as a means to invoke memories of the wartime Grand Alliance *and* more recent memo-ries of the Falklands. This was the place of D-Day in British memory by the early twenty-first century. Mixed and meshed with memories of the South Atlantic and reshaped by Britain's return to overseas military intervention (the Gulf, Iraq, Afghanistan, Sierra Leone), D-Day could be deployed by politicians to reassure Briton's of their "great" wartime past, while also reminding them of the extent to which they could still find that greatness in the present, particularly when they went into battle with the time-honored American ally. As Blair himself was reported as saying: "D-Day for me is a symbol of the liberation of Europe, the strength of the British and American alliance and the change in Europe since the Second World War. It is a celebration of all those things. So it is a tremendously uplifting and optimistic commemoration."[106] Anticipating this Blairite appropriation of the D-Day past in an attempt to lend legitimacy to the controversial Anglo-American wars of the present, one aggrieved *Guardian* columnist pointedly declared, however, that "Bush's war has nothing to do with the spirit of D-Day."[107]

In the early twenty-first century, therefore, a British narrative of D-Day remains alive and well. Take, for instance, the sustained interest among British publishers and public in popular histories of the allied landings: Robin Neillands, *D-Day, 1944: Voices from Normandy* (1993); Stephen Ambrose, *D-Day: June 6, 1944* (1994); Robert Kershaw, *D-Day: Piercing the Atlantic Wall* (1994); David Stafford, *Ten Days to D-Day: Countdown to the Liberation of Europe* (2003); Martin Gilbert *D-Day* (2004); Andrew Williams, *D-Day to Berlin* (2004).[108] So, too, many of these histories privilege a rather Anglo-centric reading of the events. Thus, Martin Gilbert's narrative lingers on the idea that the success of the landings owed much to a British predilection for technical ingenuity and skill in the work of deceit and distraction, while the structure of David Stafford's history actually focuses explicitly on events *in* Britain during the days before the invasion.[109] Seen in this light, Anthony Beevor's recent (2009) history of the landings is but the latest in a well-established historiographical trend, although it must be noted that it also represents an attempt explicitly to challenge aspects of the American and Ambrosian narrative of the landings that came to the fore in the late 1990s.[110]

Elsewhere, contemporary British interest in the Normandy landings is more than apparent in the tone and tenor of responses to the release of *Saving Private Ryan* (1998) and *Band of Brothers* (2001), together with the tabloid outrage that followed the initial French failure to invite the Queen to the D-Day commemorations in June 2009. For several media commentators, the two Spielberg projects represented an attempt to Americanize the D-Day story and entirely eliminate the British role.[111] Indeed, these complaints, first raised in response to *Saving Private Ryan*, ensured that shortly before the release of *Band of Brothers* public relations executives took great care to make it clear that while American soldiers took center stage, the series was nonetheless a joint Anglo-American production (by HBO and the BBC), filmed in Britain, with many of the leading characters played by British actors.[112] In a similar vein, much of the tabloid press saw the 2009 "snub" as a cynical and Anglophobic attempt to recast the landings as solely an expression of Franco-American solidarity. The royalist *Daily Mail* even declared that the French government's failure to invite the Queen to the commemorative ceremonies in Normandy was not simply a regrettable neglect of diplomatic etiquette; rather, it was nothing less than an "insult" to all Commonwealth troops buried along the Calvados coast; she is, after all, the head of state of both Britain and Canada.[113] In both cases, the controversy was the extent to which the vision of D-Day offered for public consumption flew in the face of the narrative of the landings that Britons had been constructing and re-constructing since the 1950s. Simply put, neither Spielberg's 1998 film nor Sarkozy's 2009 guest list acknowledged the *British* story of D-Day.

Moreover, if left unchallenged, such Franco-American neglect of the British D-Day story might unravel the wider narrative of the nation's war experience. In popular memory, which remains stubbornly Euro-centric, Britain's war begins with a principled stand against German aggression in Poland, it then moves through the defeat and despair that accompanied Dunkirk until a moment of supreme heroism by the Few secures a reprieve from the threat of invasion. Bombing and Blitz follow, before American entry into the conflict and victory at El Alamein turn the tide. On 6 June 1944, the forces of the British Empire then return to the Continent and, with the American ally, begin the destruction of the Nazi war machine in

Western Europe. Final victory against Germany follows within the year. D-Day, therefore, occupies a crucial position in British memories of World War II. All stories need a satisfying conclusion, and for the British, D-Day is just that—a reassuring end to the nation's war story. For in place of a postwar picture of decline and retreat, commemorating D-Day privileges the idea of a selfless sacrifice for France; of Dunkirk redeemed; of Imperial might unleashed; and of blood brotherhood with the cousins beyond the sea. To question, challenge or undermine Britain's D-Day, therefore, is to tamper with the grand conclusion to a story of World War II, and of Empire, deeply entrenched in British memory.

NOTES

1. The author would like to thank Nicola Bishop, Michael Dolski, John Buckley and the staff at the Centre for Historical Research at the University of Wolverhampton for their comments and criticisms on earlier drafts of this chapter.

2. *The Mail on Sunday*, 16 Nov. 2003.

3. Three good general discussions of British memory of World War II are: Mark Connelly, *We Can Take It! Britain and the Memory of the Second World War* (London: Pearson, 2004); Lucy Noakes, *War and the British: Gender, Memory and National Identity* (London: I. B. Tauris, 1998); Malcolm Smith, *Britain and 1940: History, Myth and Popular Memory* (London: Routledge, 2000). Although not yet published when this book went to press, judging from the names of the editors and the list of contributors involved, another new publication about British war memory looks set to be a valuable addition to this field of study: see Lucy Noakes and Juliette Pattison, *British Cultural Memory and the Second World War* (London: Continuum, 2013). See also Geoff Eley, "Finding the People's War: Film, British Collective Memory, and World War II," *American Historical Review* 106 (2001), 818–38; John Ramsden, "Myths and Realities of the 'People's War' in Britain," in *Experience and Memory: The Second World War in Europe*, eds. Jorg Echternkamp and Stefan Martens, 40–52 (Oxford: Berghahn, 2010); Mark Connelly, "'We Can Take It!' Britain and the Memory of the Home Front in the Second World

War," in eds., Echternkamp and Martens, *Experience and Memory*, 53–69. For a discussion of Dunkirk in British memory, see Penny Summerfield, "Dunkirk and the Popular Memory of Britain at War, 1940–58," *Journal of Contemporary History* 45 (2010), 788–811; Penny Summerfield, "Divisions at Sea: Class, Gender, Race and Nation in Maritime Films of the Second World War, 1939–60," *Twentieth Century British History* 22 (2011), 330–53. For details about efforts to commemorate the Battle of Britain and the RAF, see Garry Campion, *The Good Fight: Battle of Britain Propaganda and the Few* (Basingstoke: Palgrave Macmillan, 2009); Paul Addison and Jeremy A. Crang, eds., *The Burning Blue: A New History of the Battle of Britain* (Pimlico: London, 2000), esp. 163–263; Martin Francis, *The Flyer: British Culture and the Royal Air Force, 1939–1945* (Oxford: Oxford University Press, 2008). For the place of the Home Guard in British Memory, see Penny Summerfield and Corinna Peniston-Bird, *Contesting Home Defence: Men, Women, and the Home Guard in the Second World War* (Manchester: Manchester University Press, 2007). For the Blitz, see Lucy Noakes, "Making Histories: Experiencing the Blitz in London's Museums in the 1990s," in *War and Memory in the Twentieth Century*, eds., Martin Evans and Ken Lunn, 89–104 (Oxford: Berg, 1997); Angus Calder, *The Myth of the Blitz* (London: Cape, 1991); Graham Dawson and B. West, "Our Finest Hour? The Popular Memory of World War Two and the Struggle over National Identity", in *National Fictions: World War II in British Films and Television*, ed., G. Hurd, 8–13 (London: BFI Books, 1984).

4.   For some details about the place of the Holocaust in British memory, see Judith Petersen, "How British Television Inserted the Holocaust into Britain's War Memory in 1995," *Historical Journal of Film, Radio and Television* 21, no. 3 (2001), 255–72.

5.   For a discussion of the problematic legacy of Bomber Command, see Mark Connelly, *Reaching for the Stars: A New History of Bomber Command in World War II* (London: I. B. Tauris, 2001), esp. 137–57. For information about the Bomber Command Memorial, dedicated in June 2012, see Robin Gibb, Steve Darlow, and Jim Dooley, *The Bomber Command Memorial: We Will Remember Them* (London: Fighting High, 2013).

6.   See the second quotation at the very start of this chapter. Robert Ryan, *After Midnight* (London: Review, 2005), 23. As Ryan's character suggests, the fighting in Italy, culminating with the fall of Rome on 5 June 1944, was

quickly side-lined by the campaign in Normandy. The events in Asia and in the Pacific Theatre of operations have been even more overlooked, with the British formation that fought in Burma (the 14th Army) known as the "Forgotten Army." That is not to say, however, that the war against Japan has failed to attract *any* attention in British culture. See, for example, the popularity of films such as *The Bridge on the River Kwai*, dir. David Lean (Columbia Pictures Corporation, 1957) 161 min., as well as the television comedy *It Ain't Half Hot Mum*, created by Jimmy Perry and David Croft(British Broadcasting Corporation, 1974–1981), 56 eps. But popular memory of the war in Britain nonetheless remains heavily Euro-centric.

7. Eley, 818–38.

8. See, "Mountbatten, Admiral Lord Louis," in ed., I. C. B. Dear, *The Oxford Companion to the Second World War* (Oxford: Oxford University Press, 1995), 763. For details about the Allied invasion, especially regarding the plans and approach, see Carlo D'Este, *Decision in Normandy* (Old Saybrook, CT: Konecky and Konecky, 1994). See also Olivier Wieviorka, *Normandy: The Landings to the Liberation of Paris*, trans. by M. B. DeBevoise (Cambridge, MA: The Belknap Press of Harvard University Press, 2008), 182–200.

9. See, "COSSAC," Ibid., 272–73.

10. See, "Overlord," Ibid., 848.

11. Ibid., 848–51.

12. Ibid., 853.

13. Max Hastings, *Overlord: From D-Day to the Liberation of Paris* (London: Pam Books, 1999), 35.

14. Indeed, one recent history of the battle for Omaha Beach suggests that one of the key problems behind the strategic concept of the landings was precisely its "Anglo-American" qualities. That is, the overall strategy was neither a true reflection of the American "way" of war, nor of the British way. Hence it was, at root, a fudge that tried to accommodate the strategic visions and tactical capabilities of two very different militaries. See Adrian R. Lewis, *Omaha Beach: A Flawed Victory* (London: The History Press, 2004).

15. See, "Overlord," *Oxford Companion to the Second World War*, 853.

16. Hastings, *Overlord* (1999), 27.

17. See James Chapman, "'The Yanks Are Shown to Such Advantage': Anglo-American Rivalry in the Production of the 'True Glory'(1945)," *Historical Journal of Film, Radio and Television* 16, no. 4(1996), 541–42.

18. Ibid.

19. Winston S. Churchill, "Statements to the House of Commons on the Liberation of Rome and the Landings in France, Jun 6 and 8, 1944," in *The War Speeches of the Right Honourable Winston S. Churchill*, vol. 3,ed. Charles Eade (London: Cassell, 1964), 157; *The Times*, 7 June 1944, 4.

20. Quoted in Mark Connelly, *We Can Take It!* (London: Pearson, 2004), 218. For a detailed discussion of British documentary footage of the D-Day landings, see Michael Paris, "Reconstructing D-Day: 6 June 1944 and British documentary films," in ed., John Buckley, *The Normandy Campaign: Sixty Years On* (Abingdon, Oxon: Routledge, 2006), 201–12. See also Michael Paris, "Picturing D-Day," *History Today* 54 (2004).

21. *The Daily Mirror*, 7 June 1944, 3.

22. Ibid.

23. *The Times*, 7 June 1944, 4.

24. Ibid, 5.

25. John Keegan, *Six Armies in Normandy: From D-Day to the Liberation of Paris*(London: Pimlico, 2004), 18–19.

26. Hastings, *Overlord* (1999), 35.

27. See Carlo D'Este, *Warlord: A Life of Churchill at War, 1874–1945* (London: Allen Lane, 2009), 759–766. See also Wieviorka, *Normandy*, 182–200.

28. *The Times*, 7 June 1945, 4.For details, see Kate Lemay's chapter in this volume.

29. *The Times*, 7 June 1948, 4; *The Times*, 7 June 1948, 8, and *The Times*, 7 Dec. 1948, 6.

30. Pierre-Laurent Pizy, "Commémorations du débarquement de la bataille de Normandie à travers le journal *Ouest-France* (1954–1994)," Mémoire de maitrise, Université de Caen (2003), 95.

31. *The Times*, 16 May 1951, 2.

32. For details about the origins of this museum, see Celebration of 10th Anniversary of D-day landings in Normandy: Opening of Mulberry Harbour Exhibition at Arromanches-les-bains, 1954: FO 371/112815, National Archives, London. See also CAB 21/3250: French establishment of a museum to commemorate D-Day landing: request for information about units of British Army, 1952–53, NA, London. Today, the museum is one of the key visitor attractions in Normandy. It includes exhibits of military uniforms and equipment, but the centerpiece is a display about

the Mulberry Harbor, the rusting remains of which can be seen through a special viewing window.

33. *The Times*, 7 June 1954, 6.

34. William Fotheringham, *Roule Britannia: Great Britain and the Tour de France* (London: Yellow Jersey Press, 2012), 23.

35. *The Times*, 7 June 1947, 4 and *The Times*, 7 June 1954, 6.

36. See correspondence between the British Embassy, Paris, and the Western and Southern Department of the Foreign Office, 24 Apr. 1954. Ceremonies to celebrate the 10th Anniversary of D-day landings in Normandy: FO 371/112818, NA, London.

37. For an example of this British-centered approach to the landings in postwar historiography, see David Howarth, *Dawn of D-Day: These Men Were There, 6 June 1944* (London: Collins, 1959; London: Greenhill and Mechanicsburg, PA: Stackpole Books, 2001). See also John Frayn Turner, *Invasion '44: The Full Story of D-Day* (London: George G. Harrap & Co. Ltd., 1959). For a discussion of Canadian efforts to assert their role in D-Day, particularly through commemoration, see "D-Day in Canadian Memory," by Terry Copp and Matt Symes in this volume.

38. The only French combat troops involved in the D-Day landings were Free French Commandos, members of No. 4 Commando of the British Army. They landed at Sword Beach under the command of Phillipe Kieffer. During the battles of 1944–45, however, most Free French forces served under American command, and were supplied with American equipment.

39. Winston S. Churchill, "Statements to the House of Commons on the Liberation of Rome and the Landings in France, June 6 and 8, 1944," in ed., Eade, 158

40. For some details about the post-1945 work of the IWGC, see P. Longworth, *The Unending Vigil: A History of the Commonwealth War Graves Commission, 1916–1967* (London: Constable, 1967), 187–213. For full details about the Commission's cemeteries in Calvados, see the Commission's website, accessed 6 Aug. 2012, http://www.cwgc.org/.

41. Chester Wilmot, *The Struggle for Europe* (London: Collins, 1952).

42. Field Marshal The Viscount Montgomery of Alamein, *Normandy to the Baltic* (London: Hutchinson and Co., 1947). Montgomery did, however, attempt to offset claims of a British bias by including a sentimental foreword in which

he proclaimed his belief in the fighting ability of the American soldier. See v–vi.

43. Dwight D. Eisenhower, *Crusade in Europe* (London: Heinemann, Ltd., 1948).

44. *D-Day the Sixth of June*, dir. Henry Koster, (Twentieth Century-Fox, 1956; Twentieth Century-Fox Home Entertainment, 2002), DVD, 106 min.

45. Lionel Shaprio, *D-Day: Sixth of June* (London: Collins, 1955).

46. For the details of British decline in the immediate postwar period, see Peter Clark, *The Last Thousand Days of the British Empire* (New York: Bloomsbury Press, 2012).

47. Winston Churchill, quoted in David Reynolds, "Rethinking Anglo-American Relations," *International Affairs* 65 (Winter, 1988–1989), 94.

48. The historiography of the Anglo-American Special Relationship is volumi-nous. See, for example, H. C. Allen, *The Anglo-American Relationship Since 1783* (London: A & C Black, 1959); C. J. Bartlett, *"The Special Relationship": A Political History of Anglo-American Relations Since 1945* (London: Longman, 1992); John Dumbrell, *A Special Relationship: Anglo-American Relations from the Cold War to Iraq* (London: Palgrave Macmillan, 2006); W. R. Louis and H. Bull, *The Special Relationship: Anglo-American Relations Since 1945* (New York: Oxford University Press, 1986); Kathleen Burke, *Old World, New World: The Story of Britain and America* (London: Abacus, 2009). A useful survey of this historiography can be found in Reynolds, 89–111, and Alex Danchev, *On Specialness: Essays in Anglo-American Relations* (*St. Anthony's Series*)(London: Palgrave Macmillan, 1998), 1–13.

49. Cornelius Ryan, *The Longest Day* (New York: Simon and Schuster, 1959).

50. *The Longest Day*, dir. Ken Annakin, Andrew Marton, Bernhard Wicki and Darryl F. Zanuck, (Darryl F. Zanuck Productions, Inc., and Twentieth Century-Fox Film Corporation, 1962; Twentieth Century Fox Home Entertainment, 2006), DVD, 178 min.

51. For a discussion of the American response to the Suez Crisis, see Walter LaFeber, *The American Age: US Foreign Policy at Home and Abroad, 1750 to the Present* (London: W. .W. Norton & Company, 1994), 556–60. For a more detailed history of the crisis, see W. S. Lucas, *Divided We Stand: Britain, the US and the Suez Crisis* (London: Hodder and Stoughton, 1991).

52. Jeffrey Walsh, "Remembering Desert Storm: Popular Culture and the Gulf War," in *War and Memory*, eds. Martin Evans and Ken Lunn, 205.

53. For a reference to the British response see, for instance, *Look*, 25 Feb. 1964, United States Army Military History Institute, Louis Lisko papers. See also *The Times*, 4 August 1963, 7. For the Eisenhower documentary, which was eventually screened in the United States during the twentieth anniversary commemorations, see *D-Day Plus 20 Years: Eisenhower Returns to Normandy*, (CBS Reports, Columbia Broadcasting Systems, Inc., 1964 (filmed Aug. 1963), Ambrose Video Publishing, Inc.), VHS, CFDM, 123 min.; *The Times*, 8 June 1964, 8, 10.

54. For a more detailed discussion of Franco-American tensions during the 1964 commemorations, see Kate Lemay's chapter in this volume.

55. For details about de Gaulle's use of the phrase "Anglo-Saxons" when discussing the American and British, see John Newhouse, *De Gaulle and the Anglo-Saxons* (London: Andre Deutsch, 1970); Andrew Pitt, "A Changing Anglo-Saxon Myth: Its Development and Function in French Political Thought, 1860–1914," *French History* 14 (2000), 150–73.

56. *The Times*, 8 June 1964, 10.

57. *The Times*, 7 June 1969, 1.

58. For a discussion of the wartime origins of this myth, see Michael Paris, *Warrior Nation: Images of War in British Popular Culture*, 1850–2000 (London: Reaktion Books, 2000), 186–221. See also Connelly, *We Can Take It!* (London: Pearson, 2004), 156–93. The phrase and idea of a "People's War" consolidated in the years before and after the publication of Angus Calder's *The People's War: Britain, 1939–1945* (London: Jonathan Cape, 1969).

59. See, for example, two popular feature films of this era: *Dunkirk*, dir. Leslie Norman (Ealing Studios, 1958), 134 min. and *Battle of Britain*, dir. Guy Hamilton (Spitfire Studios, 1969), 132 min. For details about the place of Dunkirk in British memory, see Summerfield, "Dunkirk and the Popular Memory," 788–811. For the Blitz and British memory, see Noakes, "Making Histories," in *War and Memory*, eds. Evans and Lunn, 89–104; Calder, *The Myth of the Blitz* (London: Cape, 1991); Dawson and West, "Our Finest Hour?" in *National Fictions*, ed. Hurd.

60. Viscount Montgomery, quoted in *The Times*, 7 June 1948, 4.

61. John Frayn Turner even begins his history of the Normandy invasion with a chapter on Dunkirk and Dieppe. See Turner, *Invasion*, 13–22.

62. See Connelly, *We Can Take It!* (London: Pearson, 2004), 234–39. For *Up the Marines* and *Close Range*, see Steve Holland, ed., *No Surrender*, a War Picture

Library anthology (London: Prion, 2010). For the portrayal of the landings in the Commando series, see George Lowe, ed., *Commando: Fight or Die: The Ten Best Commando D-Day Comic Books Ever* (London: Carlton Books Ltd., 2011). Significantly, neither the *War Picture Library* nor *Commando* series of comics had much time for acknowledging the multi-national make-up of the allies. Representatives of Commonwealth and Empire forces occasionally got some recognition (especially the Australians), but Americans barely featured at all. For generations of British school boys raised on these comics, therefore, the Second World War was won by square-jawed and resolute Tommies who were more than a match for the rather two-dimensional Germans (many of whom seemed incapable of anything other than screaming "Achtung" or "Himmel" when confronted in combat).

63. *The Times*, 24 May 1971, 3. For a reference to local opposition to the memorial, see *The Times*, 21 Apr. 1965, 12.

64. For a discussion of the restrained nature of the thirtieth anniversary of D-Day, see Pierre-Laurent Pizy, 97.

65. *The Times*, 13 June 1974, 19; *The Times*, 20 June 1974, 19.

66. *The Times*, 8 June 1974, 8.

67. Ibid.

68. For some details about this series, see James Chapman, "Television and History: The World at War," *Historical Journal of Film, Radio and Television* 31, no.(2011), 247–75.

69. *The Times*, 7 June 1975, 3.

70. For a discussion of the First World War in British cultural memory, particularly in the 1960s and 1970s, see Daniel Todman, *The Great War, Myth and Memory* (London: Hambledon , 2005).

71. For details regarding British protests against the postwar American military presence, see Duncan Campbell, *The Unsinkable Aircraft Carrier: American Military Power in Britain* (London: Paladin, 1986); and Simon Duke, *US Defence Bases in the United Kingdom: A Matter for Joint Decision?*(London: Macmillan, 1987).

72. See Connelly, *We Can Take It!*, 276–78.

73. *Overlord*, dir. Stuart Cooper, Joswend and Imperial War Museum, 1975, 83 min.

74. For a detailed discussion of the various ways—conscious and unconscious—through which the Falklands Conflict of 1982 was understood with

reference to the Second World War, see Lucy Noakes, *War and the British*, esp. 103–33.

75. Connolly, *We Can Take It!* (London: Pearson, 2004), 271.

76. Ibid.

77. John Ramsden, "Myths and Realities," in *Experience and Memory*, eds. Echternkamp and Martens, 44.

78. Ibid., 273.

79. Quoted in Connelly, *We Can Take It!* (London: Pearson, 2004),273; *The Daily Mirror*, 7 June 1982, 3

80. *The Times*, 6 June 1984, 15.

81. *The Times*, 6 June 1984, 2.

82. *The Times*, 12 April 1984, 2 and 6 June 1984, 1. See also *The Daily Mirror*, 6 June 1984, 3.

83. *Yomped* is a British Royal Marines slang term for a forced march that came into common use during the Second World War as meaning any physically difficult task requiring endurance. *Humped* is an equivalent term in the US Marine Corps.

84. Hastings, *Overlord* (1999), 16.

85. For an excellent discussion of the reputation of the British military in historiography, see John Buckley, "Victory or Defeat? Perceptions of the British Army in Northwest Europe, 1944–5," *Global War Studies* (forthcoming).And for a comprehensive challenge to the thesis of Hastings, see Russell A. Hart, *Clash of Arms: How the Allies Won in Normandy* (Norman: University of Oklahoma Press, 2004).

86. Exercise Tiger, which took place in April 1944, met disaster when a small number of German E-Boats broke through the protective screen provided by Royal Navy destroyers. The E-Boats duly attacked and sank several unprotected landing craft, with the result that 946 American servicemen were killed. The bitter irony was that the troops in question were destined to land on Utah Beach, where casualties on D-Day itself were only around two hundred (killed, missing, wounded and taken prisoner). For details about Exercise Tiger, and the memorial eventually established on Slapton Sands, see Ken Small, *Forgotten Dead* (London: Bloomsbury, 1999).

87. For details about this organization, see *NVA Friends*, The Normandy Veterans' Association, accessed 6 Aug. 2012, http://www.nvafriends.nl/index.php?cid=36.

88. For information about some of the Normandy activities of the Suffolk Regiment Association, see "Programme for Commemorating the 40th Anniversary of the Normandy Landings, Bayeux," GB 554/B13/40, Suffolk Regiment, 1685–1959, Suffolk Records Office, Bury St. Edmunds.

89. For a far more detailed discussion of American appropriation of D-Day in the 1980s, see Michael R. Dolski's chapter in this volume.

90. For some details, see *D-Day Museum and Overlord Embroidery*, Portsmouth Museum and Records, accessed 6 Aug. 2012, http://www.ddaymuseum.co.uk/.

91. *The Times*, 31 May 1982, 8.

92. *The Times*, 6 June 1988, 9.

93. See, for example, the website run by "Les Amis du Suffolk Regiment" who maintain the memorial to the regiment erected at site "Hillman," accessed 6 Aug. 2012, http://www.amis-du-suffolk-rgt.com/index.php/en/. For more examples of British war memorials in Normandy (and indeed American and Canadian memorials) see Tonie Hold and Valmai Holt, *Normandy Landing Beaches: Battlefield Guide* (Barnsley: Leo Cooper, 1999).

94. *The Times*, 2 Mar. 1991, 6.

95. See, for example, *The Times*, 2 October 1990, 12 and 16 Jan. 1991, 11.

96. For a discussion of the attempt to draw parallels between World War II and the Gulf War, see Jeffrey Walsh, "Remembering Desert Storm: Popular Culture and the Gulf War," in *War and Memory*, eds. Martin Evans and Ken Lunn, (Oxford: Berg, 1997), 205–22.

97. *The Times*, 16 May 1994, 18. The following is not an exhaustive list, but to my knowledge, British D-Day memorials can be found at: Portsmouth/Southsea (1948, 1984, 1994), Plymouth (US Navy Memorial), Plymstock (2004), Weymouth (1947 and 2002), Southwick (1994), Sandown, Isle of Wight (2004), Saltash Passage (1947 and 1958), Tiverton (2011). Memorials to the Normandy Veterans Association can be found at several locations, including Whitehaven, Carrisbrooke Castle, Leeds, Glasgow, Chatelherault Country Park, Packington, Newport. For an extensive and detailed discussion of British involvement in the D-Day commemorations in Normandy in June 1994, see Tony Longland, "The 50th Anniversary Commemorations of D-Day," in ed., W. G. Ramsey, *D-Day: Then and Now*, vol. 2 (London: After the Battle, 1995), 638–85.

98. Mark Connelly, "The Longest Days: A Personal View of the Television Coverage of the Fiftieth Anniversary of D-Day," *Contemporary Record* 8 (1994), 602–9. The Channel Four documentary was *D-Day: As It Happens*, dirs./prods. Martin Gorst and Joe Myerscough (Windfall Films and Channel 4, 2013).

99. See, for example, *The Daily Mirror*, 7 June 1944, 23.

100. Fotheringham, 212.

101. For details of some of these memorials, and information about recent efforts to preserve sites in the UK connected to the D-Day operation, see John Schofield, "D-Day Sites in England: An Assessment," *Antiquity* 75 (2001), 77–83. See also Henry Wills, "Archaeological Aspects of D-Day: Operation Overlord," *Antiquity* 68 (1994), 843–45.

102. See Holt and Holt.

103. For a discussion of war tourism in Normandy, see Sam Edwards, "Commemoration and Consumption in Normandy, c. 1945–1994," in *War Memory and Popular Culture: Essays on Modes of Remembrance and Commemoration*, eds. Michael Keren and Holger H. Herwig, 79–61 (Jefferson, NC: Macfarland, 2009).

104. This docudrama was later released as a DVD. See *D-Day: 6.6.44*, dir. Richard Dale (British Broadcasting Corporation, Discovery Channel, ProSieben, France 2, Telfrance, Dangerous Films, 2004; British Broadcasting Corporation, 2004), DVD, 120 min.

105. *The Observer*, 7 June 2004. See also *The Guardian*, 6 June 2006, accessed 6 Aug. 2012, http://www.guardian.co.uk/politics/2004/jun/06/past.interviews.

106. *The Guardian*, 6 June 2006, accessed 6 Aug. 2012, http://www.guardian.co.uk/politics/2004/jun/06/past.interviews.

107. *The Guardian*, 1 June 2004.

108. Robin Neillands, *D-Day, 1944: Voices from Normandy* (London: Orion Books, 1993); Stephen Ambrose, *D-Day: June 6, 1944* (London: Pocket Books, 1994). Ambrose was of course American, and his history gave relatively little space to the British and Canadian beaches, but his book was nonetheless very popular in Britain; Robert Kershaw, *D-Day: Piercing the Atlantic Wall* (London: Naval Institute Press, 1994); David Stafford, *Ten Days to D-Day: Countdown to the Liberation of Europe* (London: Little, Brown, 2003); Martin Gilbert, *D-Day* (London: John Wiley & Sons, 2004); Andrew Williams, *D-Day to Berlin*, (London:

Hodder, 2004). Many of these histories have also been through multiple editions.

109. Significantly, the histories of both Stafford and Williams were also later filmed and aired on British television. See: *Ten Days to D-Day*, dir. Marione Milne (3BM Television, 2004), 90min.; *D-Day to Berlin*, dir. Andrew Williams, (British Broadcasting Corporation, 2005), 150min.

110. Anthony Beevor, *D-Day* (London: Viking, 2009).

111. See Connelly, *We Can Take It!* (London: Pearson, 2004), 295. Despite press criticisms, however, *Saving Private Ryan* proved popular with British cinema audiences.

112. Ibid.

113. *Daily Mail*, 29 May 2009, accessed 6 Aug. 2012, http://www.dailymail.co.uk/news/article-1188515/D-Day-snub-Queen-Palace-fury-Sarkozy-refuses-invite-royals-65th-Anniversary--Brown-wont-act.html. See also *The Sun*, 27 May 2009, accessed 6 Aug. 2012, http://www.thesun.co.uk/sol/homepage/news/2450681/Nicolas-Sarkozy-in-D-Day-snub-to-Queen.html.

Chapter Three

Canada's D-Day:
Politics, Media, and the Fluidity of Memory

Terry Copp and Matt Symes

When the idea of developing a book on the ways in which various nations had constructed a memory of D-Day was first proposed, we were pleased to have an opportunity to contribute a chapter. We have been involved in projects designed to "improve everyman's memory" of Canada's role in the Second World War for many years and have witnessed the process by which government and the media transform selected events into markers in a patriotic story of nation building. This analysis begins with an account of the Canadian role in the D-Day landings and then reviews the ways in which these events were portrayed to the public. While French civilians and some regiments in Canada placed emphasis on the commemoration of 6 June, D-Day only began to emerge as a major symbolic moment in Canadian history in 1994, reaching iconic stature in 2004. The changing political climate in Canada has led to increasing government emphasis on other events in Canada's military history, especially the battle for Vimy Ridge in 1917.

Canadians on D-Day

When the 3d Canadian Infantry Division was selected for the assault phase of Operation Overlord, the lessons of the disastrous Dieppe Raid of August 1942 were on everyone's mind.[1] Could surprise be achieved? Would there be enough air and naval support to overcome fortified defensive positions? Would the tanks be able to get off the beach? Could the Allied air forces prevent the enemy reserves from reaching the beachhead on D-Day? These and other questions worried the planners, but as the details of the operation were developed a new mood of confidence took hold.

The sector of the Normandy coast, code-named "Juno," that was allotted to the Canadians bore no resemblance to Dieppe. The five miles of coastline, at low tide bounded by wide sandy beaches, was defended by one major strongpoint and two smaller resistance nests. In between these fortified positions the Germans relied on flooding, a narrow band of minefields, a continuous line of beach obstacles, and the rocky shoals just off the shore to defend the coast. The entire area was held by just three battalions of a static coastal division, the 716th.

With the US Eighth Air Force and Royal Air Force's Second Tactical Air Force attacking the beach defenses, air power alone seemed to promise a rapid breakthrough. Instead of the six small destroyers at Dieppe, the Royal Navy was to provide cruisers, fleet destroyers, and a host of support vessels, including landing craft with rockets to destroy the minefields. The 3d Division's own field artillery was to add support, firing over the heads of the infantry during the final thousand yards. Duplex Drive (DD) Sherman tanks were to "swim" ashore ahead of the Infantry, while Royal Engineers armored vehicles (AVREs) helped to destroy obstacles and create beach exits. Centaur Mark IV tanks of the Royal Marine Armored Support Group (RMASG), mounting 95mm guns, could take on fixed defenses and burst through concrete. The planners, determined to avoid the kind of slaughter that had taken place at Dieppe, had tried to think of every contingency. Gen. Bernard Law Montgomery was convinced that given operational surprise the British and Canadians ought to be able to breach the coast defenses quickly and begin to advance inland early on D-Day.[2]

The Canadians, landing two brigades in the first wave, were supposed to break through the Atlantic Wall and gain control of their intermediate objective by midday. The reserve brigade would then lead the way to the Caen–Cherbourg railway ten miles inland. Most of this double-track rail line was above or below grade, with a limited number of crossing points. The Canadians had been warned about counterattacks from one of two armored divisions, and detailed orders for defending the railway, a ready-built antitank barrier, were issued two weeks before D-Day.[3]

The Royal Navy's Force "J" reached its anchorage off Juno at 0300 hours on 6 June. If the enemy was aware of the date of the invasion, a very dangerous moment would come when the big transports lowered the assault craft just seven miles from the shore, well within the range of German coastal batteries. The US Navy had elected to unload eleven miles out to sea to avoid this threat, but the calculated risk taken by the British and Canadians cut almost an hour off the time required to reach the beaches.[4]

As the bombardment of the French coast began, the troops were roused from seasickness and sleep and offered a cold breakfast along with a shot of rum. Everyone then moved to their assigned positions and began climbing down netting into the swaying, tossing LCAs (Landing Craft, Assault). By this time RAF Bomber Command, including No. 6 Group, Royal Canadian Air Force, was completing its attack on the coastal batteries. As the LCAs formed up, the aircraft of the US "Mighty Eighth" Air Force were on their approach routes to begin bombing the coastal positions. The air force generals knew that even the most accurate bombing would produce few direct hits on the beach defenses. They hoped that the sheer weight of the attack would help neutralize the defenders by cutting communication links and reducing morale. Unfortunately, the weather, which contributed to the safe crossing of the Allied invasion fleet and to the achievement of operational surprise, bedeviled the bombing program. When the US Eighth Air Force arrived over the coast, cloud conditions made it necessary to use H2X airborne radar. H2X operators had been instructed to have five-to-thirty-second delays to avoid short bombing, and consequently most bombs fell some distance from the beaches and only slight damage was observed at any point in the beach defenses. The report of the Air Force Field Party maintained that "since bombs fell in many towns and villages adjacent to the beaches... [bombing] helped to demoralize enemy reserves," but admitted that no enemy positions were hit by heavy bombers.[5]

Hawker Typhoon squadrons assigned to attack beach targets found the winds and overcast skies a serious challenge and refrained from exaggerated claims. Investigators could find no evidence that the fighter-bomber air attack played any role in the destruction of the Atlantic Wall. Bomb craters and especially the shallow elongated marks left by rockets could be identified easily, and none could be found at strong points or resistance nests in the Anglo-Canadian or American sectors.[6]

For those familiar with the limitations of air power, the failure of the first part of the Allied plan was disappointing but not surprising. The real difficulty was in understanding why the naval gunfire was only marginally more effective. Maj. John Fairlie, a Canadian artillery officer attached to the 21st Army Group's Operational Research Section, conducted an exhaustive investigation of the Juno sector and concluded that naval fire had done "no serious damage to the defenses." Examination of the physical evidence coupled with cross-checked testimony revealed that the enemy's concrete emplacements were "overcome by DD tanks, engineer, and infantry assault." Fairlie noted that the damage credited to naval fire was difficult to assess because of the German method of sighting guns to enfilade only the beach area.[7] In any event, the defenses were substantially intact when the Allied troops reached shore and the Germans were able to deliver a great quantity of lethal fire against them.

The Royal Navy's report on Overlord agreed that the pattern of the coastal defenses "allowed [the enemy] to present a solid front of concrete to seaward of his pillboxes against which naval gunfire had no destructive effect. On the straight Normandy coastline, with shallow water off shore, ships could not be berthed so as to enfilade these pillboxes."[8] The plan also called for the field artillery regiments to add weight to the attack by firing from landing craft during the run-in to shore. Unfortunately for the Canadians, accuracy from the pitching decks of LCTs (Landing Craft, Tank) was impossible even when correction could be made through the dust and smoke of battle.[9]

At the eastern end of Juno the LCAs carrying the North Shore (New Brunswick) Regiment hit the right beach at the right time. Tanks of the Fort Garry Horse, released from their LCTs within 2000 yards of the shore, joined the infantry to clear the string of houses west of the village. The resistance nest, an elaborate series of trenches and tunnels surrounding a 50mm gun, had not been hit by any part of the elaborate bombardment and the struggle to subdue the defenders lasted all morning. The reserve companies followed orders and bypassed the battle, advancing inland.[10]

At Nan White Beach in front of the Bernières-sur-mer, the Queen's Own Rifles had the roughest time of all the Canadian assault battalions. The DD tanks and the specialized armor were late and played no role in overcoming the resistance nest. The QORs were supposed to land well to the west and take the position from the flank but the landing craft were pushed downwind and Baker Company was faced with a frontal assault on a fortified position some 300 yards in length. Half the company were killed or wounded in the first minutes of the battle and only the extraordinary valor of the men who rushed the pillboxes stopped the slaughter. Everything that could go wrong did go wrong at Bernières-sur-mer but the infantry came through.[11] At Courseulles, a small useful port, the German defenses were classified as a strongpoint, the only such position on the Juno sector. The companies of the Royal Winnipeg Rifles and Regina Rifles tasked with overcoming the strongpoint suffered heavy casualties but on either flank assault companies got off the beach quickly and were able to help overcome the main defenses.[12]

No one who examines the events of the first hours of D-Day can fail to be impressed with the accomplishments of the assault battalions. At Juno, as at Omaha and elsewhere, the almost total failure of the elaborate air and naval bombardments had left the beach defenses intact, forcing infantry, combat engineers, and individual tank crews to overcome the enemy by fire and movement. It took incredible courage just to keep going. For most Allied soldiers, seasick and sleep deprived, D-Day passed in a blur. Men interviewed in the following days could rarely recall even approximate timings. The sight of comrades lying face down in the water or sprawled lifeless on the sands registered but there was no time to mourn.[13]

By late afternoon, the reserve brigade was clear of the inevitable traffic jams and ready to advance to the railway and Carpiquet. There were still many hours of daylight left and the brigade probably could have reached its objective if the army commander, Lt. Gen. Miles Dempsey, had not ordered his three assault divisions to stop at their intermediate objectives and dig in. Dempsey's decision was based on the situation confronting the 3d British Division at Sword Beach. Shortly after 1600 hours, the scout troop of the Staffordshire Yeomanry reported that enemy tanks were advancing from Caen. A battle group from the 21st Panzer Division had launched the first major counterattack of D-Day.

The British divisional commander, Maj. Gen. T. G. Rennie, ordered one of his brigades to dig in and ensure that the Sword bridgehead could not be rolled up from the west. The brigade antitank guns turned back an attack by German armor which then moved north to within sight of the coast. By early evening, the German battle group had lost about one-third of its tank strength but was still a formidable force. With other enemy forces holding out in Lion-sur-mer and the radar station at Douvres-la-Délivrande, the threat to both Sword and Juno was very real; however, the arrival of hundreds of aircraft bringing reinforcements to the British 6th Airborne spooked the German corps commander, who ordered the panzers to withdraw to their start line. General Dempsey concluded that more armored counterattacks could be expected, and thus ordered all three assault divisions to take up defensive positions.[14]

This decision was to prove costly to the Canadians for, during the night of 6–7 June, the lead elements of 12th SS Panzer Division began to arrive at Caen. Their commander, Col. Kurt Meyer, established his headquarters at the Abbaye d'Ardenne, an *Ancienne Abbaye* dating from the twelfth century. When the Canadian advance began on the morning of 7 June, he was able to observe their movements from the church tower. Despite orders to wait and mount a coordinated counterattack with the 21st Panzer Division, Meyer, an experienced veteran of the Eastern Front, believed the Canadians should not be permitted to reach the railway.

Meyer deployed his regiment across the extended Canadian flank and struck with overwhelming force. The North Nova Scotia Highlander's losses of 110 killed, sixty-four wounded, and 128 prisoners were much higher than any Anglo-Canadian battalion suffered on D-Day. The violence of this brief encounter did not end when the fighting stopped. In Authie, Hitler Youth, described by a witness as "wildly excited," began murdering Canadian prisoners while the battle still raged and continued killing prisoners after the fighting ceased. Yet more Canadians were executed in cold blood in the courtyard of the Abbaye d'Ardenne, and on the grounds of the Chateau d'Audrieu.[15] The counterattack forced the 9th Canadian Brigade to withdraw to a position less than five miles from the coast. The 25th Panzer Grenadier Regiment also suffered heavy losses and for the next month was committed to holding ground domi-nated by Allied artillery and naval gunfire—not the best use of elite Panzergrenadiers.

AN EARLY DISTANCING OF D-DAY

The news that Canadian soldiers were part of the Allied forces that landed in Normandy on 6 June 1944 reached Prime Minister William Lyon Mackenzie King at 0430 hours. An RCMP constable knocked on his door relaying the message "the invasion has begun." King was told that Eisenhower had announced that Canadian troops were involved and shortly thereafter he learned that both the Royal Canadian Navy and Royal Canadian Air Force had been committed to action. King was caught off guard as he had been led to believe the invasion would not take place before the third week of June. His diary records a characteristic complaint about lacking time to prepare a full statement for the press and the House of Commons. He was, however, pleased with the warm reception his statement received and proud of his words. He made "No effort at exhorta-tion or making of the moment an occasion for eloquence, personal prominence or glorification of country, etc., but simply direction of attention of the House to essential points."[16]

The press and the Canadian Broadcasting Corporation (CBC) were a little less restrained, but given British insistence that no units could be named for security reasons the available information was too general to allow for human interest stories, the essential element in publicity. Ross Munro, who went ashore on D-Day as the representative of the combined press of Canada, filed his first dispatch on 7 June reporting that "the Canadians won and established their beachhead in two hours and forty-five minutes and pushed inland." Munro arrived after the beach defenses had been overcome and his personal memories of D-Day focused on the monstrous traffic jam created when the reserve brigade began to land on the narrowing beach.[17]

Subsequent reports on the events of D-Day were too general to catch anyone's attention, a consequence of the tight censorship demanded by Gen. Bernard Montgomery. This led Canadian reporters to draw comparisons with Dieppe, which they could describe, and to reproduce a statement from Lt. Gen. H. D. G. Crerar claiming that while the Canadian contribution to the successes of the invasion was "impossible to exaggerate," no details were available. As the battle of Normandy progressed, censorship restrictions were relaxed and Canadians were allowed to learn the names of the regiments involved in the landings, but neither Ross Munro nor other Canadian reporters sought out stories about D-Day. The struggle beyond the beaches, including the counterattacks of 7–10 June and the battles for Caen in early July, were seen as much bigger stories. In August, the "Falaise Gap" incident dominated press coverage.[18]

Canadians learned a bit more about the events of 6 June when Ross Munro published *Gauntlet to Overlord* in 1945. His D-Day chapter, "The Lightning Strikes," was a mixture of personal observation, material from press briefings, and interviews with civilians and soldiers in Bernières, which he reached on the afternoon of D-Day. After briefly sketching the events of the morning he turned to the advance inland and the German counterattacks. For Munro, D-Day was a success: "The Allied invasion forces had achieved practically everything the High Command had hoped..." It was the fight for the beachhead perimeter and the advance to Caen "that required immense endurance, stamina, and courage..."[19]

The relative neglect of D-Day in Canadian accounts was particularly evident when the Canadian official historian C. P. Stacey published his one-volume "historical summary" in 1948. He devoted thirty-eight pages to Dieppe and ten to planning the invasion of France with just three pages outlining the Canadian role on 6 June. Stacey was working toward a far more comprehensive history of the campaign in Northwest Europe but there was little support in Ottawa where the new Minister of Defense, Brooke Claxton, insisted that "nobody would be interested in reading about the Second World War." Claxton was wrong. The "historical summary" sold more than 15,000 copies—a best seller by Canadian standards.[20]

Stacey turned to a much more ambitious project, published in 1955 as *Six Years of War: The Army in Canada, Britain, and Asia*. The Canadian fascination with tragic defeat was evident in the detailed fifty-two-page account of the Hong Kong expedition and the ninety-eight pages devoted to the Dieppe Raid.[21] Finally, in 1960 *The Victory Campaign* appeared offering a detailed account of the planning of Overlord with sixteen pages devoted to the Canadian role on D-Day.

Unfortunately, Stacey chose to editorialize:

> The D-Day achievement was magnificent…Nevertheless, reviewing the day as a whole, fifteen years after, one may be permitted to inquire whether it is conceivable that we could have accomplished more on the 6th of June. Was it really impossible to reach the inland objectives? Could not a more sustained effort in the later phases have produced deeper penetration and the seizure of ground which we later had to purchase with weeks of bloody fighting?

Stacey then introduced the theme that would shape his writing and influence other historians for the next several decades:

> We shall see in this volume that the British and Canadian forces—and the same is probably true of those of the United States—were usually better at deceiving the enemy and achieving

initial success in an assault than they were at exploiting surprise and success once achieved. Perhaps they were too easily satisfied.[22]

Stacey quoted the commander of the 716th German Infantry Division, a formation that had yielded thousands of prisoners and ceased to function by the end of D-Day, who told interrogators that the Canadian infantry were too "hesitant and careful." This comment, so typical of German generals taken into captivity, led Stacey to conclude that "we could certainly learn something from the Germans about 'maintaining the momentum of the attack,'" an observation completely unrelated to the events of D-Day.[23] Stacey's approach contrasted sharply with the one adopted by Gordon Harrison in *Cross Channel Attack* (1951) and L. F. Ellis, *Victory in the West* (1962), the American and British official historians who both offered a straightforward analysis of the challenges and achievements of the day. Neither author indulged in speculation about whether there was a lack of "sustained effort." While the official historians were researching their versions of the Battle of Normandy, Cornelius Ryan published his 1959 best-seller *The Longest Day*, later turned into a blockbuster movie in 1962 by Darryl F. Zanuck.[24] The book included aspects of the Canadian story but no major Hollywood star was cast as a Canadian and their contribution to the success of the invasion was ignored. Reviewers in Canada complained about the Americanization of D-Day but no one came forward to develop a film or television program to tell a different story.

Stacey and the team of historians at the Directorate of History, Department of National Defense, retained access to the War Diaries and other records until the late 1970s when a thirty-year rule was implemented. In 1981 Terry Copp and the late Robert Vogel began a "new reading" of the primary sources, German, British, and Canadian, related to D-Day and the Battle of Normandy, launching a five-volume series on the campaign in Northwest Europe with *Maple Leaf Route: Caen* published in 1983.[25] Neither author had any previous background in operational or tactical military history but as tenured professors they could ignore the negative reaction of colleagues who shared the view that military history was not a legitimate field in Canadian academia. There was so little interest in the project that the books were self-published, achieving commercial and critical success only in the latter years of the decade.[26]

An Ambivalent Engagement with Canada's D-Day

Showing a degree of renewed interested in D-Day, the Canadian War Museum commissioned Reginald Roy to write *1944: The Canadians in Normandy*, a narrative account of the campaign to be published in time for the fortieth anniversary in 1984. Roy, an army veteran and author of several regimental histories, noted that there are "no accounts of Canadian brigades or divisions...nor have there been biographies of Canadian generals," a sharp contrast to the many accounts by "American, British, and German historians."[27] Roy's book followed Stacey, devoting just ten of its 320 pages to D-Day, focusing instead on the battles for Caen and the advance to Falaise.

The fortieth anniversary was also marked by Ronald Reagan's speech to "the boys at Pointe du Hoc." This brief, beautifully crafted talk, timed to coincide with the morning television programs, was heard by millions including Canadians who responded warmly to Reagan's reference to "the unsurpassed courage of the Canadians who had already seen the horrors of war on this coast. They knew what awaited them here but they could not be deterred, once they hit Juno Beach they never looked back."[28] The audience at Pointe du Hoc included European leaders and the Prime Minister of Canada, Pierre Trudeau. It would have been entirely out of character for Trudeau, who was on the verge of retiring and engaged in a quixotic world tour promoting peace, to offer such sentiments and he did not try.[29] Apart from Reagan's speech, the anniversary passed without any special impression on Canadian memory.

The first initiatives to memorialize Canadian participation in the invasion came from residents of the area. In Bernières-sur-mer there stands one of the early monuments erected to the Allies, and at St. Aubin-sur-mer a monument in honor of the North Shore

(New Brunswick) Regiment and the 48th British Commandoes was erected shortly after the war in 1947. Both were local initiatives. Roger Alexandre was just fourteen when the Queen's Own Rifles and the First Hussars suffered devastating losses in his hometown hamlet of Le Mesnil Patry. Since the 1950s he has dedicated a great deal of time to safeguarding the Canadian memory in Normandy, even when Canadians showed little interest.[30]

The early commemorative effort focused on Le Regiment de La Chaudiere or the "French Tommies" but garnered little attention in Canada. The Chauds, in reserve behind the Queen's Own Rifles in Bernières-sur-mer, charmed the locals with their old Norman accents and were fondly remembered. In fact, until 1984 many of the locals were sure the Quebec regiment had liberated their seaside town. Monuments and street names bear the regiment's name. A 1970s plaque in honor of the Chauds at a former German bunker in Bernières-sur-mer has the time of the landings wrong and places the regiment at the front end of the assault. While the Canadian military and the population of Quebec always shared a deeply divisive relationship, the 1960s represented the height of the Quiet Revolution and with it a complete rejection of any positive memory of the Québécois during either World War.

In 1984 a chance meeting between veterans of the Queen's Own Rifles and the owners of the first house liberated in Normandy led to further informal commemorations.[31] Bernières-sur-mer was the site of one of the seaside houses that laid claim to being the first to be liberated on D-Day. The Queen's Own Rifles veterans hail from Toronto, Ontario, one of the wealthiest cities in Canada. By 1984 most had reached retirement age and had also lived through one of the most prosperous times in human history. With commitment, money, and time, the regiment began to develop relationships with local citizens and an agenda to commemorate their own sacrifice. Their efforts since their first meeting in Normandy have led to the construction of several monuments in areas of significance to the Regiment at Bernières-sur-mer and Le Mesnil-Patry. After 1994 the Queen's Own Rifles made arrangements with the owners to have "Maison Queen's Own Rifles" become a center of activity every 6 June.[32]

Also in 1984, Jacques Vico, who grew up on the grounds of the Abbaye d'Ardenne, organized a ceremony to unveil a memorial to the Canadian soldiers executed by the 12th SS on 7 June 1944. The Canadian Minister of Veterans Affairs, who was in Normandy for the public events, attended the ceremony and heard Vico describe how the graves of the men buried in the Abbaye garden were discovered when his mother noticed changes in the pattern of the spring flowers.[33]

Canadians had learned about the murders at the Abbaye through press coverage of the trial of Kurt Meyer who was accused of responsibility for the killings and found guilty in the only Canadian trial of a Nazi war criminal. The prosecutor, Col. Bruce Macdonald, published a detailed account of the trial in 1954 but it took the intervention of Vico and his neighbors who used the simple memorial and informed talks about the incident to transform the Abbaye garden into a site of memory and a place of pilgrimage.[34] A Canadian soldier serving in Germany as a member of the 4th Canadian Service Battalion designed the memorial plaque for the garden and he subsequently published a pamphlet, later expanded into a book titled *Murder at the Abbaye*.[35]

"Le Comité Juno Canada-Normandie" was established in 1985 and began to mark routes visitors could follow from the landing places to the Falaise battlefields. This enterprise helped to tie together a number of memorial plaques erected by regimental associations and to encourage visitors to explore the Juno sector, but neither the Canadian government nor media showed much interest.[36]

In 1992 there was an attempt to construct a modern Canadian memory of D-Day when representatives of a new museum in Caen, *Le Memorial*, visited Ottawa to encourage Canada to develop a memorial garden on the grounds of the museum in time for the fiftieth anniversary of the Normandy landings. The American Battle of Normandy Foundation, founded in 1985, was sponsoring an elaborate American memorial garden and proposed a "Wall of Liberty" listing the names of all Americans who lost their lives in the battle.[37] Neither the Canadian government nor the Canadian War Museum was willing to become directly involved but Hamilton Southam, a Second World War veteran and prominent member of the family who owned the Southam newspapers, began to organize the Canadian

Battle of Normandy Foundation to respond to the invitation from Caen. Southam consulted Public Works Canada and accepted a suggestion that the Foundation engage "students of architecture and landscape to bring their particular sensibilities and creative energies to the study and design of the project."[38]

A student design competition was organized with teams drawn from the French language Université de Montreal and Ottawa's Carleton University. The students in the graduating year were the age of many of the soldiers in 1944. Before leaving for a site visit in France, they met with veterans who had joined the board of the new foundation and were encouraged to develop their own approach to the project. Professor Nan Griffiths, who with her colleague Professor Bernard Lafargue supervised the students, described the process of creating the garden in a 1999 article:

> On arrival in Normandy it became apparent that there was no agreement on what the project should be, where it should be located, or what funding might be available to build it. A model of the American garden, designed by professional architects with a budget of millions, offered little guidance and the students began their work as individuals developing ideas before forming three teams for the competition. A site was then selected, partly for its remoteness from the American garden and partly because it lent itself to the symbolic, metaphorical approach the students preferred.

Professor Griffiths offered this view of the design selected:

> Remembrance is implied rather than literal...The space of the valley evokes a sense of the fearsomeness of the space of landing, of time and waiting, of exposure in a large site and a large situation...A theatre of war is transformed into a theatre of memory.[39]

A British academic and author, Paul Gough, visited the space shortly after it opened and provided a "reading" of the garden that drew upon his studies of other sites of memory. Gough had visited the Vimy memorial and Beaumont-Hamel where he was "fascinated by the fusion of abstract and figurative elements, and speculated that this combination of hard modernist edges with dramatic use of statuary seemed to be a particular strength of Canadian war memorials." The Canadian Memorial Garden presented a very different, highly original, and controversial installation, "more of a peace garden than a monument." Gough suggested visitors should begin their visit inside the grove of trees where an "incessant flow of water" runs over sixteen black stones inscribed with the Latin text *Nulla dies umquam memori vos eximet aveo* (No day will erase your generation from our memory).

Figures 6 & 7. The Canadian Memorial Garden from bottom (left) and top (right). Photos courtesy of Terry Copp and Matt Symes.

For Gough, the water was intended "to act as a metaphor for the Atlantic crossing, a point somehow reinforced by the grid-like structure of the slabs, which seem to mimic the longitude and latitude lines on Admiralty charts." The visitor leaves the symbolic landing area and crosses an empty valley, 38 meters wide, before following a winding path up a slope to a narrow passage in a polished marble wall. Inscribed above this entrance to the terrace are the words "Liberation Comes From The Sea / La Libération Vient Par La Mer." Gough suggests that "the design team seem to have used the topography of the valley to suggest a complex series of ideas about distance from one's home country, about the painful progress of a combatant through exposed tracts, up an arduous and disorienting climb, to a hard-won breach in an impregnable stonework, and finally to an eventual triumph." The garden, he insists, "sets a benchmark for future designs of memorial landscapes."[40]

There were other attempts to create a public memory of Canada's role in the Second World War. In January 1992 the CBC broadcast a three-part television series titled *The Valor and the Horror*. Episodes on Hong Kong, Bomber Command, and Verrières Ridge were all characterized by poorly researched scripts and claims that the producers were telling the real and previously hidden truth about Canada's war. A major controversy quickly developed as veterans and historians who had studied these campaigns offered sharp criticism of the series. A sub-committee of the Canadian Senate held hearings that were derided as a witch hunt or applauded as an opportunity for the public, including veterans, to have their say.[41] Most journalists rallied to support the producers while a number of veterans led by a former Defense Minister, Barney Danson, a Normandy veteran, raised funds to develop a new television series under the title "No Price Too High."

The result was a six-part series that included a program on D-Day, a topic entirely ignored in *The Valour and the Horror*. Using letters and diaries actually written by participants and read aloud by actors, the producer, Dick Nielsen, provided a respectful, straightforward account of events in a slow-paced style that contrasted sharply with the CBC programs.[42] The programs were originally broadcast on cable; many Canadians had to wait until PBS stations located close to the border ran the program to attract Canadian audiences.

D-Day's (Partial) Return

The fiftieth anniversary of D-Day was marked by a remarkable recreation of the airborne assault on Normandy with more than 1,000 American and 1,400 British and Canadian paratroopers, old and young, jumping from low-flying Hercules aircraft into the landing zones of 1944. Dignitaries including Queen Elizabeth, President Bill Clinton, and Prime Minister Jean Chrétien sailed to Normandy from the south coast of England in commemoration of the original cross-channel attack. The *Globe and Mail*, Canada's self-styled "national newspaper," allowed one of its senior reporters, Murray Campbell, to write a front-page story to appear on the Saturday edition before D-Day. Titled "D+50: The Fight for Juno Beach," Campbell focused on the Regina Rifles, a battalion his uncle, an accountant and unlikely citizen-soldier, had commanded on D-Day. This was the first time a major newspaper had offered readers a lengthy, well-researched essay on the "death and confusion of that terrible morning in Normandy."[43]

Campbell's articles were an exception. The 1994 anniversary was a television-centered extravaganza. The international ceremony, organized by the government of France with elaborate security arrangements, was centered on Omaha Beach with a smaller British event in the Queen's presence at Arromanches-les-bains. There were also activities scheduled in the Juno sector and the CBC televised these as well as the main ceremonies. Canadian television networks also covered the unveiling of a striking memorial to Anglo-Canadian friendship in the two World Wars located in London's Green Park. The presence of Princess Diana, who "emerged from self-imposed retirement" to attend, made Green Park a major media event in Britain and Canada, rivaling D-Day.[44]

Prime Minister Jean Chrétien's speech in London was innocuous but the words he used in Normandy, claiming to recall an era when Canada was a "young nation" with soldiers who "did not live as Anglophones or Francophone, easterners or westerners, Christians or Jews, immigrants or natives." They died, he insisted, "as Canadians."[45] This attempt to use the sacrifices of D-Day to promote national unity angered Quebec nationalists who were campaigning for the election of a separatist government in the province and making the case for Quebec independence in the House of Commons. Lucien Bouchard, the leader of the *Bloc Québécois*, condemned Chrétien, insisting that "It is not for anyone else to say what they thought when they died on those beaches far away from their families." A Federal cabinet minister further stoked the controversy claiming, "She was 'hurt' to see someone whose goal is to break-up the country lay a wreath at the D-Day ceremonies in Ottawa."[46] The success of the 1994 commemoration as a media and tourist event led the French government and various local authorities in Lower Normandy to encourage development of new facilities and attractions that would draw visitors to Normandy by making the landing beaches into a permanent tourist circuit. Initially Canadians, faced with the election of separatist government in Quebec and a referendum on Quebec independence in June 1995, had other things in their mind. The marginalization of D-Day was evident in May 1995 when the Prime Minister returned to Normandy to officially open the Canadian Memorial Garden. The media reported on Chrétien's participation in ceremonies marking the anniversary of Victory in Europe held in the Netherlands but the garden rated only brief inside page coverage.[47]

D-Day was not entirely neglected. The early efforts of French civilians, Regimental Associations, and the Comité Juno meant that key locations were marked with signs so battlefield tourists could visit. The Canadian Battle of Normandy Foundation co-published a guidebook, *A Canadian's Guide to the Battlefields of Normandy* in 1994, and established a national program offering university students bursaries to participate in a Normandy-focused battlefield study tour. From 1995 onward, Canadian students were present at the annual D-Day ceremonies at the garden and in the three "Juno" villages, but the foundation's major commemorative activities were focused on the Abbaye d'Ardenne and on the liberation of Caen in July. Subsequently the foundation worked with military historians at Wilfrid Laurier University to create additional battlefield memorials at Verrières Ridge and St. Lambert-sur-Dive, drawing visitors to the sites of two of the major battles fought by Canadians in Normandy.[48] The foundation also began to include First World War battlefields as well as those in Belgium, Holland, Germany, and Italy, changing its name to The Canadian Battlefields Foundation to reflect the broader mandate. This approach did not appeal to Garth Webb, a D-Day veteran who had returned from the 1994 commemoration determined to establish a bricks and mortar Canadian presence on Juno.

Garth Webb and his partner Lise Cooper, like many other visitors to the Canadian Memorial Garden, found the space too abstract and impersonal. They also resented the almost total failure of the curators at *Le Memorial* to include references to Canadians in their exhibits. Webb, with modest funding from a financial company, developed a project to transform the railway station at Bernières-sur-mer, a small building featured in many photographs of the village on D-Day, into a museum.[49] Plans in Bernières-sur-mer faltered when the seaside hamlet voted against a larger permanent installation.

Webb switched his attention to the village of Courseulles-sur-mer and began to plan a new modern building on the beach where the Royal Winnipeg Rifles landed. The Canadian government wanted nothing to do with this private initiative until Webb persuaded Walmart to take up the cause and encourage Canadians to donate to a Juno Beach Centre. Enlisting the support of Walmart was a stroke of genius. Many Canadians opposed the entry of the company into Canada when it purchased the Woolco chain of stores in 1994. Walmart sought to counter criticism of its low wage and aggressive anti-union policies with community involvement and responded to the opportunity to identify the company with Canada by persuading customers to donate one dollar each to help build the Juno Beach Centre. Ultimately, Walmart donated $1.8 million in addition to the several hundred thousand received from customers.[50]

Garth Webb employed an abrasive, take-no-prisoners approach to fundraising that offended many people. Neither he nor any of his core group of supporters had any experience in building or running a museum and they were unwilling to seek advice. Officials at Veterans Affairs Canada, the Canadian War Museum, and other organizations with an interest in war commemoration were ignored as the fundraising campaign proceeded. Walmart's well-publicized role embarrassed the Canadian Federal and Provincial Governments. When construction began in 2001, government contributions accounted for 40 percent of the $10 million budget with a further $2.2 million from the regional governments in France.[51] Despite this, the Juno Beach Centre remained fully under Webb's control.

The controversies over the ownership of war memory reached a new level of intensity when the Canadian War Museum announced a plan to expand and revitalize their sadly neglected facility by adding a larger exhibition space devoted to the Holocaust. The proposal was developed without any consultation with veterans groups, the Canadian Jewish Congress, or historians, and quickly became a cause célèbre. The same Senate sub-committee that had provided a platform for critics of *The Valour and the Horror* began hearings in February 1998 and discovered that no one except the Canadian Museum of Civilization Corporation that had gained responsibility for the War Museum favored the inclusion of a Holocaust gallery in a museum dedicated to Canadian military history from the colonial period to the present. It was agreed that a Holocaust memorial ought to stand alone.[52]

The Federal government quickly seized control of the controversy, announcing that funds for a completely new war museum along with a site in suburban Ottawa were available. Jack Granatstein, a prominent and outspoken historian, was appointed as Director and together with an Advisory Board chaired by Barney Danson, concepts for the new museum—which the Prime Minister insisted must be located in the city proper—were developed. Once the new site was chosen an architectural competition was held and a design selected. The Canadian War Museum opened in May 2005 and became the major component of the transformation of the nation's capital that now included "four other memorializing projects associated with Canadian military history."[53] None of these (a memorial to Aboriginal Soldiers, a rebuilding of Confederation Square providing better access to the National War Memorial, a peace-keeping memorial, and a newly established Tomb of the Unknown Soldier, the remains taken from a cemetery at Vimy Ridge) had any specific relation to D-Day or the Battle of Normandy.

It is difficult to estimate how much of an effect this series of Ottawa-based projects had on popular opinion, but what we do know is that when *Saving Private Ryan* reached Canadian theaters in 1998, curiosity about D-Day and Canada's role in this iconic event reached a new high. Many Canadians complained that the film, like *The*

Longest Day, ignored their countrymen but as one reviewer recalling *The Valour and the Horror* put it:

> The unschooled may emerge from *Private Ryan* asking what Canadians were doing on 6 June while the American soldiers were pushing ashore through a barrage of Nazi shells, mines and bullets. Those who know that nine battalions of Canadian troops were busy assaulting German-held beaches in Normandy might ask instead what Canadian film and TV producers were doing while Spielberg made this movie.
>
> The answer is, worse than nothing. Our pop-culture elite at the CBC, the National Film Board, and the private production houses have been obsessively exposing Canadian war efforts as unmitigated disasters and frauds. A quick survey of Canadian film and TV treatments of the Second World War suggests that if we'd made *Saving Private Ryan*, the Allies never would have gotten off the beach. Private Ryan himself would have been flattened by a German Tiger tank, with the rescue squad dead to the last man in a circle around him.[54]

Canadians had never attempted to tell a story of heroism and achievement.

The short-term effect of *Saving Private Ryan* was enormous and may account for the extraordinary selection of D-Day as the number one "Canadian" story of the twentieth century in a top ten list compiled by print and broadcast journalists in November 1999. D-Day did not really fit the criteria—"an event that was major news the day it occurred, but also went on to endure with Canadians beyond that moment, or an ongoing news event that over a period of time was judged to have been of major significance in the country's development or history"—but Steven Spielberg had created a memory that was still going strong in 1999.[55]

The culmination of a newfound interest in Canada's military past, mass public interest in the 1994 D-Day celebrations, and no doubt the lasting impact of *Saving Private Ryan* caught most officials off-guard and forced the government to reexamine its overseas commemorations. The result was an extension of the Historic Sites and Monuments Board's mandate to include overseas sites. In 1999 Roger Sarty, then chief historian at the Canadian War Museum, led a battlefield tour on behalf of Veterans Affairs which included the Minister of Heritage, Sheila Copps. On the tour Copps unveiled the first official Canadian monument in Normandy.[56]

Construction of the Juno Beach Centre began the next year and, when it opened in 2003, television and press coverage was extensive. Visitors entered the display via a simulated landing craft with audio and visual cues to the D-Day experience, but once inside the exhibits provided little insight into the events of 6 June 1944 or the Battle of Normandy. A room devoted to Pre-War Canada appeared to have been developed by a left-wing Quebec nationalist determined to portray the country that went to war in 1939 in the most negative light possible. The rest of the galleries offered photos and captions depicting various aspects of the Canadian war effort. One historian who toured the facility complained that "what little military history there is contains numerous errors."[57]

The public response was very different. The Centre was a striking building located on the edge of a stretch of coast that contained several intact bunkers lending the area a unique air of authenticity. As preparations for the 2004 anniversary began the Canadian officials selected the Centre as the site for an elaborate sixtieth anniversary ceremony that was to include the presence of the Queen. Veterans Affairs Canada, which after the fiftieth anniversary had begun a program called Canada Remembers, brought sixty veterans and a number of school children to Normandy for a five-day "pilgrimage" that received wide coverage in Canada. Over 6,000 people attended the ceremonies at the Juno Beach Centre that included a flyby of a Lancaster bomber escorted by two Spitfires. The day ended with a line piper playing a lament at the edge of the beach.[58] In his remarks, Prime Minister Jean Chrétien said, "The world needed a memorial so that the memory and the story of Canada's military and civilian contribution and efforts during the Second World War would never be forgotten. Until now there has been no significant Canadian Memorial to mark their achievements."[59] That need was relatively new.

Jonathan Vance, in a recent study on memory and the Second World War in Canada, convincingly argues that there was little time for elaborate commemoration. "Social memory" Vance contends "is all about the creation of a usable past but in the two decades after the Second World War Canadians did not have much need for the past." There was no debate over the war's necessity. Instead, most Canadians enjoyed a "booming economy, the most generous veteran's benefits in the world" and a materialistic wealth that was simply impossible to fathom only a few years before.[60] Canadians commemorated the war in utilitarian memorials like parks, hospitals, and arenas. The government and local communities added the dates 1939–1945 (and 1950–1953 after the Korean War) to existing First World War Memorials and no official attention was given to overseas commemoration of the Second World War until 1999.

In 2009, Canada Remembers and the new Canadian Prime Minister, Stephen Harper, had to compete with President Obama and in a sense it was a case of déjà vu all over again. The Canadian role in the war in Afghanistan had taken center stage, especially in Ontario where a spontaneous movement to show respect for soldiers who lost their lives in Afghanistan developed. By lining the overpasses on the route from the air force base at Trenton, Ontario, to the coroner's facility in Toronto, scores, then hundreds, then thousands of Canadians displayed their pride and sorrow. The stretch of Highway 401 between the two points was renamed the "Highway of Heroes" in 2007 and remained a focal point of patriotic expression until Canada's combat mission in Afghanistan ended.[61]

A recent study of the discourse surrounding Canadian discussion of the national experience of war by Noah Richler argues that the government of Prime Minister Stephen Harper has used Afghanistan to create an image of Canada as a warrior nation rather than one committed to peacekeeping.[62] Richler is not alone in protesting the "Vimy Effect," or the attempt to make the battle for Vimy Ridge a "foundational myth." There is considerable opposition to the millions of dollars allocated to celebrations of the War of 1812, described by the Heritage Minister James Moore as "a defining moment in Canadian history." In Moore's simplistic account, "English and

French militias and Aboriginal Canadians worked together with British military forces" to repel an American invasion.[63] The current struggle over who will construct and control the social memory of Canada's military past barely mentions D-Day. June 2014 will mark the seventieth anniversary of the Normandy landings, but with the one hundredth anniversary of the beginning of the Great War and the current government's fixation on rebranding the nation with a focus on moments when conservative governments were in power, D-Day will have to compete for attention.

Notes

1. C. P. Stacey, *The Victory Campaign* (Ottawa: 1966), 5–12.

2. L. F. Ellis, *Victory in the West, Volume I: The Battle of Normandy* (London: H. M. Stationary Office, 1962); C. P. Stacey, *The Victory Campaign* (Ottawa:The Queen's Printer, 1960); and Terry Copp, *Fields of Fire: The Canadians in Normandy* (Toronto: University of Toronto Press, 2003).

3. I British Corps Instructions, 28 May 1944, Library and Archives of Canada (LAC), Record Group 24 (RG24),volume 10790.

4. Gordon Harrison, *Cross Channel Attack: United States Army in World War II* (Washington: US Army Center of Military History, 1951).

5. United States Strategic Air Forces in Europe, "Survey of Effectiveness of Bombing of the Invasion Coast," July 1944, United States Army Military History Institute Library.

6. Terry Copp, ed., *Montgomery's Scientists: Operational Research in Northwest Europe* (Waterloo: Wilfrid Laurier University Press, 2001).

7. Ibid., 381–84.

8. Combined Operations Headquarters (COHQ), "Naval Fire Support in Operation Overlord," LAC, RG 24,vol 10, 673.

9. Copp, *Montgomery's Scientists*, 385.

10. Marc Milner, *From D-Day to Carpiquet: The North Shore Regiment and the Liberation of Europe* (Fredericton: Goose Lane Editions, 2007).

11. C. P. Stacey, *The Victory Campaign* (1960), 103.

12. L. F. Ellis, *Victory in the West, Vol. 1: The Battle of Normandy* (London: H. M. Stationery Office, 1962), 201–3.

13. Gordon Brown and Terry Copp, *Look to Your Front: Regina Rifles 1944–45* (Waterloo: LCMSDS Press 2001).

14. Copp, *Fields of Fire*, 63

15. Howard Nargolian, *Conduct Unbecoming: The Story of the Murder of Canadian Prisoners of War in Normandy* (Toronto: University of Toronto Press, 1998).

16. William Lyon Mackenzie King, Diary Entry, 6 June 1994, LAC Online.

17. Ross Munro, "Canadians Push Inland 1,000 yards," *Globe and Mail*, 7 June 1944. Ross Munro, interview by Terry Copp, September 1984, Copp Papers.

18. We are grateful to Brendan O'Driscoll who surveyed a number of Canadian newspapers to analyze press reaction to this and other events.

19. Ross Munro, *Gauntlet to Overlord: The Story of the Canadian Army* (Toronto: Macmillan, 1945), 47.

20. C. P. Stacey, *A Date with History: Memoirs of a Canadian Historian* (Ottawa: The Queen's Printer, 1948), 197.

21. C. P. Stacey, *Six Years of War: The Army in Canada, Britain, and the Pacific* (Ottawa: The Queens Printer, 1955).

22. C. P. Stacey, *The Victory Campaign*, 118.

23. Ibid., 119.

24. Cornelius Ryan, *The Longest Day* (Greenwich: Fawcett Publications, 1959).

25. Terry Copp and Robert Vogel, *Maple Leaf Route: Caen* (Alma: Maple Leaf Route, 1983).

26. Terry Copp, "Workers and Soldiers: A Memoir," *Canadian Historical Review* 93 (Sept. 2012): 463–86.

27. Reginald Roy, *1944: The Canadians in Normandy* (Ottawa: Macmillan, 1984), xi.

28. Quoted in Kate Delaney, "The Many Meanings of D-Day," *European Journal of American Studies*, Special Edition(2012): Doc. 13, http://ejas.revues.org/9544. For further treatment of Reagan's performance in 1984, see Michael Dolski's chapter in this volume.

29. John English, *Just Watch Me* (Toronto: Knopf Canada, 2009), 600–3.

30. Roger Alexandre, interview by Matt Symes, 10 Feb. 2007, Le Mesnil-Patry, Calvados department, France, recorded.

31. M. Hoffer, interview by Matt Symes, 12 Feb. 2007, Bernières-sur-mer, Calvados department, France, recorded.

32. Matt Symes, "The Personality of Memory: The Process of Informed Commemoration in Normandy" in *Canada and the Second World War*, eds. Geoffrey Hayes, Mike Bechthold and Matt Symes, 444–60 (Waterloo: Wilfrid Laurier University Press, 2012).

33. Vanessa McMackin, "Rearranged Snowdrops: The Construction of Memory at the Abbaye d'Ardenne,"*Canadian Military History* 20 (2011), 30–42.

34. Bruce MacDonald, *The Trial of Kurt Meyer* (Toronto: Clarke, 1954). For a full account of the trial including the transcript see P. Whitney Lackenbauer and C. W. Madsen, *Kurt Meyer on Trial: A Documentary Record* (Kingston: Canadian Forces Leadership Institute, 2007).

35. Ian S. Campbell, *Murder at the Abbaye: The Story of Twenty Canadian Soldiers Murdered at the Abbaye d'Ardenne* (Ottawa: The Golden Dog Press, 1966).

36. See Comité Juno Canada-Normandie, www.comitejuno.org.

37. The American Battle of Normandy Foundation was in difficulties by 1994. See United States Government Accountability Office, "Battle of Normandy Foundation: Uncertainties Surround its Future Viability," November 1994.

38. Nan Griffiths, "The Canadian Memorial Garden Caen, Normandy, France: Two Views—Memory, Monuments, and Landscapes,"*Canadian Military History* 8 (1998), 76.

39. Ibid., 82.

40. Paul Gough, "A Difficult Path to Tread,"*Candian Military History* 8 (1999), 80.

41. David J. Bercuson and S. F. Wise, *The Valour and the Horror Revisited* (Montreal: McGill-Queen's University Press, 1944).

42. Co-author Terry Copp was the historical advisor, on-camera historian for the series and author of a book published as *No Price Too High: Canadians in the Second World War* (Toronto: McGraw-Hill Ryerson, 1994).

43. *Globe and Mail*, 4 June 1994.

44. Ibid., 4 June 1994.

45. Ibid., 7 June 1994.

46. *Toronto Star*, 8 June 1994.

47. The *Toronto Star* offered a one-paragraph note in its travel column.

48. Terry Copp was co-chair of the Foundation's Education Committee and author of *A Canadians Guide to the Battlefields of Normandy* (Waterloo: LCMSDS, 1994).

49. Terry Copp worked closely with Garth Webb in the first phase of the project but was not involved in the final development of the Juno Beach Centre.

50. See www.junobeachcentre.org/centre/pdf/jbc_press_document_2011.pdf.

51. Ibid.

52. Report of the Senate Subcommittee on Veterans Affairs, "Guarding History," May 1998.

53. Reesa Greenberg, "Constructing the Canadian War Museum / Constructing the Landscape of Canadian Identity," in *(Re)Visualizing National History: Museums and National identities in Europe*, ed. Robin Ostcow (Toronto: University of Toronto Press, 2003), 189.

54. *Globe and Mail*, 24 Aug. 1998.

55. "Canadian News Events of the 20th Century" *Canoe.ca*, http://www.canoe.ca/RemembranceDay/991107_dday3.html.

56. "Sheila Copps Unveils Plaque at Normandy," News Releases and Backgrounds, *Parks Canada*, 6 June 1999, http://www.pc.gc.ca/APPS/CP-NR/release_e.asp?id=23&andor1=nr.

57. *The National Post*, 18 June 2004.

58. Terry Copp was present throughout the ceremony.

59. See the whole speech at http://www.ctv.ca/CTVNews/TopStories/20030607/juno_beach_memorial_030606/ accessed November 2011.

60. Jonathan Vance, "An Open Door to a Better Future: The Memory of Canada's Second World War" in *Canada and the Second World War*, eds. Geoffrey Hayes, Mike Bechthold, and Matt Symes (Waterloo: Wilfrid Laurier University Press, 2012), 475.

61. Pete Fischer, *Highway of Heroes: True Patriot Love* (Toronto: Dundurn, 2011).

62. Noah Richler, *What We Talk About, When We Talk About War* (Fredericton: Goose Lane, 2012).

63. Meagan Fitzpatrick, "Feds Launch War of 1812 Anniversary Plans," *CBC News*, 11 Oct. 2011.

Chapter Four

Gratitude, Trauma, and Repression: D-Day in French Memory

Kate C. Lemay

Beginning on 6 June 1944, Norman French were put into the challenging role of welcoming the Allied military forces that had inadvertently killed thousands of Normans, those citizens unfortunate enough to live in Norman urban centers used as communication hubs by the German military. For those Normans living through the bombardments of Caen and Saint Lô, among other towns such as Mortain, Vire, Falaise, Caen, Lisieux, and Le Havre, 6 June was the traumatic renewal of Norman war experience. Other Norman cities like Bayeux, undamaged by the bombardment, had to accommodate thousands of neighbor refugees.[1] In the end, no one in Lower Normandy was left unaffected: 13,000 lost their lives. After enduring the devastating bombardments, Normans warily waited for their liberation as the battle, which started on the beaches in the departments of Manche and Calvados, tore through the Cotentin Peninsula to capture the major port city of Cherbourg, then headed south, and with the brutal battle through Saint Lô, broke out into the department of Orne to finally force the German military back east. The bloody struggle had enormous cost to the Norman landscape and its civilians. Men, women, and children were eyewitnesses to a grisly combat that routed the German forces out of their cities, villages, and all expanses in between. The landscape of war duly became a battlefield of memory invested with conflicting histories of both gratitude and resentment. As a result, the memory of trauma in Normandy has continually surfaced in political, economic, and social arenas, first figuring prominently in local remembrance during the postwar period, but then evolving into repressed underground expression as French memory shifted as early as 1984.[2]

In French remembrance, D-Day represents two sides of French war experience whose gradual changes are addressed accordingly in a chronological format. One remembrance is to recall, publicly, the joyous release from the tyranny of the Nazi regime and to give thanks to the Liberators, a remembrance that is complicated by interior resentments toward the Allies.[3] The French government, on a national level, promoted this approach especially through the *Monuments Signaux,* or Signal Monuments, a group of identical, large-scale works that were organized by the *Comité du débarquement,* or D-Day Commemoration Committee, whose aim was to mark major sites of battle and commemorate the Allied forces.

Another remembrance priority, but one that until the fiftieth anniversary of D-Day remained rarely visible in material culture and was often restrained in public remembrance, is a more region-specific, Norman-driven memory, a memory that simultaneously acknowledges *and* suppresses the devastation of cities and landscapes, of homelessness and refugees, and of horrific wounds and terrible death. Indeed, the tendency to mute the terror and tragedy is even reflected in the name soon adopted by the French to describe the D-Day operation: "the landings" (*les débarquements*). In using such soft terminology, Normans give a sweeping category to what was violent combat and destruction. In many respects, this term is more appropriate to French experiences beyond Normandy where the arrival of the allies was seen from afar. Furthermore, one must not forget the agency inherent in the Liberation of the South, during which many citizens liberated themselves or at least had the help of their compatriots fighting with the French First Armored Division.[4] Yet although Marseille and other cities suffered major losses and destruction, as a region, Normandy was the main French casualty of war, and this was reflected in regional attitudes and resentments toward their Liberators. British soldier A. G. Herbert compared

Norman reception to the rest of France, describing his arrival in Paris, "We now felt at last that we had left Normandy and were meeting the real French people for the first time. Unlike the people of Normandy, these folk made us feel welcome, and it seemed worth fighting for their freedom."[5] In remembrance, 6 June remains a bittersweet day for Normans.

The second part of this chapter argues that while many Normans were able to forgive the destruction and pay public tribute to former Allied soldiers, expressions in material culture demonstrate how, elsewhere, Norman resentment evolved into underground subversion of this public gratitude. Consequently, in recent years, lingering Norman resentments have been appropriated by extreme right-wing groups and have occasionally but continuously surfaced at American commemorative sites. These tensions were even reflected on the national level, as between 1956 and 1985 the American cemetery in Normandy increasingly became the stage for a story of waning Franco-American diplomatic friendship as the memory of D-Day was contested. During this time, Norman memory of D-Day gradually evolved from region-specific to a national collective with less emphasis on trauma and more priority given to French agency in self-liberation, such as the Resistance fighters. While perplexing in its codes and silences, French remembrance of D-Day provides insight into how collective memory, while often dependent on local landmarks and site-specificity, is nonetheless capable of revising itself, thereby contributing to international relations and even functioning across national divides.

THE SIGNAL MONUMENTS AND OFFICIAL MEMORY

When the Allied forces stormed the Norman beaches and fought their way inland, they needed logistical support. Two floating harbors of British origin, code-named "Mulberries," were assembled in the waters of Vierville-sur-mer and Arromanches-les-bains between 7 and 18 June 1944, in order to service Allied supply needs until the major port city Cherbourg was captured. Originally, each harbor consisted of roughly six miles of flexible steel roadways that floated on pontoons girded in steel and concrete, comprising about 31,000 tons of steel.[6] Great piers provided access to the beach, and the artificial harbors were sheltered from the sea by lines of massive sunken caissons, sunken ships, and floating breakwaters.[7] A violent storm destroyed the port off Omaha Beach on 19 June 1944, and afterwards, its still-operable parts were towed to Arromanches, to the British-operated Mulberry, that saw continued use for the following ten months. In total, this harbor landed 2.5 million men, 500,000 vehicles and 4 million tons of goods.[8]

The floating harbors figure importantly, albeit indirectly, in French memory of D-Day. In 1946, the United States government agreed to give the salvageable materials of Omaha Beach's inoperable floating harbor to France, for the purpose of resale and profit, ostensibly to be used during reconstruction. The French government instead decided to dedicate the profits to multiple projects whose goal was to commemorate D-Day. Two hundred workers operated out of Vierville-sur-mer between 1949 and 1955, eventually packing a total of 28,000 tons of scrap metal.[9] The materials were then sold off, creating a profit of F180 million, or for 2008 standards, approximately just under $200,000,000.[10] This enormous sum was placed under the care of Raymond Triboulet (1906–2006), the sous-préfet of Bayeux and a devoted supporter of Charles de Gaulle. Under Triboulet's direction, the D-Day Commemoration Committee was established on 22 May 1945, and in coordination with American, British, and Canadian governments, this committee continually has helped to organize most of the commemorative ceremonies for D-Day in Normandy.[11] Comprised of the mayors of the small villages that dot the coastline where the Allies assaulted the beaches, the committee remains to this day the longest lasting and most effective organization in France serving the memory of D-Day.[12] Most importantly, the Committee facilitated the preservation of the sites by deeming them historic through government law.[13]

The Committee's projects began with ten almost-identical Signal Monuments, the first of which was established in 1950. Another early major commemorative effort was the marking of La Voie de la

Liberté, or Liberty Highway, consisting of cylindrical, cream-colored, stout kilometer markers bearing a design of the eternal flame along the routes taken by the Allied forces to liberate France.[14] The third early project was the posting of signs bearing names of soldiers killed on various roads, first established in 1951 and then constructed of more durable enamel in 1958.[15] Over time, other major projects came to include: numerous museums across Normandy, including those in Arromanches-les-bains (1953), Sainte-Mère Église (1964), and Benouville/Pegasus Bridge (1974). The Committee also funded some reconstruction efforts like the rebuilding of church steeples in Caen (ca. 1954) and Tilly-sur-Seulles (1963), and, until the American Battle Monuments Commission took over in 1979, the Committee oversaw the commemorative park on Pointe du Hoc (first established 1956). Finally, the Committee turned the blockhouses on Longues-sur-mer into commemorative sites (1961).

Figure 8: Borne 00, Kilometer marker for *La Voie de la Liberté*, 1946-1947. Sainte Marie du Mont, Manche. Photo courtesy of Kate C. Lemay.

The Signal Monuments are the best example of the importance of place in D-Day memory. Site or place is a key and defining characteristic of French memory of the landings. Site-specificity prioritizes the physical inseparability between a work and its site of installation. D-Day memory in France, by virtue of being the battlefield, is innately driven by a sense of the historical value of that terrain or landscape. In site-specificity, then, the significance of the memorial-as-object depends upon the bodily presence and individual experience in the here-and-now moment.[16] The experiential quality of material culture whose message is inherently wrapped up in its location—such as monuments—should not be underestimated. Before the blockbuster movies, these monuments served to mark and establish in collective memory *la plage sanglots,* or "Bloody Omaha." This term was developed by the visceral memories of veterans that the waters were colored red from blood during the assault, and also by the Normans who witnessed the trauma.

F50 million, or approximately $7 million, was allocated to produce the Signal Monuments. The first was dedicated in Bernières-sur-mer on 5 June 1950.[17] Six of the monuments mark points along the English Channel where the Allies landed; four more are inland, marking the important battles that took place in Carentan (1954), Sainte Mère Église (1954), Bénouville (Pegasus Bridge, c. 1955), and Isigny-sur-mer(1958). The monuments were designed beginning in 1948 by Yves-Marie Froidevaux, who was the Chief Architect of Historical Monuments from 1939 to 1983. The Signal Monuments' aesthetic, through the fortress-like solidity of their form and materials, visually relate Froidevaux's specialty in restoring medieval churches. Those Signal Monuments placed on the beach are the largest, reaching just under 30 feet in height and nine feet in width. Their design is heavy and blocky, yet a graceful curve in the back creates a surging forward and upward movement. Adhering to mid-century design principles allowing its overall form to be the main expression, the monument is plain and without decoration, bearing only inscriptions in block letters only in French (with additional plaques in English placed at a later date) to dedicate the works to the memory of the various military forces. The Signal Monuments are impressive for both their permanent appearance as well as for their seeming movement upwards. They resemble the dominating and aggressive prow of a ship, symbolizing the enormous force of the assault upon the beaches.

Figure 9: Yves-Marie Froidevaux, *Signal Monument*, drawing ca. 1948. Archives of the Comité du débarquement, Bayeux.

With their enduring material and mid-century expressive abstraction, the Signal Monuments reflect the official, government-sponsored memory of D-Day in France. Official culture, as historian John Bodnar explains it, involves the cultural leaders and authorities in society concerned with social unity, continuity of existing institutions and loyalty to the status quo.[18] Official culture relies on dogmatic formalism and the restatement of reality in ideal rather than complex or ambiguous terms. These monuments, however, were not sufficient as places of pilgrimage for a people devastated by war. Instead, as I argue elsewhere, the French, Normans especially, appropriated Allied war cemeteries, as places through which to channel and understand their own traumas.[19] These cemeteries dot the Norman landscape, and include twenty formal burial grounds for the Commonwealth, for which remains were collected and interred by military forces, rather than buried, likely ad-hoc or by Normans in civilian cemeteries. In keeping with the example set after the First World War, the Commonwealth never repatriated their dead, and nor did the Germans. Five cemeteries are located in Normandy for the remains of German soldiers. Two park-like cemeteries with major works of American art and architecture hold the remains of American soldiers, but until 1949, eight temporary American cemeteries were found across Manche and Orne.[20] At that time, the United States government repatriated 60 percent of their dead.[21]

In stark contrast to Anglo-American practice, the only French war cemetery in Normandy holds the remains of nineteen soldiers of Gen. Jacques-Philippe Leclerc's Free French 2d Armored Division. It is located in Écouves, a village five kilometers north of Alençon in the Orne department. But this instance of an official French site of memory is rare. Equally important, beyond such markers as the Signal Monuments, the French landscape also lacked the kind of commemorative material culture such as village and town memorials that had been such an important aspect of the French response to the death and devastations of 1914-18. Thus, in their attempt to recover from war traumas sustained during the 1940s, many Normans appropriated Allied cemeteries for their own mourning. Those living near the eight temporary American and twenty Commonwealth military cemeteries had seen them grow from the days of battle. Some Norman men even helped in recovering bodies for burial. For example, Jacques Pingnot, who at age nineteen worked with the American Graves Registration Service from June 1944 through July 1945, described the bodies that were strewn about in Norman landscape, a large amount of which had been flooded. "When the water went away" he said, "we found the bodies…we bagged them. A couple hundred of them. We got used to it, doing it every day."[22] Given the difficult visceral tragedy the Normans had witnessed and even experienced, the bland, stocky Signal Monuments were not sufficient as pilgrimage sites. Therefore, Normans covertly dealt with their own difficult and complex war history, in the context of political and social upheaval and even interpersonal violence, by becoming active caretakers of the Allied war cemeteries.

Norman women organized initial information about the fallen, including personal effects left in clothing or boots, and the metal "dog tags" tucked inside the helmet placed on a rifle crossed by the bayonet. Norman women and children were the most frequent visitors to the battlefield cemeteries, perhaps because it was more acceptable for them to play a public role in mourning the region's overwhelming loss. Working in the dirt, decorating the American grave with planted flowers and shrubs, women created symbolic memorials, not only to the fallen soldier but also to their own experience.[23] Indeed, the care-taking of graves of the Liberators provided Normans a healing ritual. One Caen resident, Marie Louise Godmer, decorated the grave of an American soldier for years and corresponded with his family. Due to the destruction of Caen, Godmerwas displaced for six months, but she still performed this commemorative service.[24] To this day, *Les Fleurs de la Mémoire,* a volunteer organization based in Saint Lô, organizes the decoration of 2,300 American graves in Normandy by 720 French families.[25]

D-DAY, THE TRAUMA

When we rose from the dirt, we saw an immense smoking cloud before us. As Saint Lô burned, we said to each other, 'those Savages!'[26]
–Saint Lô, Capital of Ruins, 1944

In other places, people are probably joyously celebrating June 6. Not here. Today, at 8pm, we will place a plaque on the prison to remember the 80 imprisoned by Nazis who were killed. Tomorrow, the dedication of a stele for firemen killed while on duty; at 10pm, mass for the remembrance of all those killed during the bombardments...[27]
–Caen, The Martyred City, 1945

On 6 June 1944, Allied planes dropped thousands of tons of bombs on the Norman cities of Caen, Saint Lô, and Liseux (among others).

By 1:30 p.m. Caen was a smoking ruin, and by the end of the day, 15,000 of its residents were homeless, 2,000 more were injured, and 2,000 were dead.[28] The "*cité martyre*," as Caen became known, endured just over ten weeks of battle, during which an estimated 5,000 to 10,000 tons of bombs were dropped.[29] Caen was not the only city in Calvados to experience terrible fate. To the southeast, Lisieux suffered the deaths of 1,200 during the 6 and 7 June bombardments. It came to be referred to as "*la cité meurtie*," meaning, "the scarred city," as it lost 75 percent of its structures, in turn leaving approximately 8,000 citizens of Lisieux without homes. To the west of Caen, Saint Lô, "*la capitale des ruines*," was 95 percent destroyed: first due to the bombardments on 5 and 6 June, and then due to battle in July. During the aftermath, in their desperation Normans often became enemies. One survivor in Lisieux recalled seeing one man who was trapped under rubble calling for help. "Someone approached him, and started to remove the rubble. In a flash, he took his wallet and moved on calmly, leaving the man stuck in the ruins."[30] The *sous-préfet* of Lisieux, P. Rossillon, pleaded in a letter published in the local newspaper on 21 June 1944, "At the moment during which we are crying for the hundreds of dead...at the moment during which Normandy has become a battlefield with an increasing amount of ruins, I ask of everyone to remain disciplined, united and in solidarity with one another during this suffering..."[31] The devastation endured by the Normans and the extreme circumstances of survival during the landings' aftermath in effect became a phenomenon revealing the worst character of humanity—of people turning against each other. The shame and the chagrin in turn have had long-lasting, if unspoken, effects on the memory of D-Day.

Given such harrowing statistics—but perhaps because of such despicable episodes—it is odd but fascinating that very few memorials (with the exception of the Mémorial de Caen, discussed later) or markers were put in place to commemorate French civilian deaths during the immediate postwar era. Prior to 1965, the grassroots association *Le Souvenir Français* placed six small steles in cemeteries or on the side of streets in Manche towns La Glacerie, Cerisy-la-Forêt, Coutances, Avranches, and Valognes.[32] During the immediate postwar era, the only large-scale memorials of which I am aware, located in Saint Lô and Falaise, were organized by and paid for by local citizens. This is likely due to government restrictions, as well as the fact that knowledge about civilian death first was published in major newspapers in 1994, during the fiftieth anniversary commemorative publications in *Ouest-France*. Until this major anniversary, rarely if ever did newspapers outside of the ruined towns address the issue.

Although as a whole, French memorials and French civilian cemeteries lacked the same kind of pilgrimage power as the Allied war cemeteries and memorials, one civilian cemetery in Saint Lô reveals the realities of *la capitale des ruines*. A large, unified plot located in the principal cemetery of the city, on the Rue du Général Gerhardt, contains 250 graves for the nearly 500 victims of the 6 June bombardment of Saint Lô. The design of this plot is simple and dignified, consisting of six rows of forty knee-high, gray-granite, rectangular headstones. The inscriptions identifying the victims, however, reveal the painful nature of the experience and its memory. On one headstone, the words read (translated into English): "9 Bodies / Rue de la Herbaudiere / Cave Sodey / Therefore Mr. Bourlier / and his children." The remains of the nine bodies, marred beyond distinction and undoubtedly intermingled, are buried together under this one stone. Other headstones bear the result of lost identities inherent in such a tragedy: "Older Woman / Rue de la Marne"; "Remains / Rue Belle Croix"; "Unknown Algerian"; "Families / Baufils-Fabre / Porcher / Cadiou / Duchemin." The sparse words describe, in the most dignified manner possible, the horror Saint Lô went through, and the miserable deaths of five hundred victims. There are no dates of birth and death for those identified. Instead, it is enough to be part of the heartrending and wretched plot, whose boundary is marked with a long stone slab set into the ground, *"Victimes du Bombardement 6 juin 1944."*

The psychological toll of the tragedy is revealed in the absence of commemorative material culture. At the center of the repression was the French government itself. Historian Henri Rousso has described how postwar era government officials considered French civilian deaths as "inappropriate" for traditional forms of commemoration.[33] Until 1968, all monuments first had to get approval from the national government, a laborious process involving two separate committees and many figureheads.[34] For example, in the Manche, memorialization efforts between 1945 and 1950 reflect the larger political tensions between Gaullists (pro-Charles de Gaulle) and Communists, who were battling each other for power in the national government. Of the twenty-nine commemorative steles put into place, thirteen were for the Resistance, and principally for those of communist politics, including Maurice Marland in Granville and Désiré Lerouxel in Avranches. During this early phase, in the Manche (the American sector), the memory of the American liberators was largely placed to the side, as only four sites were inaugurated: a monument to the 1st Engineers on Utah Beach, erected by the Americans; commemorative plaques for American soldier Rex Combs in Chef-du-Pont; Eisenhower's former headquarters in Jullouville; and a memorial in Graignes to Americans and French who were burned alive in the church. Four plaques were dedicated in the Manche to the memory of civilian victims: two in 1947 and two in 1948. Since 1968, however, the presence of material culture greatly increased in the landscape: twenty-four plaques were dedicated to civilian victims, seventy-two erected to commemorate Americans who died, and eighteen more for the Resistance. Beginning in 1968, the government loosened its control over approval of monuments, and completely relinquished it in 1982. At this point, to borrow Jay Winter's phrase, a "memory boom" started, and individuals, associations, and communes continually have engaged in commemorative efforts.[35]

The unfortunate circumstances of Caen, which lost 75 percent of its buildings and homes during bombardments and ensuing on-ground battles, remained in the hearts of the Caennais. As a result, Jean-Marie Girault, the mayor of Caen during the years 1971-1998, wished to construct a museum to commemorate the tragic consequences of the war in the region; to promote historical study of war; and to make a statement promoting world peace. At eighteen years of age, Girault had been an ambulance driver and part of the Red Cross response to the Battle of Caen, often narrowly escaping death. When elected mayor, he designated space for the Mémorial de Caen in 1972, and finally secured appropriate finances and institutional mission in 1983. Partnering with the research team, *l'Institutd'Histoire du Temps Présent*, a group operating out of the French government's *Centre Nationale des Recherches Scientifique*, the city of Caen decided to construct a history museum pertaining to World War II and the Cold War, as well as providing a center for research. Within the museum, the history of twentieth century wars were illustrated by multi-media sources, and the museum itself was designed to be a monument to the destruction of Caen.[36] The first stone was laid in 1986 by then-Prime Minister Jacques Chirac, and opened to the public in 1988. Five gallery spaces were researched and organized by various historians according to the following themes: The Fragility of Peace, 1919-1939; France during the Occupation; World War/Total War (1941-45, featuring the Holocaust); From the Landings to Victory (opened in 2010); and a film by Jacques Perrin, *Hope* (recently removed and replaced by films on the Battle of Normandy). Because visitors have traditionally come to learn about World War II history, in 2002 galleries were added covering the memory of civilian death in Normandy. In 2009, however, the scope was extended to include another gallery providing details of the Berlin Air Lift and the Cold War.[37]

The fiftieth anniversary of D-Day, meanwhile, marked the beginning of major change in French memory, catalyzing a process of continual new inquiries into the French experience of the landings and especially of the Allied bombing campaign that accompanied it. For instance, a census in January 1994, organized by the Mémorial de Caen, reveals some contemporary French attitudes about D-Day. Across France, a thousand people ages eighteen and older were asked questions about associations with D-Day and feelings about former enemies and allies. Relative to associations with D-Day, 41 percent reported thinking of the Liberation first. Eighty-five percent responded that they think first and foremost about the role played by the Americans, whereas 35 percent first reflect on the Free French 2d Armored Division who landed under direction of Gen. Jacques-Philippe Leclerc.[38] Popular films and TV-series such as *The Longest Day* (1962), *Saving Private Ryan* (1998), and *Band of Brothers* (2001) have helped American memory dominate the collective recollection of D-Day. Perhaps as a result, many of those French who experienced and survived the Battle of Normandy acknowledge the trauma but they do not dwell on it, instead choosing to exhibit acceptance and stoicism. One Saint Lô survivor wrote, "That which we suffered in Normandy was an ordeal of the time—a few unforgettable months—but it can not be compared to what other civilians in different corners of Europe and the world since have been through. Nevertheless, the ordeal profoundly marked us."[39]

Such "marking" ensured that by the 1990s the memory of civilian death due to Allied bombardment began to emerge in public consciousness through the publication of eyewitness accounts in regional newspapers. Just as importantly, in 1994, French laws regarding the construction of municipal *monuments-aux-morts* were changed to allow the list of the dead to include not only the names of soldiers killed in action but also the names of civilian victims of the war, finally reversing the postwar failure to acknowledge civilian dead. A year later, concerted grass-root efforts also were made to commemorate civilian death, and by 2004, *l'Association Normandie mémoire* had begun organizing annual ceremonies to commemorate the civilian victims of the Battle of Normandy. Publications by French scholars have greatly facilitated the emergence of these recollections, particularly those writing in the 1980s and 1990s.[40] These historians have written provocatively and at length about the difficult humiliation postwar French society had to negotiate, and the resulting widespread denial of certain events and facts.[41] Furthermore, research teams at the Université de Caen, Basse-Normandie, among other institutions, have contributed important studies of civilian trauma during the war.[42] Finally, the Mémorial de Caen Peace Museum has become a major outlet for Caennais and other Normans to speak about their war experiences and participate in scholarly events, in addition to functioning as a national field trip destination for students in grammar and high school.[43] The success of the museum is apparent in its effect on the surrounding commemorative landscape: already by 1984, as Serge Barcellini argues, there was a shift in primacy of location and site-specific memory, from Bayeux, the seat of the *Comité du débarquement,* to Caen.[44]

It is crucial to note that Normandy is not the only region to address its losses. In 2008, the major port city of Brest in Brittany converted the Abri-Sadi-Carnot—a former mile-long tunnel that functioned as bomb shelter, hospital, and Nazi arms storage, which tragically exploded in 1944, killing more than 400 French and Germans—into a peace museum.[45] Moreover, by the early twenty-first century the deaths of Norman civilians during the summer of 1944 were also increasingly recognized—and understood—in the context of the national catastrophes and traumas of the war, including: the French fight and defeat, 1939–40; the deportation of Jewish people; the internment camps located in France for gypsies and nomads; and the forced labor camps for the Todts and others.[46] For the whole of France, historians estimate that between 150,000 and 270,000 civilians died by bombardment, execution, massacre, deportation, or internal combat, a number equivalent to nearly half the losses of American soldiers of World War II, but one that until recently has largely been unacknowledged.[47]

In concert with the increasing visibility given to the traumas of the past, the late-twentieth century also saw D-Day tourism become an official, government sponsored endeavor. To be sure, veterans and local communities had long been involved in commercially-oriented memorial activities. But by the 1990s, such activities were increasingly initiated by regional and national government. In 1994, for instance, the municipal government in Lower Normandy began to organize and coordinate tours with historical markers, while by 1997 the organization SETEL, *Société d'études touristiques et d'équipement de loisirs,* had realized eight thematic circuits following the progression of battle after D-Day: *Overlord l'assaut; Cobra la percée; la contreattaque; l'encerclement; le dénouement; D-Day le choc; Objective un port;* and *l'affrontement.* Big, blue information panels called *totems* mark the circuits, and signs along the roads guide tourists to points of interests and the direction of the next totem. In addition to these circuits, the regional government has funded the renovation of several of those museums initially built by the D-Day

Commemoration Committee, such as the Pegasus Bridge Museum (2000) and the Paratroopers Museum in Sainte Mère Église (2011), as well as the construction of new exhibits at the Utah Beach Museum (2011). The most recent D-Day tourism efforts have attempted to integrate technology, such as the website with an interactive map and photographs pertaining to historical sites, "Les chemins de la mémoire". As historian Stéphane Cachard has acknowledged, all efforts are rituals of knowledge pertaining to the past, participating in the construction and identity of a region, a nation, and even of Europe. Effectively, Cachard links historic tourism of Normandy to the valorization of French identity and patrimony. He and others understandably are concerned about the rather inappropriate celebratory spirit and partying nature in the behavior of the re-enactors, those men and women who dress in American "GI" uniforms and camp out in the fields around Hiesville, Amfréville, and Sainte Mère Église. Responding to the circus-like atmosphere one sees today in Sainte Mère Église on 6 June, Cachard states that "memory tourism" must be given an ethical and moral direction by the local museums to sustain memory of the serious nature of the combat.[48]

By the 1990s, memory tourism had become connected to the commemorative activities of veterans as increasing numbers of old soldiers returned to visit their Normandy battlefields. American veterans, for example, have erected several private memorials to fallen comrades, often with local help and support. Agnès Bouffard, the mayor of Hiesville, is one of those community leaders who has been involved in these activities. In 1987, Bouffard was enlisted to help a group of Americans who had organized to fund the construction of a monument to honor GEN Don Forrester Pratt, the highest-ranking American soldier who died on D-Day, victim of a glider crash. With Bouffard's help, they were able to locate and secure the donation of a small corner of land in Hiesville for their monument. Since 1987, every 6 June, Bouffard coordinates a commemorative ceremony in Hiesville at the Pratt Memorial, which every other year is part of the official commemoration ceremonies organized by the *Comité du débarquement*. Bouffard stated that this memorial is one of the few monuments completely paid for by an American group; most in her area, like the stele commemorating the first American hospital on the Columbières farm, are funded by French Associations or Communes, or even by groups like re-enactors from Belgium and Holland.[49]

In summary, French memory of D-Day has recently evolved from one characterized simultaneously by both public gratitude and repression of painful trauma into one that is more openly inclusive. But this is also a memory more accessible for appropriation into regional tourism and domestic politics.

POLITICS AND THE SUBVERSION OF D-DAY MEMORY

As we now understand, over the years, the construction of the many monuments and memorials to the Allied Forces complicate French memory of D-Day. Yet initially, during the immediate postwar, the Norman French appropriated Allied war cemeteries as sites to channel grief and at which to recover from the war. Even during this early period, however, Normans felt lingering resentments against their Liberators, which would eventually surface in local and national politics. The tombstone of Louis Guérin, located in the village of Quibou in the department of the Manche, reflects a rare protest against Americans. After being forced to witness the rape of his wife, thirty-one-year-old Louis Guérin was murdered by at least one American soldier on 25 August 1944.[50] The same year, his father had the following inscription inscribed on his son's grave, "Tué par les noirs," meaning, "killed by the blacks."[51] The racist underpinnings of the inscription reveal that the Normans, a largely white, Catholic population—most of whom who had never seen racial minorities prior to World War II—would know instinctively, given the date and the racial description, that the murderers were American soldiers.

The grave of Louis Guérin is the only funerary site of which I am aware that was constructed during the immediate postwar era in protest of the American presence in Normandy. Even so, other strains of resentment and resistance have emerged, particularly as praise for American efforts during D-Day has often dominated commemorative rhetoric, problematically creating, as historian Olivier Wieviorka has pointed out, a remembrance of American soldiers as "demigods."[52] On occasion, the Normandy American cemetery has been a focal point for the expression of these resentments. Although intended, among other things, as a powerful public statement of transatlantic solidarity, American memorials in Normandy were available for local, regional and national appropriation. As a result, the Normandy American Cemetery, a formal presentation of sacrifice adorned by major works of American-designed art and architecture, has come to displace the French Signal Monuments in French memory. Few visitors to Omaha Beach today go to the Signal Monument, whereas millions every year walk through the American cemetery, drawn to the moving experience of visiting seemingly endless rows of individual graves. By moving through such a space, the visitors, the majority of which are European, and most of whom are French, are *experiencing* rather than looking. For them, the symbolic monument in the form of a ship's prow no longer suffices. As part of the shift in French memory, landscapes of American war memory have become enmeshed with French collective memory and even, at times, French national identity.

For instance, even during the inauguration of the Normandy American cemetery in 1956 there were hints that some in the French government might seek to use the site in ways not anticipated. Indeed, although offering the appropriate degree of gratitude, President Coty's 1956 speech was, at least in part, inspired by the Gaullist politics of the moment. This was a political creed keen to emphasize, indeed rehabilitate, French power and grandeur, a political movement largely driven by Charles de Gaulle's formidable efforts to rally French nationalism in the postwar period. Seen in this context, the American war cemetery and the memory of American sacrifice for French liberation in World War II clearly did not serve Gaullist ambitions.[53] As a result, French political speeches given at the American cemeteries dating from 1956-1978 vacillated between being highly critical of the United States and appropriating American war memory for their own explicitly nationalist terms.

These Franco-American tensions came to head in the 1960s, a

controversy more than apparent during the twentieth anniversary commemorations of June 1964 that de Gaulle refused to attend. In fact, his absence created a tension so extreme that the American ambassador to France, Charles E. Bohlen, later would quip that for de Gaulle, "The greatest amphibious military operation of all time was un-history."[54] Many of the American veterans present at the ceremony grumbled scornfully when the French representative, Jean Sainteny, Minister of Veterans Affairs, stated, "It is thanks to the French Résistance that the landings were successful." The same Americans were outraged when Sainteny reproached the Allies for not having sufficiently armed the French Resistance.[55] From Sainteny's speech especially, it would seem that the French were embittered by the attention that the Americans received, especially within the context of contemporary Franco-American tension. Bohlen reflected in 1968, "I feel that de Gaulle's basic interpretation of American power—which compels the French to withdraw from support of us in any given circumstance short of all-out war—really does not offer much hope or room for improvement...in Franco-American relations."[56]

De Gaulle's commemorative politics reveal his ambitions: after failing to pay tribute at the Normandy American Cemetery, two months later de Gaulle attended the ceremonies in the south of France to honor the actions of the Free French Forces during the Mediterranean landings of August 1944, thereby emphasizing the French role in the liberation of the South. His itinerary included twelve stops along the Mediterranean coast.[57] During the August commemorative ceremonies, he described how during the Third Republic and pre-war era, France had not put its defense first, and argued, "We must have modern arms and our own force of dissuasion. We must have our own national defense development. France must be strong as well as prosperous and hence a country that will be listened to in world affairs."[58] De Gaulle duly acted on these ideas in 1966 when he announced the French withdrawal from NATO and requested that the American bases in France to be closed by 1 April 1967. Continuing Franco-American disagreements over the conflict in Vietnam, together with a re-energized French commitment to build a powerful European Union, ensured that tensions between Washington and Paris lingered well into the 1970s, despite the departure of de Gaulle from office in 1968.

Finally, in January of 1978, after the end of the Vietnam War, Franco-American relations began to improve. French President Giscard d'Estaing received American President Jimmy Carter at Omaha Beach and the Normandy American Cemetery, and both presidents made speeches while standing in front of the cemetery's massive colonnade framing the bronze statue of the American youth ascending to heaven. Photographs of the two presidents were widely published in both France and the United States, and the resulting impression was that of a harmonious alliance and working relationship between the United States and France. The French responded to Carter's tour by becoming more aware of the diplomatic effect such a visit might make, a point that became evident again in June 1984 when President Reagan paid his official visit to the D-Day beaches. The positive diplomatic influence of these two trips in France was so effective that, since Carter, every American president has been invited to reenact a similar visit to the Normandy American Cemetery.[59] Farther to the north and east, along the British and Canadian sectors of the D-Day beaches, a similar synthesis of commemorative activities has also been apparent in Franco-British and Franco-Canadian commemorative activities, with the result being the emergence of locally distinct war memories among the communities near Gold, Juno, and Sword Beaches. But the contemporary power of American-sponsored D-Day narratives—especially on film, television, and in the literature of popular history—has ensured that American commemorative sites, specifically the Normandy Cemetery, have been the focal point of French efforts to appropriate and re-script the story of the D-Day landings.

Indeed, on occasion the Normandy American Cemetery has been a forum for historical revisionism: in 1985, for example, it was used by an extremist right-wing group seeking to challenge the very ideas and values that the cemetery is designed to commemorate and communicate. Anonymous neo-Nazis vandalized the colonnade of the Normandy American Cemetery a month before the

D-Day anniversary. The colonnade, the architrave of which bears the inscription, "This Embattled Shore, Portal Of Liberation Is Forever Hallowed By The Ideals, The Valor And The Sacrifices Of Our Fellow Countrymen," was defaced by writing in black graffiti that used the context of civilian death to question the Liberation: "Mai 1945, Libération? Dresde! 200,000 morts. Caen! St. Lô! Normandie Martyres!"[60] Although this was the aggressive act of an extremist group, it signaled the emergence of long-repressed memory, critical memory that recalled civilian death finally emerged from the Norman vernacular consciousness into the public, albeit through an extremist right wing gesture. With the memory of D-Day politicized and appropriated, formerly underground reminiscence of civilian death has evolved to be prominently featured in today's collective Norman memory. It even plays a role in current French visitation of German war cemeteries. During my field research in June 2011, I noted identical anonymous entries by "Michel" in the Visitor's Book at two different German Military Cemeteries from World War II located outside of Marigny and Lisieux. The remarks state, "You, brave German soldiers, you killed less French than our 'Allies,' the *'Ricains.* Caen 15000 dead...St. Lô, Condé, Rouen, Le Havre...I witnessed the landings at Hermanville."[61]

CONCLUSIONS

By noting first the French government's tendency to encourage the repression of unpleasant war experiences, and by tracing the shift in French memory toward the inclusion of civilian loss, we see how collective memory of the Norman war experience has been intertwined with politics and site-specificity. Due to official French control of monument construction prior to 1968, memory was restrained by design, most notably seen in the Signal Monuments program run by the *Comité du débarquement.* Contemporary Cold War tensions and a resurgent Gaullist nationalism ensured that in the 1950s and 1960s American war cemeteries and memorials became ripe fodder for political propaganda: for some, they were forums for invocations of diplomatic transatlantic relations; for others they were hindrances to Gaullist ambition. However, starting in 1968, with the loosening of restrictions on the number of French-designed memorials, French memory also began to shift, becoming more inclusive but also more subversive. In particular, by the 1990s, long-repressed elements of the Norman war experience were granted more commemorative space, and more public visibility: the civilian deaths that accompanied the allied landings were finally confronted and acknowledged. Yet this "loosening" of official control also created space for rebellious critiques, sometimes making the American cemeteries targets of anti-Americanism. By outlining these evolutions, it is clear that material culture should be considered as an important influence and even forceful agent in French memory of D-Day, as well as in the political theater of Franco-American relations.

Notes

1. William I. Hitchcock reports 100,000 Calvadosiens fled their homes. See Hitchcock, *The Bitter Road to Freedom: A New History of the Liberation of Europe* (New York: Free Press, 2008), 41.

2. For numbers of civilian deaths and military casualties from all nations, see Luc Capdevila and DanièleVoldman, *War Dead: Western Societies and the Casualties of War* (Edinburgh: Edinburgh University Press, 2002), 29. Numbering civilian dead at 13,000 is probably the best estimate for Lower Normandy; in all of Normandy (Upper and Lower) the total number of civilian dead is around 20,000. See Michel Boivin, Gérard Bourdin, Bernard Garnier and Jean Quellien, *Les Victimes Civiles de Basse-Normandie dans la Bataille de Normandie* (Caen: Éditions-Diffusion du Lys, 2009); Michel Boivin and Bernard Garnier, *Les victimes civiles de la manche dans la bataille de Normandie* (Caen:Éditions du Lys, 1994); and Michel Bourdin and Bernard Garnier, *Les victimes civiles du Calvados dans la bataille de Normandie* (Caen: Éditions du Lys, 1995).

3. It should also be noted that in the southern provinces, there was a "second" D-Day, consisting of the August 1944 landings from the Mediterranean Sea. However, due to the tourism and vacation attraction of this area, this

second D-Day has almost been entirely wiped from the landscape, with only a handful of memorials in existence specific to the landings.

4. In Operation Dragoon, the American Seventh Army swept north as fast as it could, to meet with the Third Army and Allied forces in the Vosges and Metz, then pushing the German military north and east.

5. Hitchcock, 43. Hitchcock demonstrates the warmer receptions that Allied soldiers received once outside of Normandy, citing Herbert and others. See Hitchcock, 19–46.

6. The harbors were fabricated in secrecy in Britain and floated into position immediately after D-Day.

7. The shelter consisted of concrete caissons (also known as "Phoenixes") sunk in line offshore, as well as floating steel tanks of cruciform shape ("Bombardons") moored about three miles out to sea. The uploading facilities ("Whales") comprised of floating pier-heads, which adjusted to the ebb and flow of the tide; these were connected to the shore by roadways which were laid on floats and secured to moorings attached to anchors in the seabed. See Guy Hartcup, *Code Name Mulberry: The Planning, Building and Operation of the Normandy Harbours* (New York: Hippocrene Books, Inc., 1977), 15.

8. Chris Trueman, "The Mulberry Harbour," *History Learning Site*, accessed 5 June 2012, http://www.historylearningsite.co.uk/mulberry_harbour.htm.

9. Thierry Houvel, quoted in *La Renaissaince*, 6 June 1994.

10. All money conversions from francs into dollars from this point on are of 2008 standard.

11. Archives of the Comité du débarquement, "Monuments Signaux." Bayeux, France.

12. The master list kept by the Committee reveals the most important political figures and associations for the memory of D-Day; among this list are approximately eighteen other important and viable associations that have sustained effective efforts to the remembrance, including *l'Association nationale des enfants et petits-enfants des évadés et rescapés du Vel d'Hiv 16 juillet 1942; l'Association franco-américaine des aérodromes normands de la 9e US Air Force*, and so forth.

13. French law of 21 May 1947 outlined the responsibilities of the D-Day Commemoration Committee. According to this law, vestiges of the floating harbor off Arromanches-les-bains were preserved as a historic site. Lacking a preservation law pertaining to the Mediterranean assault in August 1944,

vestiges of the battle that led from Toulon to Saint Raphael are no longer visible. This stretch of coastline comprises the French Riviera and has long since been developed into commercial and residential real estate.

14. For Comité du débarquement and tourism, see Sam Edwards, "Commemoration and Consumption in Normandy, c. 1945–1994," in *War Memory and Popular Culture: Essays on Modes of Remembrance and Commemoration*, eds, M. Keren and H. H. Holger, 76–91, (Jefferson, North Carolina: McFarland, 2009). Edwards attributes the initial idea for the *Voie de la Liberté* to French officer Guy de la Vesselais, who thought the road would "pay 'homage' to the 'traditional fraternity of the Franco-American armies'..." See Edwards, "Commemoration," 78.

15. Archives of the Comité du débarquement, « Monuments Signaux. » Bayeux, France. In 1957, F2,000,000, or $32,568, was allocated to the construction of eighty-six panels bearing the names of American soldiers killed in action. Made of enamel and reflective material, this permanent signage is located in the Manche along service routes of the landings.

16. On site-specificity and art, see Miwon Kwon, "One Place after Another: Notes on Site Specificity," *October* 80 (Spring 1997): 85–110.

17. Archives of the Comité du Débarquement, « Monuments Signaux » folder, Bayeux, France. For this monument, the architect earned three million francs, or about $48,849.

18. For the role of official culture in public memory, see John Bodnar, *Remaking America: Public Memory, Commemoration, and Patriotism in the Twentieth Century* (Princeton: Princeton University Press, 1992), 13–20.

19. I address how the American war cemeteries figure prominently in the evolution of French memory in my dissertation, "Forgotten Memorials: The American Cemeteries in France from World War II." (Indiana University, 2011).

20. The cemeteries included the following: Saint Laurent-sur-mer (3,797 graves); Marigny (3,070 graves); Le Chêne Guérin (1,202 graves); La Cambe (4,534 graves); Sainte Mère Église Number 1 (2,095 graves); Sainte Mère Église Number 2 (4,098 graves); Saint James (4,367 graves); and Blosville (5,766 graves).

21. This percentage of repatriation is taken by the American Battle Monuments Commission, the government agency that designed the permanent military cemeteries overseas. See the pamphlet brochures pertaining to the overseas

cemeteries available at "Cemeteries," ABMC, http://abmc.gov/cemeteries/index.php

22. Interview by the author, June 2011. Also quoted in Jeff Stoffer, *Mother of Normandy: The Story of Simone Renaud* (China: Iron Mike Entertainment, 2010), 64.

23. I have not found archival sources relating specific numbers of Normans who adopted American graves during the postwar era, but judging from interviews I have conducted with Normans who worked in the cemeteries, I estimate a conservative ten to twenty women per cemetery. Today there are several groups organized for the adoption of graves, including: Association Thanks-GI (Lorraine) headed by Elizabeth Gozzo, Souvenir Franco-Americain Draguignan (Provence) headed by Maurice Dreclerc, and Les Fleurs de la Memoire (Normandy). See Eleanor Beardsley, "French Families Adopt US Graves in Normandy," *National Public Radio*, 26 May 2008, accessed 5 Mar. 2012, http://www.npr.org/templates/story/story.php?storyId=90824280; and Antonin Dehays, "'Blosville': Un Cimetière américain provisoire en Normandie," *39–45 Magazine* (Bayeux: Éditions Heimdal, 2011), 46–51.

24. Marie-Louise Godmer to an unknown American recipient, 10 May 1946. Collection of Antonin Dehays.

25. *Ouest France*, 13 and 14 Apr. 2002.

26. Jacqueline Lecaplain's journal entry, 7 Nov. 1944.See Jean Poupard, ed.,*Témoignages des Saint Lois de 1944* (Saint Lô: Association « Saint Lô 44 », Responsable éditions, Octobre, 1994), 38.Translated from French to English by Kate C. Lemay.

27. Letter, Jean Dupuis, 6 June 1945, republished in *Ouest-France*, Apr.1994. Translated from French to English by by Kate C. Lemay.

28. Jean-Pierre Azéma, Robert O. Paxton and Philippe Burrin, *6 juin 44*, (Caen:Editions Perrin/Le Mémorial de Caen, 2004), 132–134; Henri Goupil, interview by the author,27 Feb.–1 June 2011.

29. *Liberté de Normandie,* 10 July 1945; and *Liberté de Normandie,* 9 July 1954.

30. *Ouest-France,* 8 Sept. 1984.

31. P. Rossillon, "À la population meurtrie," *Le Lexovien,* 21 June 1944; reprinted in *L'Eveil de Lisieux,* 31 March 1994.

32. Jacqueminede Loizellerie, "Les lieux de mémoire de la Seconde Guerre mondiale dans la manche," (Mémoire de maitrise, Université de Caen, 1998), 44.

33. Henri Rousso, *The Vichy Syndrome: History and Memory in France since 1944*, trans. Arthur Goldhammer (Cambridge, MA: Harvard University Press, 1991), 22–24.

34. A departmental commission for the purpose of approval of a monument was consulted, and they in turn counselled by a national commission. Each commission had more than sixteen members, and had only two months for the approval process, leading to the prioritizing of memorials according to politics rather than an even-handed consideration of all memorials. Loizellerie, "Les lieux," 34–36.

35. For monument statistics prior to 1965, see Loizellerie, 133–37. For statistics up to 1995, see Loizellerie, 10. For French law history, see Loizellerie, 30–38. For the importance of the French *commune* or village, which was like an extension of the family, in paying tribute to the memory of individual loss, see Serge Barcellini and Annette Wiewiorka, *Passant, souviens-toi! Les lieux du souvenir de la Seconde Guerre mondial en France* (Paris: Plon, 1995), 14–20. For the definition of the memory boom as part of tourism and leisure time, see Jay Winter, *Remembering War: The Great War between Memory and History in the Twentieth Century* (London: Yale University Press, 2006), 38–39.

36. Architect Jacques Millet designed the structure, a block-like building with an entrance of vertically-oriented rough stones made to look like a large crack in the Earth. Across the facade, the following text written by Norman poet Paul Dorey is inscribed: *"La douleur m'abrisée; la fraternité m'arelevée; de ma blessure a jailliun fleuve de liberté,"* (translated by Kate C. Lemay: Pain has broken me, brotherhood has raised me, from my wound flowed a river of freedom).

37. Historians who have worked on these galleries include Etinne Fouilloux and Denis Peschanski (The Fragility of Peace 1919–1939); Jean-Pierre Azéma and Henri Rousso (France during the Occuption); Robert Franck and Denis Maréchal (World War/Total War); and Philippe Buton and Dominique Veillon (From the Landings to Victory). Recently, Jean Quellien has curated the gallery on the Battle of Normandy and World War II history. Prior to the renewed focus on World War II history, the Mémorial de Caen found itself unable to succeed in attaining the predicted 600,000 visitors per year. Eighty percent of the public visits the gallery spaces dedicated to D-Day and the Second World War; mostly secondary school students (rather than general

tourists) on field trips visited the other galleries. The gallery featuring the Nobel Peace Prize Winners was taken down in the fall of 2011. Recent additions include Cartooning for Peace, a gallery of critical opinions of war as demonstrated in the graphic arts; and finally, a section on the Cold War, featuring Berlin. Like all museums, these gallery-exhibitions are regularly changed and updated. See "Histoire de l'Institution et du Concept," Archives of the Mémorial de Caen.

38. Questionnaire, "Les français et le cinquantenaire du débarquement Allié de juin 1994," from *1994_50e Anniversaire: Presse France*, Archives of the Mémorial de Caen.

39. Jacqueline Lecaplain, reflecting in 1994; quoted in Poupard, 34.

40. Scholarship by Henri Rousso in particular has had a long-lasting influence on the recovery of French memory though a brave acknowledgement of French denial. See Rousso.

41. See, among others: Barcellini and Wieviorka; Capdevila and Voldman; Mechtild Gilzmer, *Mémoires de Pierre: Les monuments commémoratifs en France après 1944*, trans. Germaninto, French by Odile Demange, pref. Serge Barcellini (Paris: Éditions Autrement, 2009); Pierre Laborie, *Le chagrin et le venin: La France sous l'occupation, mémoire et idées recues* (Paris: Bayard, 2011); Jean Quellien, *La Normandie au coeur de la geurre* (Rennes: Éditions Ouest-France, 1992); Daniéle Voldman, *La reconstruction des villes françaises de 1940 à 1954* (Paris: L'Harmattan, 1997); Olivier Wieviorka, *Normandy: The Landings to the Liberation of Paris*, trans. M. B. De Bevoise (Cambridge, MA: The Belknap Press of Harvard University Press, 2008); and Olivier Wieviorka, *La mémoire désunie: Le souvenir politique des années sombres, de la libération à nos jours* (Paris: Éditions du Seuil, 2010).

42. Recent analysis of French civilian death includes virtual monuments to civilian victims. See Jean Quellien "Memorial des Victimes Civiles: Basse-Normandie," *Centre de Recherched'HistoireQuantitative*, n. d., accessed 13 Feb. 2012, http://www.crhq.cnrs.fr/1944/Basse-Normandie.php. See also Stéphane Cachard's tourism and memorial project, "Les victimes civiles," *NormandieMémoire*,n. d., accessed 13 Feb. 2012, http://www.normandi-ememoire.com/histoire.page.php?rubrique=normands&page=victime s_civiles.

43. Stéphane Simonnet, the Director of Scientific Research at the Mémorial de Caen, and his team have organized soirées for Caen citizens to discuss their

experiences during the war, as well as scholarly initiatives including the 2011 conference, "Rencontres internationales: Normandie, 6 juin: L'émergence d'unemémoire collective?"

44. See Serge Barcellini, "Diplomatie et commémoration: Les commémorations du 6 juin 1984: Une bataille de mémoire,"*Guerres Mondiales et conflits contemporains*47, no. 186 (Apr. 1997), 121–46.

45. For more on the museum, see *Ouest France,* 6 juillet 2007. For a description of the fire's aftermath, see Joseph James Shomon, *Crosses in the Wind: The Unheralded Saga of the Men in the American Graves Registration Service in World War II* (New York: Stratford House, 1947), 45–46.

46. Most remembrance relating to the French battle and defeat during 1939–1940 have been repressed in the material landscape in France. For example, prior to 1965 and the rise of Gaullism, only four communes in the Manche commemorated de Gaulle's 18 June 1940 appeal to the French to fight on and resist. See Loizellerie, 86. For internment camps and Jewish deportation, see pages 130 and 175.

47. See Voldman, 25.

48. Cachard is the director of tourism in Sainte-Mère Église and its surrounding communes. See Stéphane Cachard, email message to the author, 25 Sept. 2012.

49. Phone interview with Agnès Bouffard, 25 Sept. 2012.

50. The American soldier responsible for the rape and murder is identified in French documentation as Mr. Mogann. In American archives, I have not found any reference to this person, nor has J. Robert Lilly (see email correspondence between author and J. Robert Lilly, 21–23 Sept. 2011). For record of Mogann, see Préfecture de la Manche, "Commandations à Mort des Militaires Américains," No. 2820 B; archives of the Mairie de Quibou, Quibou, Manche, France. For more information on the rapes committed by American soldiers in Europe, see Patrick Cabouat and Alain Moreau's documentary film, *La face cachée des libérateurs,* dirs. Patrick Cabouat and Alain Moreau (France 3, 2006), 54 min.; also Alice Yaeger Kaplan, *The Interpreter* (New York: Free Press, 2005); J. Robert Lilly, *Taken By Force: Rape and American GIs in Europe During World War II* (New York: Palgrave Macmillan,2007); Stéphane Lamâche, *La Normandie Américaine* (Paris: Larousse, 2010); and Mary Louise Roberts, *What Soldiers Do: Sex and the American GI in WWII Europe* (Chicago: University of Chicago Press, 2013). For discussion of the

design of the burial plot for executed American soldiers of World War II in Europe, see Kate C. Lemay, "Forgotten Memorials: The American Cemeteries in France from World War II" (PhD Diss., Indiana University, Bloomington, 2011), 152–59.

51. Historian Antonin Dehays interviewed the daughter of Guérin on 19 Mar. 2012, and generously shared the information with me that the inscription was ordered by the father of Louis Guérin.

52. Wieviorka, *Normandy*, 11.

53. Bohlen wrote, "Above all, [de Gaulle] restored France's morale after the shattering blows of World War II. France was humiliated far more by the dreadful defeat of 1940 than those of us on the outside realized." See Charles Bohlen, *Witness to History, 1929–1969* (New York: W. W. Norton and Company, 1973), 502, 514–15.

54. Bohlen, *Witness to History*, 517.

55. *Paris-Presse*, 9 June 1964.

56. Bohlen, *Witness to History*, 520.

57. De Gaulle attended ceremonies in Fréjus, Dramont, Nartelle, Boulouris, St. Raphael, Sainte Maxime, La Croix Valmer, Cavalaire, Le Ayol Canadel, Hyères, Mont Faron, and Toulon. See "Le Général de Gaulle préside aujourd'hui," *Nice-Matin*, 15 Aug. 1964. During this visit, he was thirty to forty minutes by car from the Rhône American Cemetery in Draguignan, Provence, which was hosting commemoration ceremonies as well. His absence from the Rhône American Cemetery commemoration ceremony was seen as an affront by American diplomats.

58. *The New York Herald-Tribune*, 15 Aug. 1964. See also *Paris-Presse*, 1 Sept. 1964.

59. Recently, perhaps attempting to increase his popularity among conservatives, the French President François Hollande visited Normandy, but attended ceremonies in Ranville, the British sector, and not the American cemetery overlooking Omaha Beach.

60. *Ouest-France*, 3 May 1985; and *Courrier de l'ouest*, 3May 1985.

61. In French, the term 'ricains' is pejorative slang for American.

Chapter Five

"Sie Kommen":
From Defeat to Liberation—German and Austrian
Memory of the Allied "Invasion" of 6 June 1944

Günter Bischof and Michael S. Maier[1]

The Battle of the Bulge was the bloodiest battle on the Western Front in World War II. Yet the Western Allies' invasion of Normandy "has become the symbol of World War II in Europe" and is at the forefront of the former Allies' remembrance culture and politics of history.[2] For Germans and Austrians, meanwhile, the Normandy "invasion" marked a decisive defeat; only recently have the Germans begun to talk about the beginning of their "liberation" from Hitler's terror regime in their remembrance of the Normandy campaign.[3] While American and British D-Day veterans have been flooding the beaches of Normandy, German and Austrian veterans have quietly and unobtrusively visited the bunkers of the "Atlantic Wall," or paid tribute to their fallen comrades at one of the six German cemeteries in Normandy (in which 77,976 Germans and Austrians are interred). The largest of these is La Cambe, where 21,500 soldiers are buried.[4] Austrian soldiers made up roughly one-tenth of Nazi Germany's armed formations of approximately twelve million soldiers. Proportionally we may speculate that among these fallen German *Wehrmacht* and SS soldiers buried in Normandy there may be as many as 8,000 Austrian nationals.

While the victorious Allies engage in cults of intense *public memory* regarding this decisive turning point of World War II, especially the Americans and British, there is no such intense public and institutional memory among Germans and Austrians; the German and

Austrian "memory booms" of World War II have concentrated on the final solution, after a long period of denial, their victimization in the bombing war, the Germans' expulsions from the East, and the criminal campaigns of the *Wehrmacht* on the Eastern Front.[5] As Robert G. Moeller has suggested, West Germans preferred to see themselves as victims in the 1950s and again in the 1980s–1990s; by and large the same is true of the Austrians.[6] The Western Allies' commemorations have constructed a distinct public memory of D-Day, with their heads of state gathering on the beaches of Normandy in 1984, 1994, and 2004, defining collective national memories in their speeches, and with thousands of veterans gathering for somber commemorations of their fallen comrades. The first German chancellor admitted to the exclusive club of D-Day victors, Gerhard Schröder, took part in 2004.

Similarly, while *individual memories* of Allied D-Day soldiers have been collected assiduously and the soldiers' sacrifice and patriotism defined with gusto as "the greatest generation," the same has not been true for those who were defending the Norman coast on the morning of 6 June 1944.[7] To be sure, German and Austrian Normandy veterans have often been eager to tell their stories and travel to Normandy when asked; their memories largely revolved around the enormous advantages of the Western Allies in materiel and the devastating bombardments they endured from the air, sea, and land. But no specific oral history collections of Axis Normandy veterans have been published.[8] Likewise, the *cultural memory* landscape of Normandy is littered with American, British, and Canadian memorials, museums, and cemeteries; in fact, Normandy cemeteries have mutated to "American places."[9] Germans, in contrast, have treaded carefully with modest memorials and burial grounds. There is no distinct Austrian presence in Normandy. Major D-Day museums have been built in New Orleans and Portsmouth, defining and cultivating American and British national collective D-Day memories; Germans and Austrians have no such exquisite temples of memory. At best, the Normandy invasion might get honorable mention in national military museums and/or special exhibits. There is little German and no Austrian scholarly literature on the historical memory of the Normandy invasion.[10]

In this essay, therefore, we are suggesting a first outline for such a memory trajectory by analyzing the media discourses of the 1984, 1994, and 2004 commemorations toward the formation of a *collective memory*. We will also briefly summarize individual memories of German and Austrian veterans, and note that a public, or institutional, or collective memory of this turning point in World War II history hardly exists in Germany and Austria.

Silence, Suppression, and Victimhood: D-Day in Germany and Austria

There has been a "surfeit of memory" of World War II in both West Germany and Austria in the past thirty years or so but this has not always been the case.[11] Both nations have radically different trajectories of World War II memory since 1945. Since the 1960s West Germans have developed a very critical memory of their role in World War II; East Germans and Austrians, in contrast, have suppressed their roles as perpetrators in Hitler's Third Reich, or conveniently "externalized" their guilt to the West German perpetrators—the East Germans attributing their liberation exclusively to the Red Army. After a brief period of purges in the Western zones of occupation in Germany and Austria unleashed by the occupying powers, the West Germans and Austrians silenced their World War II past in the 1950s and concentrated on their perceived victimization during the war. Scholars "raised a cordon sanitaire around Nazi war crimes" and the Axis war record also became taboo in the private sphere. Citizens of both nations "emphasized their own suffering and largely ignored the suffering they had inflicted on others." Norbert Frei has characterized this phase in German memory of World War II as the "politics of the past (*Vergangenheitspolitik*)" to be followed by a phase in the 1960s and 1970s of trying to "master the past (*Vergangenheitsbewältigung*)."[12]

In the 1960s a new generation of student rebels began to "raise the specters of the past."[13] While the myth of the chivalrous *Wehrmacht* was preserved in public memory and popular culture, the resistance movement was rehabilitated. The screening of the American TV-series *Holocaust* in 1979 put the Final Solution at the center of West German *Vergangenheitsbewältigung* and was a culmination of this phase. With the 1980s came a long phase of "preserving the past *(Vergangenheitsbewahrung)*" focused on keeping events like the Final Solution in public consciousness through the construction of new memorials, such as the Berlin Holocaust Memorial, or via commemorative ceremonies like the fortieth anniversary of the end of World War II in 1985.[14] During the latter occasion, for example, President Richard von Weizsäcker delivered a famous speech in the German Bundestag reminding the Germans that it was time to embrace 8 May as a "day of liberation"; "It liberated all of us from the inhumanity and tyranny of the National-Socialist regime."[15] No Austrian officials found similar words for what 8 May signified for the Austrian historical narrative of World War II.

Between the 1980s and 1995, West Germany went through a long series of fiftieth anniversaries connected to the events of World War II.[16] Among these, the Normandy invasion was not even a major event when compared to the Battle of Stalingrad, the assassination attempt on Hitler on 20 July 1944, or the 8 May 1945, commemorations. In fact, contemporary interest in the expulsion of thirteen million Germans from Eastern Europe and the suffering of German POWs in Soviet camps succeeded in reopening the "Germans as victims" narrative that had run parallel to the "Germans as perpetrators" narrative of the 1960s and 1970s.[17] Taken together, these anniversaries defined Germany's efforts to establish and preserve an acceptable World War II narrative.[18] For instance, the *Wehrmachtsausstellung*, a travelling exhibit (1995–1997), at last destroyed the myth of the "clean *Wehrmacht*" by documenting its numerous war crimes in the East and in the Balkans.[19] Elsewhere, the Kohl government showed a particular enthusiasm for memory politics, even though it blundered in instances such as the controversial 1985 visit with President Ronald Reagan to the

Bitburg cemetery where SS soldiers are buried next to *Wehrmacht* troops. At the same time, a major debate raged among German historians (*Historikerstreit*) over the ultimate meaning of the war in the East, as well as the question of German victims vis-à-vis Jewish victims.[20] Against this backdrop, Kohl's absence from the 1984 and 1994 D-Day commemorations was much discussed in the German press. He chose not to go since his older brother had been wounded there. Chancellor Gerhard Schröder's invitation to the 2004 Normandy commemorations thus signaled an "end to the postwar period." Drawing upon ideas and phrases cultivated during the preceding two decades of activity, Schröder declared the Allied campaign "a victory for Europe and Germany" and thus the country was "retroactively integrated into the antifascist community of Western nations."[21]

The Austrians, in contrast, consistently aimed at "externalizing" their responsibilities to "guilty" West Germany.[22] Based on the Allied "Moscow Declaration" of 1 November 1943, postwar Austria claimed to be "Hitler's first victim." The Allies had aimed at arousing Austrian resistance against the Nazi regime, and the Austrians tried to demonstrate such a resistance record in the official documentation *Red-White-Red Book* (1946).[23] While there was a serious effort to prosecute Austrian war criminals in the *Volksgerichte* (people's courts) in the immediate postwar years, this campaign soon ended with the onset of the Cold War.[24] Starting in the early 1950s, moreover, many agents of Austrian war memory abandoned the "antifascist" record and concentrated instead on commemorating the fallen soldiers and veterans that had "defended the *Heimat* (homeland)." Austrians clawed onto this "victim's myth" until the 1980s, when both the election of Kurt Waldheim as president and the commemorations of the fiftieth anniversary of the March 1938 Anschluss in 1988 unleashed a more complex memory of Austria(ns') World War II past. Compared to West Germans, Austrians delayed a genuine effort at *Vergangenheitsbewältigung* by hanging onto the official "victims doctrine" for two generations. Indeed, at the national level, Austrians only began seriously to address the crimes of their World War II past in the 1980s, a response, in part, to the fiasco of the Waldheim election of 1986, the fiftieth anniversary of the Anschluss in 1988, and the contentious debates that surrounded the *Wehrmachtsausstellung*—a travelling exhibition (1995–1997) on crimes committed by the *Wehrmacht* in the Balkans and the Eastern Front. When Ernst Fischer, then the President of the Austrian Parliament and now Austria's President, opened this exhibit in Graz, he reminded his audience that Austrians "were forced" to serve in the *Wehrmacht* too, committing war crimes.[25] At last, the taboos of the World War II past were tackled by historians and a reluctant public.[26] Austrians had been victims, but many Austrian "Eichmann-men" had also been perpetrators of war crimes in the vast bureaucracy of the Final Solution and in Hitler's *Wehrmacht*. On the cultural landscape, Austria's World War II memory now became defined with new controversial war monuments such as Alfred Hrdlicka's famous "Memorial Against War and Fascism" (1988) on Vienna's central Albertina Square and Rachel Whiteread's Holocaust Memorial on the *Judenplatz* (2000).[27] Today, Austrian memory of World War II continues to be characterized by ambiguity; the country only recently has turned on a path of "preserving the past" and historicizing World War II. In fact, with regard to the 1944 Normandy invasion, Austria has never turned toward viewing the German defeat as the beginning of *its* liberation from Nazi occupation. Austrian governments, the Austrian press, and the Austrian public have stayed in an autistic bubble, ignoring the global discourses raging about the important turning point of 6 June 1944, and its larger meaning for the defeat of Nazi Germany.

"This Was Bloody Murder": Veterans' Memories of the Allied Invasion

In the late 1940s and the early 1950s, many Germans either tried to suppress their memories of the recent war or, elsewhere, claimed to be victims too. Such silence and suppression was aided by the lack of information connected to the war in the public realm, a gap particularly apparent with regard to German experiences of the Normandy landings. Indeed, since Rommel had committed suicide in 1944 and von Rundstedt—the German commander on the Normandy front—wrote no postwar account of the battle, in terms of the German viewpoint on Operation Overlord we only have the memoirs of Hans Speidel and a small essay from the leader of tank forces Geyr von Schweppenburg from the late 1940s.[28] These memoirs unleashed a lively debate in Germany among generals, soldiers, and analysts about the decisions on the positioning of tank forces in France prior to D-Day and their late release to engage invasion forces; the "tank controversy" has not ceased to this day.[29] But this debate did not figure greatly in contemporary popular culture.

Nonetheless, for those veterans who served in Normandy, it was here, in the immediate postwar period, that their memories began to take shape and form, a development aided in the early 1960s by two books and a movie. Paul Carrell's bestseller *Sie Kommen* was first published in 1960 and went through many reprints; Corneluis Ryan's *The Longest Day*, meanwhile, was published just a year earlier.[30] The portrayal of the Germans in the feature film that followed soon after—*The Longest Day* (1962)—also helped shape German memories of the Normandy invasion. Well-known German actors, speaking in German, portrayed generals such as Rommel, von Rundstedt, and Blumentritt. Just as importantly, these figures were portrayed sympathetically as respectable enemies and not as Nazi-monsters—the archetypical differentiation of the "good" war in the West and the "bad" war in the East. Stephen E. Ambrose has even argued that "*The Longest* Day offered a kind of exculpation in 1962 for a worthy, chastened, and now useful former foe."[31] Ryan's and Carrell's books were fast-paced journalistic-documentary narratives, called a *Tatsachenbericht* in German, based on oral histories and few archival sources. Carrell portrayed the Germans as tough fighters overwhelmed by Allied materiel—especially the overwhelming assaults from air and sea—more than Anglo-American fighting power. Carrell had picked up the topos of devastating Allied fire-power from his many interviews with Normandy veterans and it would continue to define the individual memories of Normandy veterans to the end of their lives.[32]

The memories of Hans von Luck and Franz Gockel are a case in point.[33] Captain v. Luck, hailing from an old Prussian military family, wrote his war memoirs including his role as a battalion commander in the 21st Panzer Division north of Caen. The Normandy invasion figured as a central chapter in his detailed memoirs. His tanks were ready to roll soon after midnight, when Col. John Howard's gliders landed to take the Orne bridges, yet v. Luck's division headquarters did not get the order to move from Hitler's *Führerhauptquartier.* Von Luck agreed with Rommel that "a successful invasion was the beginning of the end."[34] Gockel, meanwhile, is the rare veteran who not only reflected about his war record but also his personal memory of this major event in his life. He regularly visited the Normandy sites after the war. Gockel manned resistance nest #62 on "bloody" Omaha Beach in Colleville-sur-mer on 6 June 1944. More than forty years after the events, Gockel's memory of the enormous assault by the Western Allies remained vivid. As he recalled, after the initial attack by Allied aircraft "explosions of gunfire from the ships could be heard, and again shells slammed into the beach." He added: "Slowly the wall of explosions approached, meter by meter. Worse than before, a deafening torrent of smoke and dust rolled toward us, cracking, screaming, whistling and sizzling, destroying everything in its path. The wall of destruction took its time, as if knowing that for us there was no escape. I prayed for survival and my fear passed."[35]

By the 1980s and 1990s, German memory culture had begun to liberate itself from the postwar guilt culture; in this context, former *Wehrmacht* soldiers like v. Luck and Gockel were able to explore their war experiences and, at times, identify their own "victimization."[36] In doing so, their individual memories of those first hours and days when the Anglo-American armies "came" (*"Sie Kommen"*) were defined by impressions of size and scale: they felt overwhelmed by the superiority in materiel of the Allied armies. As one veteran succinctly put it: "[t]his was not war anymore, this was bloody murder."[37] Not being aware of the overall strategic picture and the actual balance of forces on invasion day, these individual memories reflected the fact that battlefield experiences are always viewed from a very circumscribed perspective. Such memories are subjectively "true" but they are rarely "objective" in the historical sense. Thus, the myth of "overwhelming Allied fire power" has been serving as the explanation for the Germans' defeat in June 1944—the first serious setback in the West in World War II.[38]

The sense that the allies possessed "overwhelming" power has also left its mark on the Norman landscape: just as Allied men and materiel dominated the Cotentin Peninsula in the summer of 1944, so too do the victorious allies dominate and control the commemorative landscape. Normandy is, after all, sacred Anglo-American ground.[39] By the 1950s, dozens of Allied cemeteries, monuments, and museums had been established across the Normandy landscape. For *Wehrmacht* veterans like Gockel, however, the landscape lacked such markers and monuments of their wartime presence. To be sure, the six German cemeteries established in this part of northern France were all completed by the 1960s. But they take a rather different form to those constructed by the American Battle Monuments Commission or the Commonwealth War Graves Commission. As one German veteran has explained, "On the American side a white marble cross was set up for every individual fallen soldier; on our side there are only small markers on a giant hill with a mass grave."[40] Even so, these sites were still focal points for the small number of German and Austrian veterans who returned to Normandy in the postwar period. Gockel, for instance, recalls that when he visited in 1958 the German cemetery in La Cambe was still under construction, while the American cemetery in Colleville, where 10,000 men were buried, was a work of beauty. When he returned to La Cambe for the twentieth anniversary in 1964, the 20,000 German soldiers buried there had finally received a dignified resting place. He recognized thirty names from his unit on crosses in a La Cambe section. In 1984, meanwhile, Gockel was involved in turning resistance nest #62 into a memorial; in 1993 he added a cross to it commemorating his fallen comrades of 6 June of 3d Company, 726th Regiment, 716th Infantry Division.[41]

Figure 10: La Cambe cemetery. Photo courtesy of Melanie Boulet.

With regard to the German military and its wartime presence in Normandy, memorials of this sort are the exception. Yet
if memorials to the Axis military are, understandably, lacking,
the physical remains of the German occupation are more than
apparent because the Nazi regime left miles and miles of Normandy
beaches covered with the "architectural ruins" of the formidable
Atlantic Wall. Rommel's "asparagus" that dotted the Normandy
countryside and the beach obstacles were removed after the war,
but the massive concrete bunkers, "resistance nests" like Gockel's,
and vast defense installations remain as stark reminders of these
decisive June 1944 battles, littering the Normandy landscape.
GEN George Patton called these concrete fortresses "bulwarks
of human stupidity."[42] In the 1990s, one Munich paper published
a series of bunker pictures and mused that these structures of
steel and concrete were "reminiscences of a past that does not
vanish"; these bunkers were "monuments of human hubris that
will last for a long time." They had become characteristic of the

Figure 11: The ruined remains of Hitler's Atlantic Wall. Photo courtesy of
Melanie Boulet.

Normandy landscape radiating an "adverse fascination (*widrige
Fascination*)."[43]

Paul Virilio, a French philosopher and urbanist, argues in his
essay on the Atlantic Wall bunker archeology, illustrated with stunning black-and-white photographs, that these concrete symbols of
the war embody the "homogenization of conflict." In Virilio's mind,
the geopolitics of a Germanic Europe produced "an architecture of
the continent's great military heritage were combined in seductive,
dynamic concrete forms."[44] The 15,000 bunkers of Hitler's Atlantic
Wall stand as massive monuments for German empire building, far
removed from German territory. Just as the memoirs of those such as
v. Luck and Gockel are beleaguered outposts of veterans' individual
memory in the public realm, these derelict and decaying bunkers
are outposts of German cultural memory. Sinking into the sands
and the ocean, these massive concrete structures of the Atlantic
Wall symbolize the shifting memory landscape of the Normandy
invasion.[45]

Liberation, Reconciliation and Historicization: D-Day as Political Discourse in the Post-Cold War Period, 1984-2004

In 1984, American and Western European politicians began to use the Normandy beaches as a stage for World War II commemorations and for elevating the attending D-Day veterans to the status of an exceptional generation of national heroes. The German press showed a lively interest in the 1984 D-Day ceremonies, especially the high-profile visits by the American, British, and French heads of state to the beaches of Normandy that served to transform the proceedings into a "cinemascope production" and a veritable "victors' spectacle."[46] French President François Mitterand had "felt out" Chancellor Helmut Kohl with regard as to whether he wanted to attend the commemorative events. But the latter declined—his older brother Walter had been badly wounded on 6 June.[47] Theo Sommer, in a front page commentary of the high-brow weekly *Die Zeit*, felt that an opportunity was missed by not inviting Kohl. The former enemies could have jointly acknowledged the devastating conflicts of the era of European "civil wars" (1914–1945). Maybe it was too early, Sommer mused, for "national memories kept alive to be turned into common memories as a matter of course."[48] One French veteran was quoted as saying that he did not mind that the Germans were absent, for 6 June was a victory of the Allies against Nazi Germany and "it would be disrespectful to invite the Germans to a celebration of their defeat."[49]

Contemporary affairs always cast their long shadows over major D-Day commemorations. By the 1980s, the Federal Republic of Germany had been a NATO ally for nearly thirty years and, as a result, always felt marginalized when its contemporary allies gathered in Normandy to remember their victory over the Nazis. Theo Sommer stressed that Eisenhower's great crusade was a "deeply moral mission" that liberated the Old World from its nemesis, Hitlerite totalitarianism. Sommer reminded his readers that the success of the D-Day invasion eventually ensured that the West Germans enjoyed a much better life than the East Germans did across the barbed wire.[50] In the conservative daily *Die Welt*, meanwhile, Kohl was quoted as saying he would not have accepted an invitation to the Normandy commemorations even if he had been invited. State Secretary Alois Mertes from Kohl's Christian Democratic Party warned the Western Allies that their D-Day celebrations must not mark a "day of alienation" between the Germans and their NATO friends by giving them the impression of being a "guilty nation of losers."[51] Thomas Kielinger's *Welt*-commentary also fretted about the current German NATO allies evoking their "alliance of victors against Nazi Germany." The past was clashing with the present in the Normandy commemorations and the Federal Republic's absence might produce "disappointment and shame" among Germans. Yet it was difficult to transform the memory of an invisible brotherhood of heroes into a reconciliation ceremony with the Germans. Kielinger reminded the Germans not to forget the thousands of German soldiers who perished in Normandy but still to be thankful for the "liberation" that has allowed the Germans to become members of the democratic community of nations.[52]

Compared to the thoughtful German commentaries, the stories in the Austrian press were shallow matter-of-fact reportage about the gatherings and speeches in Normandy—no larger meanings were found in the D-Day commemorations. The reports stressed the "invasion of prominent people" and the spectacle of the commemorations. Austrian reports also stressed the attacks in the Soviet press against the "propaganda show" of the D-Day commemorations where the Russians were also absent. Soviet newspapers complained about the late opening of the "second front" in 1944 at a time when the Red Army had already seized the strategic initiative from the Nazis after enormous sacrifices of Soviet soldiers.[53] The *Salzburger Nachrichten* poked a bit of fun of the British veterans who were the "stars in the TV-shows." It also flogged the old topos that the British and American veterans won the battle due to their logistical superiority and their "enormous deployment of men and materiel."[54] There was no debate in the oblivious Austrian press as to whether D-Day might have represented the beginning of Austria's postwar liberation from the Nazi yoke too. Nor did commentators ponder the fact that thousands of Austrian soldiers died in the Normandy battle. Nor did anyone question whether the Austrian chancellor ought to have been in Normandy to remember these Austrian dead and offer gratitude and reconciliation to the victors of 1944. Such gestures of reconciliation might have been transformative for Austria; but forty years after the end of the war, the myth of Austria as "Hitler's first victim" still served the Austrians as their primary defense against a more introspective memorial culture of World War II. Austria's cozy official and institutional amnesia over the role of Austrian soldiers and perpetrators would be shattered in 1986 with the "Waldheim Affair."

Ten years later, during the "fiftieth anniversary invasion", the commemorations on the beaches of Normandy were even more spectacular. Forty-five thousand veterans attended the ceremonies.[55] Winfried Mönch argues that the 1994 commemorations might be seen as a "victory ceremony of the Cold War."[56] The larger context looming over the commemorations concerned the Cold War that had ended in 1989, the re-unification of Germany in 1990, the breakup of the Soviet Union in 1991, and continued efforts toward European integration. The German press extensively reported on President Bill Clinton's visits to the Nettuno battlefield in Italy as well as to Portsmouth and London in England, before he then crossed the Channel in the aircraft carrier USS *George Washington* to deliver his speech above Point du Hoc on 6 June. Well briefed by the historian Stephen E. Ambrose, Clinton asserted that the Normandy landings were a "turning point of the war maybe of the century."[57] He also thanked the French for their sacrifices and tactfully called the erstwhile enemy "Nazi troops," not Germans. Elsewhere President François Mitterand invoked postwar French reconciliation with the Germans as the basis for European integration.[58]

Meanwhile in Germany, the national press was preoccupied with whether or not Chancellor Kohl should have been invited to the commemorations—he had declined again.[59] The Frankfurt paper argued that Kohl's absence in Normandy was fine: "From a historical perspective it was justified, from a human one it was understandable, from a German perspective it was even thoughtful." Germany's allies of today did well to mark a clear dividing line between the National Socialist regime of the past and the close partnership in democracy of today.[60] Heribert Prantl, the *Süddeutsche Zeitung*'s witty commentator, thought Kohl would have felt misplaced in the midst of the spectacle geared toward the veterans.[61] Two foreign policy heavy-weights, one from France and Germany each, argued forcefully that Kohl should be present in Normandy to take the commemorations as an occasion "to celebrate the victory of democracy in Europe—all countries, after all, were liberated from Nazism, including Germany."[62] Karl-Heinz Janßen, also a trained historian, asserted in a lead article in *Die Zeit* that the Germans were "incapable of celebrating," referencing the Mitscherlichs' 1960s charge of the German *"Unfähigkeitzutrauern."* Kohl's ambiguity about not being invited to Normandy was only covering up the much larger German problem of including D-Day in their World War II narrative. While some now saw the Normandy invasion as "liberation," still more perceived it as defeat. Moreover, for some, Germans were as much out of place in the Normandy celebrations as they are out of place in Auschwitz commemorations.[63] Stephen E. Ambrose suggested that the victors' "refusal, in June 1994, to allow the Germans to participate in the fiftieth anniversary celebrations of D-Day suggests that Zanuck [the director of the 1962 epic *The Longest Day*] offered greater forgiveness in 1962 than proved possible thirty years *after* the film was made."[64]

The national press also provided extensive coverage of the actual events of 6 June 1944, including commentary by leading historians such as Gerhard Weinberg who labeled it "the decisive day of World War II."[65] *Der Spiegel*, for instance, dedicated a three-part historical series to the Normandy events. The "chaos in the leadership of the *Führerstaat*" was laid out in the opening cover story. While Rommel argued that the strategic reserve, including the tank forces, should be committed to battle immediately, Hitler dithered for days and missed an opportunity to stop the descent into catastrophe. Hitler's 6 June comment, after waking up at noon, suggested his total confusion: "At last, now we have them where we can beat them."[66]

Theo Sommer's front-page story in *Die Zeit* and Josef Joffe's column in die *Süddeutsche Zeitung* provided some of the most penetrating reflections on the larger meaning of these fiftieth anniversary ceremonies for Germans—suggesting in this new phase of *Vergangenheitsbewahrung* what kind of memory needed to be preserved for Germany's longtime historical narrative.[67] The trained historian Sommer felt that the Germans did not need to be part of the commemorations—"let the veterans be among themselves," he declared. He also reminded the Germans that they ought to be grateful for their liberation, beginning with the Normandy invasion. As Sommer explained, the 1944 victory "against the Germans" was the "beginning of the end of the Hitler dictatorship." Seen in this light, it was a victory "for the Germans." Elsewhere, Sommer reminded the Allies of 1944 that the young generation of Germans could no longer be held responsible for the crimes of their fathers.[68]

Exploring similar themes, Josef Joffe, with a Harvard doctorate in political science, wrote a thoughtful commentary in the *Süddeutsche Zeitung*, the major Munich paper. He concentrated on the end of American isolationism, the stabilizing American presence on the Continent, and the *Pax Americana* built in Europe after the war; needed as much in 1994 after the end of the Cold War and with a unified Germany as it was needed in 1954 at the height of the Cold War. Since the end of World War II America had served both as a "protector" and "pacifier" of Europe (*Beschützer* and *Befrieder*) and protected the West Europeans both "from others and themselves." The American presence, remarked Joffe, preserved European stability, first against Russian strength during the Cold War, and then against Russian weakness after 1991. Joffe concluded with a final comment on the meaning of D-Day for Germans: "D-Day indeed was [the] beginning of liberation, especially for the Germans."[69] French historian Joseph Rovan followed Joffe's commentary with a similarly deep analysis. Rovan had been a prisoner of the Gestapo on 6 June 1944, and saw the Allied landings as the distant beginning of his liberation, an idea he was also content to apply to contemporary Germans. Rovan also reminded Europeans that 6 June allowed the process of European unity to mature after the war.[70]

Significantly, the German press profusely reported on the French, and particularly on postwar efforts directed toward Franco-German reconciliation. In Caen, for instance, 6 June was celebrated as a "festival of peace," while a contemporary opinion poll concluded that 54 percent of the French surveyed would have welcomed German participation as a signal of reconciliation.[71] Elsewhere, French schoolchildren and British veterans joined 300 German veterans who visited the cemetery at La Cambe, final resting place for 21,500 German soldiers. A German official taking care of these cemeteries was quoted as saying that the dead were mostly eighteen-year-old boys: "Their life was just beginning. They did not want this war."[72] German commentators were also keen to acknowledge President Mitterand's efforts to lessen the diplomatic impact of Chancellor Kohl's absence in Normandy: Mitterand invited him to the French national holiday parade on 14 July on the Champs Elysées. Moreover, on 8 June, only two days after the Normandy commemorations, Mitterand attended a French and German youth festival in Heidelberg.[73] Both Kohl and Mitterand stressed their continued commitment to European integration as a means to prevent the return of nationalism as Mitterand had already done in his Bayeux speech.

Austrian press reportage on the fiftieth anniversary D-Day commemorations continued to be as shallow as in 1984. Austrians were still engaged in "mastering" their own World War II past and had not yet reached the phase of "preserving" and historicizing it. Much of the reporting concentrated on the events of 6 June in Normandy. Austrian journalists quibbled about the Germans and Russians not being invited to the D-Day commemorations and again made fun of the excessive tourist kitsch that accompanied the celebrations. But no one asked why Chancellor Franz Vranitzky was not invited to the Normandy ceremonies, nor whether the thousands of Austrian *Wehrmacht* soldiers buried in Normandy, or still suffering from traumas they brought back from the Normandy battles, deserved some attention from the public. So, too, academic experts remained silent about the meaning of 6 June for the trajectory of postwar Austrian memory, and this at the very time when Austria was joining the European Union. Clemens M. Hutter penned an ill-tempered commentary on the front page of the *Salzburger Nachrichten* and complained that the victors of 1944 gathered among themselves.

The Russians, stated Hutter, had carried "the main weight of the war against fascism and had made enormous sacrifices," and yet they were not invited to Normandy. Neither were the Germans who had to digest an enormous defeat and still adopted a democratic regime from the victors; these same Germans in 1989-90 had rid themselves admirably from leftist totalitarianism "without a bloodbath." Hutter concluded that a great opportunity was missed "to highlight the equality of the victims next to the clash of systems, statesmen, and strategists." The next opportunity to do so would come on 8 May 1995.[74] Thomas Chorherr, the editor-in-chief of *Die Presse*, criticized Germany's allies in a similar vein for not inviting Kohl. "How should one imagine a new Europe, if some indulge in their old victor's nostalgia and fail to embark on steps toward reconciliation?" he asked.[75]

The Salzburg paper also reported about Russian veterans of World War II who did not want to be treated as second class victors; they felt "humiliated and alienated" by the Anglo-Americans celebrating the defeat of the Nazis in Normandy. "Do they want to cast into oblivion our sacrifices?" A Russian general, who had been a liaison officer in Normandy in 1944, was quoted: "We all have contributed to the victory over Hitler." A Russian Foreign Ministry spokesmen noted that the Anglo-Americans wanted the Nazis and the Soviets "to decimate each other" and only intervened when they feared they were "losing territory and influence to the USSR."[76]

A *Kurier* commentary, in a typically Austrian neutralist-pacifist vein, mocked the fact that the Normandy invasion was supposed to replace Stalingrad and Moscow as the decisive battles. The D-Day production showed that the Anglo-Americans were not willing to learn: "Not a day of reconciliation between the former enemies but a fest for the victors. Not a quiet commemoration of the victims, but a history spectacle in the vein of Disney World. Not a day of warning about the suffering and misery of war, but the glorification of military achievement." These Sunday speakers did not "learn from history." The commentator concluded: "They celebrate in Normandy, while people get murdered and tortured in the Balkans."[77] Felix Ermacora, a law professor at the University of Vienna and conservative

Member of Parliament, was the only politician who commented on Normandy in the veterans' publication *Der Kamerad*. Ermacora's anemic comment worried about the effects of Austria joining the EU on her neutral status at a time when the victors engaged in their "odd" commemorations in Normandy.[78] For him the sacrifices of the soldiers on 6 June only made sense if they paved the way for a unified and peaceful Europe.[79] Elsewhere, an unnamed commentator again fretted in the same publication over the "missed opportunity" to use the D-Day commemorations as a forum of reconciliation with Germany. After all, given that the postwar peace in Europe had been built on Franco-German reconciliation, it was a "political mistake and a moral failure" not to invite the Germans.[80]

It is remarkable that both the German and Austrian press largely ignored the presence of veterans in their midst who had fought in Normandy on 6 June. It may be that the fierce public discourses over the "crimes of the *Wehrmacht*" in the East—particularly as portrayed in the travelling exhibit (*Wehrmachtsausstellung*)—cautioned the media against acknowledging Normandy veterans during these anniversary celebrations. The *Süddeutsche* interviewed the British airborne veteran David Tibbs who has regularly visited the Bayeux cemetery to visit his fallen comrades,[81] while the Graz daily, *Kleine Zeitung*, juxtaposed two veterans who fought on opposite sides in the early hours of D-Day. COL Henry Sweeney was a member of the special operations glider team that took the two bridges over the Orne River north of Caen; the Austrian Lt. Hans Höller, had commanded a small unit of the 21st Panzer Division and defended these bridges and the beach exits of Sword Beach. Höller was one of those veterans who had often been drawn back to Normandy; in 1989 the mayor of Caen had even invited him and some of his comrades for an official visit. He attended the fiftieth anniversary ceremonies with some "old comrades"—"uninvited by the victors," as he put it, "who were wallowing in their memory cult."[82]

For the sixtieth anniversary of D-Day in June 2004, the victors "wallowed in their memory cult" again. Twenty-two heads of states and some 15,000 veterans met in more than a dozen ceremonies to commemorate the sacrifices of the Normandy landings. Yet French

President Jacques Chirac finally made a major gesture toward reconciliation by inviting German Chancellor Gerhard Schröder and Russian President Vladimir Putin to the Normandy commemorations. The time had come to historicize D-Day. The international context was even more complicated than in 1994. As a result of the 9/11 attacks on the World Trade Center and President George W. Bush unleashing a war against Iraq, the NATO alliance split down the middle. The French and the Germans, and the neutral Austrians, did not join Bush's "coalition of the willing," poisoning Franco-American and US-German relations. President Bush's visit to Italy, France, and the Normandy commemorations also served as a reconciliation mission of sorts between the divided NATO Allies. Presidents Bush and Chirac did not mention Iraq in their speeches at the joint Colleville-sur-mer ceremony. Chirac praised two hundred years of close Franco-American relations and thanked those men who had made the ultimate sacrifice "to liberate our land from Nazi barbarism."[83]

Schröder's speech in the Caen Peace Memorial, where Putin was also present, and his failure to visit the German cemetery in La Cambe was at the heart of the German public discourses of the sixtieth anniversary events. In the speech and in subsequent interviews, Schröder repeatedly noted that the participation of a German chancellor in the Normandy commemorations signaled "the end of the postwar era."[84] Like others before him, Schröder stressed that the successful landings on D-Day signaled not only the liberation of Europe but also the liberation of Germany. He noted that he represented the new Germany that had "found its way back into the community of civilized nations," not the old Germany of the "grim years." This was, of course, familiar stuff by 2004, but this was the first occasion at which a serving Chancellor had made such a pronouncement during the Normandy commemorations. As if to drive home the message, President Chirac welcomed Schröder and the Germans as "friends and brothers." Schröder then joined the heads of state in their main ceremony at the Arromanches-les-bains cemetery, where 322 German soldiers were buried next to 2,000 Allied soldiers. Schröder deposited two flower arrangements—one in memory of

the German soldiers, one for the Allied soldiers. But the controversies and difficulties surrounding an official German presence in
Normandy remained: British veterans denounced Schröder's presence as a "sacrilege," while Conservative German groups criticized
Schröder for not visiting La Cambe, the largest German cemetery
in Normandy.[85] Some German veterans even remarked that there
was no reason for Schröder "to celebrate." For these, it was fine for
the Allies to celebrate their victory, but the defeated should not
be at the center of attention.[86] The Christian Democratic opposition party, meanwhile, launched some heavy political artillery at
Schröder's Caen speech, criticizing him for failing to thank the
Americans explicitly for their sacrifices. While the Germans threw
barbs at their chancellor, the British *Guardian* newspaper praised
him for "drawing a symbolic *Schlussstrich*" under this contested past,
and *Die Welt's* Eckhard Fuhr similarly recognized a new political
symbolism in Europe replacing the old constellations.[87] The Franco-
German closing of ranks against President Bush's Iraq war suggested,
said Fuhr, that the "unilateral-imperial logic of the Americans was
shattered by the European resistance inspired by Franco-German
solidarity."[88] As such, Schröder's "recoding of the past" signaled both
a clear distancing from the "old Germany of the grim years" and also
a new German patriotism.[89]

Yet the Iraq War and, especially European critiques of Bush's policies, often overshadowed these joint appearances on beaches and
cemeteries. Josef Joffe, now the editor-in-chief of the high-brow
weekly *Die Zeit*, continued his incisive D-Day commentaries. Two
deep divides had transformed the old NATO alliance, he noted. First
the end of the Cold War changed the alliance and then the 9/11–Iraq
War fiasco. In this post-Cold War world, argued Joffe, Europe had
failed to put the American superpower—"Gulliver Unbound"—into
chains in multilateral arrangements. While the Americans responded
to the terrorist attacks with military power, 1945 had muffled the
"military reflexes of the Europeans and made the EU an institutional-
ized club of the peaceful." Joffe correctly predicted that D-Day 2004
would not bring about a divorce among Americans and Europeans
but they will not now enter into "new vows of fidelity" either.[90]

On the weekend when former president Ronald Reagan passed away, Austrian commentators welcomed Schröder's invitation to Normandy and celebrated the reconciliation with former enemies demonstrated by the commemorative events of 6 June 2004. It was the presence of the German chancellor that "brought tears to the eyes" of many TV audiences around the world, explained one commentator. Elsewhere, German veterans were interviewed on French television and shook hands with Allied veterans on the beaches.[91] Even so, the Franco-German celebration was neither an anti-war demonstration nor wiping the slate clean (the famous "*Schlussstrich*") as the Germans had long wanted, at least according to Danny Leder in the *Kurier*.[92] The *Wiener Zeitung*, meanwhile, disagreed, arguing that Schröder's visit meant the drawing of the famous "*Schlussstrich*" under the "grim past and a new chapter in Franco-German friendship." "D-Day is history," noted the commentator, and "the enemy image of Germany has been banned to the archives."[93]

For the first time too, a leading Austrian politician publically commented on the meaning of D-Day for Austria. Chancellor Wolfgang Schüssel made references to the sixtieth anniversary Normandy commemorations both in speeches in Parliament and in front of the annual "European Forum" in Göttweig Monastery. D-Day "liberated Europe from the horrors of National Socialism." The vision of a peaceful united Europe was built on the 20,000 men who died in Normandy and the 25 million dead who perished in World War II. Schüssel concluded: "This is the reason why European Union must succeed as a peaceful power (*Friedensmacht*)."[94] In the Göttweig Abbey, Schüssel evoked the rebuilding of transatlantic bridges after the divisive policies of the Iraq War. He rejected any comparison between the "historic and mighty" Normandy offensive and the Iraq War and made fun of the fancy metaphor of an American commentator about pacifist Europeans being from Venus and martial Americans from Mars.[95] Schüssel's "never again war (*Niewieder Krieg*)" rhetoric was standard Austrian neutralist-pacifist cant as was the "EU-*Friedensmacht*" metaphor. He spoke of "Europe" being liberated by the victorious Anglo-American D-Day invasion, not Austria. These years also saw the Schüssel government initiate a remarkable "politics of history" when it came to Austria coming to terms with some difficult World War II legacies, including restitution efforts toward former slave laborers and Jewish victims of "Aryanization."[96] Yet despite such activities, Schüssel strangely reaffirmed the old "victim's doctrine" in an interview with the *Jerusalem Post* and failed to make the switch from Austrian "mastering" to "preserving" the World War II past, even though historians had started the process twenty years before.

Conclusion

"D-Day" initiated the end of World War II and contributed to the victory of the Allied powers over the Nazi regime. The entire territorial, ideological, and institutional reordering of the world after World War II came as a consequence of the successful Normandy landings in June 1944 *and* the rapid advances of the Red Army into Hitler's Germany in early 1945.[97] World War II brought about the collapse of old empires, ended the European control of much of the world, and firmly placed the American military on the European Continent, thereby marking the beginning of their postwar superpower status. They remain, albeit in small numbers, even today.[98] For Josef Joffe, therefore, the American commitment to Europe—as expressed in D-Day, as well as in the protection the US military offered during the Cold War and after—thus helped the Continent overcome its previously blood-drenched history.[99] Seen in this context, D-Day initiated German liberation, rehabilitation and, ultimately, reunification. It is thus astounding that place of "D-Day" in German memory has not yet found a historian.[100]

This first attempt at such a history suggests that the complex trajectory of German historical memory after the war began to integrate the significance of the Nazis' D-Day defeat into the nation's historical narrative only with reluctance, and with caution. It was not until the spectacular fiftieth anniversary of D-Day in 1994 that German media discourses at last came around to the realization that this hard and bloody military defeat also was a blessing in disguise—it marked the "beginning of the end" of both Europe's *and* Germany's liberation from the Nazi regime. President Weizsäcker's iconic 8 May speech of 1985 fortified this "liberation" thesis, providing the foundations upon which Kohl and Schröder would later build. Thus, when Chancellor Schröder was invited to the sixtieth anniversary of D-Day in 2004, he thanked the victors for this *liberation*; by now it was easy to embrace this narrative. These public German discourses always reflected the contemporary geopolitical discourses of their times; the Cold War in 1984, German unification in 1994, the Iraq War in 2004.

In the meantime, the individual—often traumatic—memories of the veterans grated against these public discourses of the elites. They had a harder time recognizing that the postwar democratic order in Germany and Austria began with their defeat in Normandy. German and Austrian veterans' memory of Normandy 1944 was largely associated with enormous firepower the Western Allies came to pour on them. The Nazis had evoked "total war" in 1943—and now it came their way.

Austrian memory of D-Day has been even more absent, if not non-existent, in public discourses. Austria's peculiar postwar "victim's doctrine" produced a silenced and stunted memory of World War II. Confronting the crimes Austrians committed while wearing the uniforms of Nazism came after much delay in the 1990s. The veterans of the *Wehrmacht* were shunned in postwar Austrian public life—they stayed among themselves in reunions and veterans' organizations. Many tried to come to terms with their own past by visiting the sites of their former fighting and defeat. *Vergangenheitsbewältigung* became an operative term late in the Austrian World War II memory regime; *Vergangenheitsbewahrung* may still be only in the initial stages.

Notes

1.   The authors would like to thank the editors of this volume, as well as Gerhard Weinberg, Heidemarie Uhl, Berthold Molden, and Rüdiger Overmans for

their valuable comments that helped to improve this essay. In the early 1990s Rolf Steininger aided the Eisenhower Center at the University of New Orleans in the collection of oral histories of German and Austrian Normandy veterans. We would like to dedicate this essay to Stephen E. Ambrose who did more than any man to single-handedly shape the American memory of D-Day through his huge effort of collecting more than a thousand oral histories of D-Day veterans, his prodigious writings on the Normandy invasion, and his founding of the American National World War II Museum, a veritable shrine also to Normandy veterans.

2. Carlo D'Este, "'The Eyes of the World': Commemoration and Memorial," in *The D-Day Companion: Leading Historians Explore History's Greatest Amphibious Assault*, ed. Jane Penrose, 257–72 (Osceola, WI: Osprey Publishing for the National D-Day Museum New Orleans, 2004), 267.

3. During the fiftieth anniversary commemorations of 1994, some "politically correct" German media began to criticize the use of the term "invasion" because the Nazis had used it in 1944; see Winfried Mönch, *Entscheidungsschlacht "Invasion" 1944? Prognosen und Diagnosen* (Stuttgart: Franz Steiner Verlag, 2001), 205.

4. D'Este, "Commemoration and Memorial," in *The D-Day Companion*, ed. Jane Penrose, 266, 270.

5. On the definitions of collective, individual, and institutional memories, see Richard Ned Lebow, "The Memory of Politics in Postwar Europe," in *The Politics of Memory in Postwar Europe*, eds. Richard Ned Lebow, Wulf Kantsteiner, and Claudio Fogu, 8–16 (Durham, NC: Duke University Press, 2006); on cultural memory, see Aleida Assmann, *Cultural Memory and Western Civilization: Functions, Media, Archive* (Cambridge: Cambridge University Press, 2011). On the changing memory regimes of the past fifteen years, see Norbert Frei, "Abschied von der Zeitgenossenschaft: Der Nationalsozialismus und seine Erforschung auf dem Weg in die Geschichte," in *1945 und Wir: Das Dritte Reich im Bewusstsein der Deutschen*, ed. Norbert Frei, 41–62 (Munich: C. H. Beck, 2005).

6. Robert G. Moeller, "War Stories: The Search for a Usable Past in the Federal Republic of Germany," *American Historical Review* 101 (Oct. 1996): 1008–48.

7. Ronald J. Drez, ed., *Voices of D-Day: The Story of the Allied Invasion Told by Those Who Were There*, fwd. Stephen E. Ambrose (Baton Rouge: Louisiana

State University Press, 1994); Douglas Brinkley and Ronald J. Drez, *Voices of Valor: Day: June 6, 1944,* including two audio CDs (New York: Bulfinch Press, 2004); Russell Miller, *Nothing Less Than Victory: An Oral History of D-Day* (London: William Morrow and Company, 1993); Tom Brokaw, *The Greatest Generation* (New York: Random House, 2004).

8. Günter Bischof and Rolf Steininger, "Die Invasion aus der Sicht von Zeitzeugen," in *Die Invasion in der Normandie 1944,* eds. Günter Bischof and Wolfgang Krieger, 89–104 (Innsbruck: StudienVerlag, 2001). This essay was based on oral histories with German and Austrian D-Day veterans and written reports solicited from them. A published collection of oral histories of German civilians and military personnel heavily concentrates on the Eastern Front, with some Normandy memoires sprinkled in between, reflecting the German soldiers' memories where *the real war* was fought; see Johannes Steinhoff, Peter Pechel, Dennis Showalter, eds., *Voices from the Third Reich: An Oral History* (New York: Da Capo Press, 1994).

9. James C. Cobb, "World War II Normandy: American Cemetery and Memorial," in *American Places: Encounters with History,* ed. William E. Leuchtenburg, 53–66 (New York: Oxford University Press, 2000).

10. Mönch's *Entscheidungsschlacht* is a notable exception.

11. Charles S. Maier, "A Surfeit of Memory? Reflections on History, Melancholy and Denial," *History & Memory* 5 (Fall/Winter 1993), 136–52. The case of East Germany is different, blaming West German "imperialists" for Nazi war crimes, and leaning on the Soviet World War II memory regime—it will not be dealt with in this essay.

12. Norbert Frei, "Deutsche Lernprozesse: NS-Vergangenheit und Generationenfolge seit 1945," in *1945 und Wir,* ed. Norbert Frei, 23–40 (esp. 26).

13. Wulf Kantsteiner, "Losing the War, Winning the Memory Battle," in *Politics of Memory,* eds. Lebow, Kansteiner, and Fogu, 102–46 (Durham, NC: Duke University Press, 2006), 110, 111, 112.

14. Frei, "Deutsche Lernprozesse," 37–40.

15. Richard von Weizsäcker, "Speech in the Bundestag on 8 May 1985 during the Ceremony Commemorating the Fortieth Anniversary of the End of War in Europe and of National-Socialist Tyranny," accessed 3 Sept. 2012, http://www.mediaculture-online.de/fileadmin/bibliothek/weizsaecker_speech_may85/weizsaecker_speech_may85.pdf.

16. Frei, "Deutsche Lernprozesse,"38.

17. Moeller, "War Stories," 1004–48; see also Wolfgang Wippermann, *Wessen Schuld? Vom Historikerstreitzur Goldhagen Kontroverse* (Berlin: Elefanten Press, 1997).

18. For memory discourses dealing with the Eastern Front and the return of the POWs, see Robert G. Moeller, *War Stories: The Search for a Usable Past in the Federal Republic of Germany* (Berkeley: University of California Press, 2001); Frank Biess, *Homecomings: Returning POWs and the Legacies of Defeat in Postwar Germany* (Princeton: Princeton University Press, 2006).

19. See the documentation of its showing in Munich (2 Feb.–4 June 1997), Kulturreferat Landeshaupstadt München, ed., *Bilanz einer Ausstellung: Dokumentation der Kontroverse um die Ausstellung "Vernichtungskrieg. Verbrechen der Wehrmacht 1941 bis 1944"* (Munich: Knaur, 1998).

20. Peter Baldwin, ed., *Reworking the Past: Hitler, the Holocaust and the Historians' Debate* (Boston: Beacon Press, 1990).

21. Wulf Kantsteiner, "Losing the War, Winning the Memory Battle," in *Politics of Memory*, eds. Lebow, Kansteiner, and Fogu,123–34 (Durham, NC: Duke University Press), 130. Schröder "wanted to make clear that Germans had reached the end of the postwar period," 144, n. 106. On the "memory battles of the 1980s," see also Charles S. Maier, *The Unmasterable Past: History, Holocaust, and German National Identity* (Cambridge, MA: Harvard University Press, 1988); Moeller, "War Stories," 1040–48.

22. On West vs. East German World War II memory, see Jeffrey Herf, *Divided Memory: The Nazi Past and the Two Germanies* (Cambridge, MA: Harvard University Press, 1997).

23. Günter Bischof, "Die Instrumentalisierung der Moskauer Erklärung nach dem 2. Weltkrieg," *Zeitgeschichte* 20 (Nov.–Dec. 1993), 345–66.

24. Claudia Kuretsidis-Haider and Winfried R. Garscha, eds., *Keine "Abrechnung": NS-Verbrechen, Justiz und Gesellschaft in Europa nach 1945* (Leipzig-Vienna: Akademische Verlagsanstalt, 1998).

25. Heinz Fischer's lecture of 12 Feb. 1997, is reprinted in Hamburger Institut für Sozialforschung, ed., *Krieg ist ein Gesellschaftszustand: Reden zur Eröffnung der Ausstellung "Vernichtungskrieg. Verbrechen der Wehrmacht 1941bis 1944,"* 203–7 (Hamburg; Hamburger Edition, 1998), 203.

26. Richard Mitten, "Bitburg, Waldheim, and the Politics of Remembering and Forgetting," in *From World War to Waldheim: Culture and Politics in*

Austria and the United States, eds. David F. Good and Ruth Wodak (New York: Berghahn, 1999), 51–84; Anton Pelinka and Erika Weinzierl, eds., *Das grosse Tabu: Österreichs Umgang mit seiner Vergangenheit* (Vienna: Verlag der österreichischen Staatsdruckerei, 1987); Helga Embacher, ed., *Umkämpfte Erinnerung: Die Wehrmachtsausstellung in Salzburg* (Salzburg: Residenzverlag, 1999).

27. Heidemarie Uhl, "From Victim Myth to Co-Responsibility Thesis: Nazi Rule, World War II, and the Holocaust in Austrian Memory," in *Politics of Memory*, eds. Lebow, Kansteiner, and Fogu 40–72 (Durham, NC: Duke University Press); Günter Bischof, "Victims? Perpetrators? 'Punching Bags' of European Historical Memory? The Austrians and Their World War II Legacies," *German Studies Review* 27 (Feb. 2004), 17–32; Meinrad Ziegler and Waltraud Kannonier-Finster, *Österreichs Gedächtnis: ÜberErinnern und Vergessen der NS-Vergangenheit* (Vienna: BöhlauVerlag, 1993).

28. On Geyr von Schweppenburg, see Winfried Mönch, *Entscheidungsschlacht "Invasion" 1944? Prognosen und Diagnosen* (Stuttgart: Franz Steiner Verlag), 93, 227; Hans Speidel, *Invasion 1944: Ein Beitrag zu Rommels und des Reiches Schicksal* (Tübingen and Stuttgart: Rainer Wunderlich Verlag Hermann Leins, 1949).

29. Mönch, *Entscheidungsschlacht*, 135–138; Hans von Luck, *Panzer Commander: The Memoirs of Colonel Hans von Luck*, fwd. Stephen E. Ambrose (New York: Praeger, 1989), 136–61; Werner Kortenhaus, *Die Schlacht um Caen 1944: Der Einsatz der 21. Panzer*-Division, 132-page-typescript in Bischof's possession; Bischof oral history with Werner Kortenhaus, 21 June 1990; Bischof oral history with Hans Herr, 26 June 1990.

30. Paul Carrell, *Sie Kommen: Der deutsche Bericht über die Invasion und die 80-tägige Schlacht um Frankreich* (Oldenbourg: Gerhard Stalling Verlag, 1961); Engl.: *"Invasion! They're Coming!"* (New York: Dutton, 1963).

31. Stephen E. Ambrose, *"The Longest Day* (1962): 'Blockbuster' History," *Journal of Film, Radio, and Television* 14 (1994), 430.

32. Paul Carrell's real name was Paul Schmidt. He had been a high ranking SS-member during the war and served as the Foreign Ministry's press spokesman; as such he became one of the Nazis' chief propagandists; he was interned for thirty months after the war—an attempt to put him on trial for war crimes against Hungarian Jews failed; see Mönch, *Entscheidungsschlacht*, 225f.

33. In the early 1990s Günter Bischof collected some three dozen reports and conducted half a dozen oral histories with German Normandy veterans as part of Stephen E. Ambrose's "D-Day Oral History Project" at the Eisenhower Center of the University of New Orleans, out of which eventually the American D-Day/National World War II Museum in New Orleans grew. Bischof has never systematically mined these oral histories but presented some initial results in his essay with Rolf Steininger, "Die Invasion ausSicht der Zeitzeugen," in *Invasion*, eds. Bischof and Krieger, 65–71.

34. Von Luck, 139. Stephen E. Ambrose encouraged v. Luck to write his memoirs and wrote a long introduction to the book, xiii–xxiv. Von Luck's voice is also prominently represented in *Voices of D-Day*, ed. Drez, 110f, 113; v. Luck also represents the breed of old German veterans in the cover story of *Time* magazine, "The Man Who Beat Hitler," 46.

35. Franz Gockel oral history, Eisenhower Center, ca. 1993.

36. Frei, 21.

37. Josef Primus interview; Letter from Curt Vogt to Bischof, 17 Nov. 1990; Bischof and Steininger, "Zeitzeugen,"66f.

38. On the problem of subjectivity vs. objectivity in oral histories, and the truthfulness ("*Wahrheitsfähigkeit*") of biographic evidence, see Hans Joachim Schröder, "Die Vergegenwärtigung des Zweiten Weltkrieges in biographischen Interviewerzählungen," *Militärgeschichtliche Mitteilungen*, 1 (1991), 9–37. Schröder argues that there is more "truth" in oral histories than the critics have it.

39. See, for example, Linda Laskowski, "Sacred Ground," *UUA View from Berkeley*, 9 Aug. 2012, accessed 22 Aug. 2012, http://pcdtrustee.blogspot.com/2012/08/sacred-ground.html.

40. Bischof interview with Paul Nagel, 25 June 1990.

41. Franz Gockel, "Normandie: Die Invasion am 6. Juni 1944 überlebt. Begegnungen und Erinnerungen aus Kriegs- und Nachkriegjahren" (Hamm 1994), 58–65 (with pictures), unpublished manuscript in the Bischof private archives.

42. Patton cited in "Ruinenromantik," *Profil*, 10 Sept. 2006.

43. *Süddeutsche Zeitung* [SZ], 3 May 1994, 11; 10 May 1994.

44. Paul Virilio, *Bunker Archeology* (Princeton: Princeton University Press, 1984). For the quotations cited here, including some bunker photographs, see "On

the Legacy and Mythology of Bunkers," accessed 22 Aug. 2012, http://www.
architizer.com/en_us/blog/dyn/30519/on-the-legacy-and-mythology-of-
bunkers-2/.

45. For such a bunker sliding into the sand, see *SZ*, 5 May 1994.

46. *Der Spiegel*, 4 June 1984, 134.

47. His brother Walter later was killed in a bombing attack, see *Der Spiegel*, 29
May 2004, 49.

48. *Die Zeit*, 1 June 1984, 1.

49. *Der Spiegel*, 4 June 1984, 137.

50. *Die Zeit*, 1 June 1984, 1.

51. *Die Welt*, 6 June 1984, 4.

52. Ibid., 6 June 1984, 2.

53. *Die Presse*, 6 June 1984; *Wiener Zeitung* [WZ], 7 June 1984, 1.

54. *Salzburger Nachrichten* [SN], 5 June 1984, 3; their Moscow correspondent
reported that the Soviets accused their former Western Allies of "practicing
historical misrepresentation" with their 6 June commemorations, ibid.

55. The previous year "only" 3,000 veterans had visited on the 6 June anniversary.
See *International Herald Tribune*, 22–23 January 1994.

56. Mönch, *Entscheidungsschlacht*, 216.

57. See picture #19 of Ambrose lecturing on D-Day to President Clinton and
officials in *Invasion*, eds. Bischof and Krieger,138.

58. *Frankfurter Allgemeine Zeitung* [FAZ], 7 June 1994, 2; *Die Welt*, 7 June 1994,
7.

59. In early March the *Süddeutsche Zeitung* reported that behind the scenes Kohl
was already maneuvering for an invitation but publically professed he was
not. The German Foreign Ministry had issued a circular that became public
wherein it prohibited German diplomats from attending war commemorations abroad. See *SZ*, 7 Mar. 1994.

60. *FAZ*, 4 June 1994, 1.

61. *SZ*, 4 Apr. 1994, 4.

62. *International Herald Tribune*, 23 Apr. 1994.

63. *Die Zeit*, 13 May 1994, 1.

64. Ambrose, "*The Longest Day*," 430.

65. *Die Zeit*, 3 June 1994, 39; *SZ am Wochenende*, 4/5 June 1994.

66. *Der Spiegel*, 23 May 1994, 178.

67. Frei, "Deutsche Lernprozesse," 38f.

68. *Die Zeit*, 3 June 1994, 1.

69. *SZ*, 4/5 June 1994, 4.

70. Ibid., 6 June 1994, 8.

71. Ibid., 1–2 June 1994, 3; *Die Welt*, 7 June 1994, 3.

72. *Die Welt*, 6 June 1994, 4.

73. *SZ*, 6 June1994, 8.

74. *SN*, 4 June 1994, 1.

75. *Die Presse*, 19 March 1994, 2.

76. *SN*, 7 June 1994.

77. *Kurier*, 7 June 1994.

78. *Der Kamerad*, no. 4 (1994), 2.

79. Ibid., no. 5 (1994), 2.

80. Ibid., no. 4 (1994), 2.

81. *SZ*, 1–2 June 1994, 3.

82. *KleineZeitung*, 5 June 1994, 30–31; Bischof has also corresponded with Höller and interviewed him.

83. *Die Welt*, 7 June 2004, 3; see also *Die Zeit*, 9 June 2004.

84. *SZ*, 7 June 2004.

85. Ibid.

86. *Die Welt*, 5 June 2004, 3.

87. Ibid., 8 June 1994, 2.

88. Ibid., 15 June 2004, 29.

89. *Die Zeit*, 21 October 2004, 3.

90. Ibid., 3 June 2004, 1.

91. *Kurier*, 7 June 2004, 4; *Wiener Zeitung*, 8 June 2004, 5; *Die Presse*, 7 June 2004, 1.

92. *Kurier*, 7 June 2004, 4.

93. *Wiener Zeitung*, 2 June 2004, 3.

94. Wolfgang Schüssel in Sixty-Fourth Session of Parliament, 4 June 2004, Stenographic Protocol. Nationalrat, XXII. GP, 64. Sitzung, 8.

95. Rede von Bundeskanzler Wolfgang Schüssel Europa-Forum Wachau, 6 June 2004, accessed 21 Aug. 2012,http://www.austria.gv.at/2004/6/9/g%C3%B6ttweig2004_final_k.pdf.

96. Günter Bischof and Michael S. Maier, "Reinventing Tradition and the Politics of History: Schüssel's Restitution and Commemoration Policies," in *The Schüssel Era in Austria*, Contemporary Austrian Studies, eds. Günter Bischof

and Fritz Plasser, vol. 18 (New Orleans/Innsbruck: UNO Press/Innsbruck University Press 2010), 206–34.

97. Wolfgang Krieger, "Der 6. Juni im politischen Denken in Deutschland und bei den Alliierten," in *Invasion*, eds. Bischof and Krieger, 173–89.

98. *Der Spiegel*, 29 May 2004, 48.

99. *Die Zeit*, 3 June 2004.

100. Maier, Herf, Moeller, Kantsteiner, Frei and Wippermann all ignore the Normandy commemorations and memory production.

Chapter Six

"Their Overdue Landing": A View from the Eastern Front

Olga Kucherenko

> One cannot but acknowledge that the history of war knows no other similar undertaking as regards breadth of design, vastness of scale, and high skill of execution...History will record this deed as an achievement of the highest order.
>
> –Joseph Stalin, *Pravda*, June 14, 1944

> At last, the Allies have landed in France to share in the victory.
>
> –Grigorii Baklanov, *Piad' Zemli*, January 1959

During a meeting of cinematographers in June 1963, the Soviet director Ivan Pyriev shared his thoughts on the Oscar-winning American epic, *The Longest Day* (1962), which he had seen while on a business trip to the United States. Noting the film's cinematographic qualities, authenticity, and attention to minute detail, the filmmaker chose to concentrate especially on its content. In Pyriev's view, the film's "underlying task" was to "falsify the history of the Second World War and to ascribe to the Western powers the main role in the victory over Hitler's military machine, simultaneously restoring the tarnished reputation of [his] generals." Pyriev found it preposterous that the American filmmakers failed to mention the fact that it had not been the sleeping pills taken by Hitler on the eve of the Normandy invasion but the "heroic Red Army" in the East that had prevented the generals from transferring additional forces to stave off the Allied "overdue landing" in the West. In Pyriev's final analysis, *The Longest Day* represented "a series of 'little truths' [that] obfuscated a huge lie."[1]

And the filmmaker was not alone in his assessment. Backed up by the Minister of Defense and the Chief of the Army's Political Administration, another film director and a veteran, Iurii Ozerov, set about creating a Soviet answer to the American blockbuster.[2] Seven years later, millions of Ozerov's countrymen flocked to see the first two out of five installments of the war epic, *Liberation* (premiered in 1970). Its claim was to show the liberation of Europe as it *really* happened from the point of view of the private and the officer, the diplomat and the state leader. What the viewers saw was the victorious war on the Eastern Front from 1943 onwards, with most of the credit for defeating the Nazis given to the Soviet Union. *The Direction of the Main Blow*, the third film in the series (1971), was to cover 1944, the year that witnessed a joint military effort by the Allies to finish off Nazi Germany. Yet the much anticipated and celebrated event at the time, the Allied landing in Normandy, received a mere forty-seven seconds in an hour-long episode. By comparison, President Roosevelt's three-minute musings about the opening of the Second Front, directly following the wartime footage of the Allies strolling purposefully along the beach, seemingly lasted for an eternity.

This lack of interest and the minimization of the significance of D-Day on the part of the film's creators—and more tellingly, their Party and Army curators—contrasted sharply with the official wartime recognition that had been accorded to the "greatest mass amphibious assault in history, unprecedented in its organization and scale."[3] Nevertheless, this should not come as a surprise in the Soviet context. Several factors predetermined this turbidity of historical memory of the Normandy landing in the postwar Soviet Union. Some of these factors derived in part from the ideological and geopolitical imperatives of the postwar period; others were psychological in nature. All of them were tightly interlinked, interchangeable, and directly dependent on each other, up to the point that it is impossible now to establish the primacy of any of them.

Thus, the failure of Soviet historiography and "historiophoty" to acknowledge wholeheartedly the positive role of the Western Allies in liberating Europe during World War II stemmed from the time-honored popular suspicion of the "class enemy," dampened down but never completely eliminated during the war; the ideological blinders and inertia of the Soviet leadership and Party ideologues; the Soviet Union's newly acquired great power status and the attendant propagandist rivalry between the former allies, especially concerning their continuous presence in Europe, as well as the growing hostility of Western historians toward the Soviet Union in the context of the Cold War.[4] Just as American opinion-makers discounted or ignored the importance of wartime operations in the East, their Soviet counterparts also minimized or depicted in unflattering terms the Allied war effort.[5] One of the tricks was to single out the Eastern Front from the overall scheme of World War II and call it "The Great Patriotic War of the Soviet Union."[6] The fact that it was not called a battle, but semantically distinguished as a parallel war, hints at the Soviet feeling of exceptionality and the uniqueness of *their* war effort. Eventually, this ensured a narrowness of view, as battles in the "East" began to dominate domestic public awareness, and people learned to appreciate *their* country's unmatched contribution to the overall victory. Albeit reservedly, the mass media did provide information on the action in other military theatres, just as it had before the German invasion. But the limited Soviet participation in the battles beyond the Eastern Front allowed the opinion-makers to focus popular attention on the events closer to home, dismissing those occurring in distant lands.[7] Besides, the horrendously traumatic war experience, which has indirectly affected several postwar generations, validated the national victimization myth.

Thus, the politically motivated scheming should not be divorced from psychological factors. The Allied contribution was much easier to dim in collective memory because it did *not* contradict the actual experience of the overwhelming majority of Soviet people who lived and fought during the war. These people were very much aware of the toll the war had taken on their community and economy. They remembered the delays in the opening of the Second Front and shared a common perception that, until the summer of 1944, the Western Allies had been fighting "to the last Soviet soldier." Even though they initially had had high hopes for the alliance, servicemen and civilians alike bore a grudge against the United States and Great Britain based on *personal* experience and *local* military realities, but also out of ignorance of the events in other military theaters. And here the dismissive attitude of Soviet opinion-makers regarding Allied material and military aid played a decisive role. To be sure, the Allies' contribution was acknowledged but always with reservation that the most damage to the Axis was done by the men and women of the Red Army, who did the bulk of the killing and dying. In this respect, a phrase uttered by a Soviet private in the opening sequence of another popular film, *The Meeting on the Elbe* (1949), is quite revealing. As he looked across the river at his American brothers-in-arms, the soldier excitedly shouted, "At least on the last day of war, let me see the Second Front." This double entendre conveyed both a jeering resentment and an overwhelming curiosity harbored by those who knew very little, if anything, about the face-off on the other side of the European continent.

Their curiosity would never be satisfied, and, while some other aspects of the war became subjects of dispute over the long postwar period, the Normandy landing and the overall context of the Second Front in Europe was one rare area where collective memory and official history converged and remained relatively constant. It was only after the collapse of the Soviet Union, the emergence of an independent scholarly community, and the arrival of the foreign films that would have been banned in Soviet times for exaggerating the contribution of the Western Allies, that the general public learned of the effects of D-Day and other battles on the outcome of World War II.

However, the resurgence of national assertiveness, which feeds off the war cult, threatens the recurrence of collective amnesia in modern-day Russia. The Great Patriotic War is ever-present among her citizens. They take special pride in their grandparents' martial achievements and link those to their national character. Especially in the post-Soviet period, the Victory in the War became a source of dignity and the kernel of national consolidation mythology. It is arguably the only event in the entire Soviet history that is capable of inducing a feeling of self-worth and self-respect among Russians. In the absence of other universally accepted, pride-inducing achievements, memory of the war becomes intertwined with identity.[8] And since D-Day rather dilutes this process, outsiders are not welcome, especially those who also claim to have been the only nation that single-handedly changed the course of the war and saved humanity.[9]

PRIMUS INTER PARES

Manipulations of public opinion were already evident during the war itself, and long before the Allied landing. Much of Soviet enthusiasm about the newly formed Alliance had died out in the course of the first year of the war, since little in terms of Allied material and military aid had been seen on the Eastern Front during this period. Even though Lend-Lease supplies began arriving in earnest afterward, the political and military leadership publicly noted the modest scale of the Allied military effort, focusing on the relative number of Axis divisions facing the Soviet Union and her allies. The Soviets did not consider the bombing of Germany and the campaign in North Africa as a second front. Stalin had been asking for one in Europe since the German invasion, and the Soviet public knew of the negotiations between the Allies, but the population was promptly informed in February 1942 that "at the moment, the Red Army and the German Fascist Army are fighting one on one."[10] The situation remained unchanged for the next two years, although the image of the Allies, especially the Americans, remained fairly positive, being further cultivated by some of the most influential writers such as Konstantin Simonov and Boris Polevoi.[11]

Nevertheless, the Soviet press kept on carefully reminding its readers of the Allies' inactivity, even deliberate foot-dragging, which allowed the Axis to concentrate their troops in the East. Simultaneously the image of the Soviet Union as a moral leader of the Alliance, its backbone, and the main fighting force was created.[12] The reports did mention the Allied contribution, especially bombing raids, but these were immediately rendered insignificant by the matchless combat performance of the Red Army.[13] The Soviet reader, meanwhile, found very little explanation as to the real reasons for the postponement of the Second Front. Nor was there a proper acknowledgement of the fact that, having shifted to the production of fighter planes and having diverted a substantial number of already operational ones to ward off Allied bombers, "the Germans reduced their bombing threat over the battlefield in the East."[14] Instead, derisive caricatures and veiled statements hinted at Western cowardice and perfidiousness.

In all fairness, some of the utterances by the Allied political and military leaders did indicate that they were playing a "wait and see game," postponing the invasion of Europe to save the lives of their own soldiers.[15] Soviet cultural figures and distinguished frontline soldiers detected this attitude while on their trips to the United States and Great Britain. Indeed, they let their feelings be known to Western audiences. In 1942, representatives of the Jewish Antifascist Committee felt scandalized when asked to repudiate the rumor of a separate Soviet-German peace agreement. They replied to this insinuation that it felt as if "so far the Soviet Union [was] leading a *separate war* with Germany," while the Allies preferred to remain ignorant of the Nazi atrocities in the East.[16] A year later, the celebrated female sniper, twenty-two year old Liudmila Pavlichenko, who had so far dispatched 309 enemy soldiers, publicly reproached her Chicago hosts for their faintheartedness and wished they would not "hide behind [her] back for too long."[17]

The public at home shared the feeling that the Allies were sitting idly and not pulling their weight.[18] Whereas the attitudes of officialdom towardthe Allied reticence to open a Second Front fluctuated depending on the situation at the front, the public mood remained constant up until the Normandy landing. The Second Front was usually a hotly discussed question among civilians and soldiers alike.[19] The majority of them, however, knew fairly little of either the scale of Allied material aid or combat in other theaters. National newspapers did not offer much in terms of critical analysis of the situation in Europe and the Pacific, while foreign newsagents, such as the popular Russian-language journals *Britanskii Soiuznik* and *Amerika*, that presented a more nuanced picture of the Allied war effort, were available only in large cities and only to a select few.[20] Thus, the major sources of information regarding the preparations for the Second Front were rumors and German propaganda leaflets claiming that "the Rumanians and Hungarians [were] better allies to [the Germans] than the English to [the Soviets]."[21] "Gradually, a misunderstanding of what was happening, and even a sense of distrust toward our allies, developed," remembers a veteran. "The Red Army was bleeding, while the Allies only shared new promises, meat stew, and army boots with us. The frontline press and our commissars cultivated this mood among the men, as only they were able."[22] Before long, the name "Second Front" was being assigned to American spam, and the much-awaited landing in France became a subject matter of biting jokes, which found their way into the press and even marching songs. The majority of the Soviet population still believed it was their country that was doing most of the fighting and suffering.[23]

All the endeavors by the British, and later Americans, to persuade Soviet audiences that the Western Allies were also extensively contributing to the overall victory were met with sneering or silent petulance.[24] Soviet ideologues spoke irritably of what they thought were British attempts to equate their war effort with that of the Soviet Union and to suggest that the latter was not in fact "bearing the brunt of war." The Soviets rejected out of hand the suggestions that the bombing campaign, or combat in North Africa and Italy, effectively represented a Second Front, and jeered at the comparison of British submariners with Soviet partisans fighting in the enemy rear.[25]

Generally, the Soviets remained very jealous of their achievements, especially as the Red Army began its westward advance, although having finally obtained the Allied commitment to open the Second Front in France in late spring of 1944, Stalin announced in his May Day speech that Soviet victories were "to a great extent" due to "our magnificent Allies, the USA and Great Britain...deflecting from us a significant part of the German army."[26] By this time, however, neither the leadership nor the public believed that the invasion of

France would actually happen and German leaflets disabused them of any hope.[27] Some even expected yet another trick on the part of the Allies.[28] There was a bitter resignation that the Red Army would fight alone until Germany's final defeat. In a British wartime correspondent's words, later corroborated by Soviet veterans, "the second front was no longer, to them, a matter of life or death. It now began to be taken for granted that the war would be won anyway."[29] After all, by mid-1944, the Red Army was no longer in a desperate situation; it stood at the gates of Europe, and, in popular view, Nazi defeat was only a matter of time.[30]

Thus, when the Allies finally landed in Normandy, the Soviets felt surprised and euphoric if grousing a little. Moscow restaurants were reportedly filled with jubilant customers; soldiers at the front fired shots in the air; there was much kissing and hugging, and much hope that "now the war [would] end soon. The Allies have plenty of strength and it [would] be easier for us."[31] But many thought the British and the Americans would have it "too easy" as well, now that the Red Army had already torn the heart out of the *Wehrmacht*; and some even expressed concern that having arrived that late in the war, the Allies would snatch the laurels of victory from the exhausted Soviet troops.[32] The public still accused Western partners of self-interest, this time of protecting themselves lest the Red Army overrun Europe, although the press discouraged such sentiments, instead propagating the idea of a joint effort.[33]

Among the first to report on the invasion of Normandy was *Pravda*. On 7 June the newspaper devoted two whole pages to the opening of the Second Front in France. Even though the news of the landing followed the reports on the Soviet bombing of Romania, the reconstruction of liberated cities, and a chess championship, the invasion was presented as not only "exceptionally important, but also massive and dangerous." It was argued that by spilling their blood in the West and in the South, the Allies helped speed up Soviet advances in the East and thereby strengthened "the great friendship of freedom-loving peoples, whose mutual blows [would] finally rid the world of Hitlerite Germany."[34] Nevertheless, when the editors of *Komsomolskaia Pravda* flatteringly compared the Western Allies'

Figure 12: A caricature by Kukryniksy from the June 17, 1944 *Pravda* issue. The caption reads: "A hopeless situation."

advance in France with that of the Red Army in Eastern Europe, they received a slap on the wrist. For such an inflation of the Allied performance at the expense of the Red Army's "decisive role" could give wrong ideas to the general public. Incidentally, the latter were prevented from watching the film footage that the Allies had rushed to Moscow in the wake of the landings in the hope that a visual image would have a much more potent effect on the general public than a written word.[35]

The Soviet primacy in this alliance remained constant, and the chess championship, as well as the reconstruction of the country, continued to dominate the news.[36] Only on 11 June did "the immense military tasks facing" the Western Allies make the first page of *Pravda* and only in the context of "the outstanding successes of the Red Army" that "had borne the bulk of the fighting against Hitler's Germany," thereby "allowing the Allies to mobilize their strength and resources" to engage "gradually" in military action. Despite the much-appreciated material aid from the West, the Soviet Union was still a paragon of virtue and military strength, that not only single-handedly averted a German invasion of America and Great Britain, but also managed to supply the former with scarce resources in her own hour of need.[37] Written by military specialists in a technical language, short matter-of-fact reports about the battles in the West continued to appear in the Soviet press. Yet under the weight of the concurrent Soviet military operations, the Normandy campaign gradually turned into a mere sideshow that did not much affect the situation on the Eastern Front considering that most German divisions were still deployed there. The general view, observers noted, was that the Allies fought an easy war without sufficient vigor.[38]

Any praise of the Alliance that did not afford the Soviet Union the lion's share of credit was deemed unfit for public consumption. Thus, on 22 June 1944, censors halted the issue of a large, colorful poster depicting Hitler and Mussolini being booted down a ladder by American and British bayonets. The absence of a Soviet blade made the poster and the accompanying poem unacceptable, for they "manifestly exaggerate[ed] the role of our allies and stray[ed] far from reality."[39] All eyes now turned to the massive offensive in Belorussia, which began the next day, 23 June, and the subsequent blows against Germany's allies in Eastern Europe. Preoccupied with their own tragedies and triumphs, the Soviet public lost interest in the Western battles.[40] The details of those operations, especially their human cost, remained obscure and thus underappreciated. Enjoying a rather limited circulation, *Britanskii Soiuznik* and *Amerika* were evidently unable to sway public opinion. The newsreels of the Normandy campaign were ordered but never screened in Soviet cinemas, possibly in response to the accelerating anti-Soviet propaganda in the West, as well as various impediments erected to everything penned by Soviet journalists there.[41] The ideologues grumbled that such an attitude led to the Western public developing a very vague idea of the hardships endured by the Soviet people. At the same time, they ignored the complaints of Western journalists who felt increasingly isolated and misinformed about the events on the Eastern Front, especially since the landing in France. The requests to establish a free flow of information—similar to the one that existed between the Western Allies—and to ensure that first-hand accounts could be "obtained by accredited correspondents at the actual front," who would then be able to "tell the story of the Soviet war effort and the achievements of its armies," were waved away.[42]

This was a telltale sign of a great socio-political friction within the alliance, which would occur shortly after the war and whose echo would reverberate with various degrees of intensity throughout the long postwar period. The two ideologically opposed camps, temporarily fused by the requirements of war but irrevocably riddled with mutual distrust, finally began to push away from each other under the weight of new political realities and the growing embitterment on both sides regarding the "Polish Question," Soviet Atomic espionage, as well as the future of postwar Europe.[43] Already in mid-October 1944, Soviet opinion-makers described the relationship with the Western Allies as "difficult and sensitive."[44] In his 6 November 1944 speech, Stalin publicly praised the Alliance partners without whom the Red Army "would not have been able to break the German resistance in such a short period of time and throw them out of the Soviet Union." But he also reminded his wartime associates whom they should thank for their victories in Western Europe.[45] The Allies were meant to feel an even stronger sense of indebtedness after their less than spectacular performance in the Ardennes in the winter of 1944-1945. The widespread opinion in the Soviet Union was that the Red Army had to save "Anglo-Americans" yet again by starting its own *Vistula-Oder* offensive more than a week earlier. The perceived Allied ingratitude, let alone America's growing presence on the European Continent, annoyed Moscow and its emissaries in the West. As the leadership deliberated an attack on Japan, the Soviet Ambassador in London, Ivan Maisky, deviously suggested letting the Western Allies try to defeat Japan on their own, in "revenge for their foot-dragging on the Second Front." In his long-term view, this "would also force America and Britain to squander additional blood and resources, thus cooling off a bit America's imperialistic ardor for the postwar period."[46]

Appropriating Victory

As the questions of the postwar settlement in Europe started to dominate the political arena, there was thus a noticeable change of attitudes toward the wartime allies on both sides of what was soon to become the Iron Curtain. Before the war was even over, the Western media had intensified its attacks against the Soviet partner, while the latter had launched a concerted propaganda campaign to discredit the Western Allies.[47] In the immediate postwar years, rumors spread that the Americans were preparing a war against the Soviet Union. The leadership, while attempting to avoid an escalation of tensions on the international arena, simultaneously encouraged anxiety at home, seeing a clear ideological and economic benefit in such fears. Propagating the old Bolshevik idea of a hostile capitalist encirclement and thereby mobilizing the populace for further sacrifices, the regime used all forms of mass media to make the former ally into an imperialist enemy, whose culture and way of life were thoroughly rotten, just like her pretenses of good faith.[48]

The tensions and conflicts that had surrounded the question of the Second Front resurfaced as the official mass media set about to give the recent war a face-lift. Not allowed to concentrate on the physical and psychological trauma, Soviet artists and historians engaged in the creation of a sanitized, heroic version of the war, in which former allies played a rather dubious role.[49] Their invasion of Europe received a purely ideological interpretation. While the Soviet Union had reportedly remained true to her wartime ideals, her Western partners had deliberately dragged out the war with the singular aim of exhausting the Soviets.[50] The tone was set by the 1947 textbook, *The Great Patriotic War of the Soviet Union*, whose author argued that the Western elites, particularly in Great Britain, had delayed the opening of the Second Front until the very end of the war, because they had not wished the Soviet Union to defeat Germany too soon and emerge as a great power. Eventually, claimed the book, to forestall the inevitable Soviet triumph, the Allies had been forced to land in France in 1944. And even then, they had managed to protract their breakout from the Normandy beachhead for two and a half months by exhibiting astonishing military ineptitude in the face of insignificant German resistance and resorting to political deviousness in seeking a compromise peace with Hitler's generals.[51] By stressing their dishonesty and poor combat performance in France, Soviet opinion-makers could thus question the momentousness of the Allied contribution to the overall victory.[52]

Moreover, such denunciation of Allied hidden motives, coupled with the quiet rehabilitation of German generals in the West, placed former Alliance partners firmly in Hitler's camp. In response to Western criticisms of the Molotov-Ribbentrop Pact, Soviet ideologues accused Great Britain and America of having encouraged Germany to attack the Soviet Union, of exhausting her by delaying the invasion of Europe, and of intentionally procrastinating on the Western Front while the Red Army did all the fighting.[53] This Stalinist conception of World War II, set out in the 1947 programmatic pamphlet, *Falsifiers of History*, survived for many decades after the war and was especially reflected in visual art that portrayed the Western Allies as eager pupils of the Nazis.[54] The image of a warmongering capitalist would usually reappear around the major commemoration dates, when Soviet artists would remind their audiences with a typical boastfulness that the Soviet Union was a battle-hardened adversary not to be challenged. Their country's victorious war record and the unfavorable accounts of Allied combat performance appealed to the Soviet public dealing with the extensive destruction and loss of life caused by Germany, and now facing a new enemy.

If wartime impressions of the Allies fighting in Europe were vague and imprecise, there was little change in Soviet public perceptions in the first decade after the war. Everything Soviet citizens knew, they learned from the official media. Alternative sources of information were rarely available. From October 1946, the publishing license for *Britanskii Soiuznik* had been cancelled, and it looked as if *Amerika* would soon follow.[55] A year later army political officers warned the ranks that it was "immoral and unpatriotic" to "listen to and read the pro-fascist junk presented by Anglo-American reactionary forces to the Soviet people."[56] The authorities also discouraged any contact with foreigners, while those few veterans who had managed to fight alongside the Allies in the West preferred to remain silent. So did historians, after one of their number had been viciously criticized for "belittling the historical role of the Soviet Union in the Great Patriotic War and exaggerating that of Great Britain and America."[57]

In his 1948 book, *International Relations during the Years of the Great Patriotic War (1941-45)*, the historian in question, G. A. Deborin, reportedly gave a non-political, and from the censors' point of view, distorted, interpretation of the Second Front. According to his critics, who evidently were more concerned about "the current international situation" than the actual course of events, Deborin had failed to adjust the past to the needs of the present and to expose "predatory aims of American imperialism." More importantly, having "overestimat[ed] the significance of the American and British role in the achievement of victory" over Germany, the historian imprudently placed the Soviet Union's contribution "on the same level with America, England and France." With the monograph withdrawn from circulation, the author was forced to apologize for his political shortsightedness (which he himself dubbed a "grave crime"), bringing down several other historians with him, including his publisher.[58]

Therefore, the Stalinist historiography of World War II set the chauvinistic tone for the way Soviet historians and the public were supposed to remember former allies for years to come. Political and administrative persecution of truth-lovers did not stop with Stalin's death, and even during a three-year intermission between 1953 and 1956, when historians and artists suddenly received much more leeway in evaluating the war, the Allies' role in it was not markedly affected by the revisionary movement. Though there were calls for a more favorable and appreciative assessment of the Allied contribution, especially the military and political significance of *Operation Overlord*, the conservatives within the Party stifled any initiative, insisting that it was the result of the massive Soviet effort which had permitted the Western Allies to land in France and to advance onto Germany.[59] Fairness and honesty toward the former allies were not high on the agenda when even the Soviet people's place in the rigid hierarchy of victors had been superseded first by Stalin and then by the megalomaniac Party.

As they claimed much of the credit for themselves, Party and military conservatives acknowledged an important role of the Allies in the defeat of Germany but made it secondary to that of the Soviet Union, which had invested incomparably more in terms of resources and lives.[60] Reviewers thought that the authors of the 1958 volume, *The Second World War 1939-1945: A Military-Historical Essay*, apportioned the credit fairly, with three-quarters of the book dedicated to events on the Eastern Front and the rest afforded to other military theaters. This, in the critics' view, reflected "the real ratio of the significance of historic events," especially when it came to the Second Front in Europe that had allegedly been opened in "exceptionally favorable conditions" created by Soviet victories in the East. Even with their technical and numerical superiority, and despite the fact that the Red Army had granted them more than enough time to prepare and execute the landing, the Allies exhibited "excessive caution and unwarranted orderliness."[61]

The slow pace of their advance, especially on the part of the British, as well as their "barbarous and futile" bombing of cities in Normandy, also came under heavy criticism in a second edition of *The Truth about the Second Front: A Memoir of a War Correspondent* by D. Kraminov. Having already caused a stir in the West in 1948, Kraminov decided to reprint his updated journal with the "modest" intention to show "what exactly was happening in Western Europe in the last year of the war" and to counter bourgeois attempts "to dictate their conception of events."[62]

The Soviets were acutely aware of the bourgeoning one-sided historiography of World War II in the West. Resentful of American and British intransigence to accept the relative significance of the Eastern Front in the overall context of the war, Soviet historians and military analysts set about to debunk the "bourgeois falsifications" aimed at depreciating Russian victories. In answer to the Western claims, both Kraminov and the army's mouthpiece, *Military-Historical Journal* (*VIZh*), propagated the idea that the Normandy landing, even though executed with skill and precision, had in actuality been "a breach in the open gates." The Allies' adversaries had allegedly represented a motley collection of demoralized, badly trained, poorly equipped and overstretched reserve troops aided by several battle hardened divisions; much of the *Luftwaffe* had been concentrated in the East thereby allowing the Allies full air superiority; the fortifications along the beach in Northern France had remained unfinished and in reality had turned out to be a far cry from what Western historians now maintained.

Such representation created an impression that the Western Allies had an easy walk across Europe until they met serious resistance in the Ardennes. At the same time, although the Canadian and American troops received special praise, they were still accused of lacking the will to "fight Russian style," which meant dealing the enemy a shattering blow and moving swiftly for 150-200 km at once. Besides, so much credit was accorded to the French resistance movement, partially sponsored by the Soviets themselves, that it sometimes obfuscated those really responsible for the operation.[63] Indeed, according to the Soviet version, the French valiantly assisted their allies despite the latter's vicious bombing of French towns. Kraminov perceived such senseless destruction of life and property as the Western Allies' true aims of "weakening not only the Russians, who continued to do most of the fighting...but also the French" so as to hinder any potential opposition to the Anglo-American plans for postwar Europe. The journalist naturally overlooked the Red Army's own track record in Eastern Europe.[64]

The old conception of the Allied culpability in provoking and dawdling over the war kept a stranglehold over Soviet historiography.[65] The Allies were accused of deliberately "fighting the fascists in the ancillary military theaters" and opening the Second Front in Europe only in June 1944 to prevent the Red Army from defeating Nazi Germany without any external help and claim victory to itself. At the same time, Allied logistical difficulties were vehemently rejected in favor of purely political explanations, which, in Soviet ideologues' views, betrayed the Allies' unwillingness to free Europe from fascist subjugation. This meant that by "consistently and actively fighting the fascists till the very last day of the war" the Soviet Union had the liberation of European peoples at heart and thus had a full right to dictate her will to the freed nations afterwards.[66] On his trip to Leipzig in March 1959, Nikita Khrushchev cultivated the feeling of indebtedness toward the Red Army and the grudge against the former allies by emphasizing Soviet altruism and suggesting that "the Allies hastened the opening [of the Second Front] so as not to allow Western Europeans, aided by the Soviet Army, to defeat occupying forces by themselves."[67]

Besides the obvious geopolitical advantages, the image-sensitive regime saw a significant benefit in amplifying and sustaining such nationalist sentiment and resentment toward the West. Soviet opinion-makers discredited the "Anglo-American" motives and performance in the war in order to promote the socialist system. By affording the Allies more credit and accepting the importance of their material help, historians risked challenging the well-established notion that the Party had prepared the Soviet Union technologically and militarily to win the war on her own. Even the first disastrous years of the war were skidded over, because they could potentially reflect negatively on the regime and the genius of its leadership, many of whom were still in power. Therefore, as they deliberately distracted popular attention from the complexities of war experience, Party censors fought doggedly against anything that could undermine the people's vote of confidence for the system. They prevented a wider distribution of foreign films which, in their view, "clearly overstate[d] the role of the US in the defeat of Hitler's Germany," and carried out a massive publishing effort to dispute Western claims that the 1944 invasion of Europe determined the outcome of the war.[68]

The legitimation drive proved especially timely when Leonid Brezhnev ascended to power in 1964. In the atmosphere of increasingly intense propagandist competition on the international arena just as the Cold War was about to take a new turn in Vietnam and the dwindling public support for the ailing regime at home, the victory in the war became the symbol of Soviet might and achievement. It proved the superiority of the socialist order over capitalism and as such became the major part of the regime's identity.[69] Moreover, as a former political officer in the Red Army, Brezhnev actively propagated his membership in the so-called "front brother-hood" whose support he needed to stay in power. Anxious to win the veterans to its side, the regime showed off the efforts to celebrate the Victory and exploited the twenty million war deaths to dispute Western claims to Europe.

To be sure, Soviet historians recognized the relative role of all members of the Coalition, placing special emphasis on the popular liberation movement in occupied Europe, but they also refuted the Western contention that it was "the Allied backing at a critical moment in the war that determined the outcome of battle on the Eastern Front."[70] It was especially important now to show that the Soviet Union would have been able to win the war in any case. So, every new Western publication prompted an instant reaction on the part of the Soviet scholarly community, who, without dismissing the value of such studies, expressed dismay at the belittling of the Soviet Union's victories, especially during the summer and autumn of 1944.[71] They stressed that it was the Allied landing in France that had been "complementary" to the battles on the Soviet-German front, not the other way around, and that in the common fight against Nazi Germany it had played no "special" role.[72] During the thirtieth anniversary of D-Day, one historian accused his Western colleagues of intentionally "diminishing in the eyes of the world the glorious achievements of the Red Army in 1944 ... by publicizing the activities of Anglo-American forces in [other] military theaters" and treating the campaign in the West separately from that in the East.[73] This could undermine the assertion that, having fought for Europe, the Soviet Union won her entitlement to a political and military pres-ence in the region, something that Western observers had already feared in 1942, predicting that it would be increasingly difficult to dislodge the Soviets from the Continent.[74]

OLD GRUDGES DIE HARD

Ten years later, in 1984, Ronald Reagan also hinted at the great power rivalry over Europe. As he stood on the Normandy beachhead, where the Allied forces had "joined in battle to reclaim this Continent to liberty," the US president stressed the continuity between the Western Allied wartime intentions and present commitments. He offered a detailed account of the landing and acknowledged the contribution of all members of the Coalition, predictably concentrating on the US role in the liberation.[75] Reagan's unambiguous thrust against the Soviet continuous occupation of Eastern Europe was promptly answered by *Pravda,*accusing him of staging a propagandistic show to mask his own country's militaristic intentions. Moreover, Soviet observers of the remembrance ceremony felt offended by the fact that in the majority of the documentaries and press releases commemorating D-Day "there was absolutely no mention of incomparably fiercer and bloodier battles on the Soviet-German front, where...the fascist beast's backbone had been broken, allowing the Western Allies to advance to the river Elbe with relatively minor losses by the end of April 1945."[76] It seemed that only the French, as well as the British historian John Erickson, showed solidarity with the Soviet cause, thereby sabotaging "the spectacle planned by Washington."[77] Although it did not say so explicitly, the June 1984 issue of *VIZh*, dedicated entirely to the Belorussian offensive, implied that if it were not for the Soviet *Operation Bagration*, the Allies would have had little chance of establishing a large-scale lodgment in Normandy.[78] A similar idea found its way into Soviet textbooks and was propagated among military cadets.[79]

Nevertheless, the official one-sided representation of the war was beginning to arouse protest from the most unexpected quarters. Revolutionary for its time, the documentary by Alexander Sokurov, *And Nothing More* (initiallycalled *The Allies*, 1982-87), cleverly subverted the heroic epos of the socialist system's victorious role. Perhaps under the influence of the ongoing Afghan campaign, the director instead presented World War II as a chaotic, tragic process involving an array of actors and intentions. More importantly, the film showed that in their humanity and aspirations, the Western Allies were not much different from their Soviet partners. Its schematic treatment of the battles in the West betrayed the general lack of knowledge about that side of the war, but the absence of ideological pathos was evident in the film as much as the celebration of a combined effort.

The documentary, in fact, became one of the first signs of the rapprochement with the West, taking place in the late 1980s–early 1990s, which also coincided with an incipient drive to demythologize (not always successfully) the last World War. Throughout the late Soviet period and its aftermath, Russian scholars exhibited a certain departure from the ideological orthodoxy of the Brezhnev school and a greater balance in treating the Allied war effort. In 1994, the Bank of Russia issued a three-ruble coin commemorating the opening of the Second Front in France.

Figure 13: A three-ruble coin minted by the Central Bank of the Russian Federation in 1994.

Reporting on the preparations for the latter's fiftieth anniversary, *Pravda* took an unexpected turn in portraying the event in human terms as acts of bravery, skill, and honor. It celebrated the wartime alliance and admitted that 6 June 1944 was a momentous date in the history of World War II that brought victory nearer. Yet old grudges died hard. The Communist-dominated newspaper could not resist the temptation to chide the Western Allies for their late entry into the war. In a typical nationalistic tone it resurrected the old idea that the Red Army could have defeated Germany on its own, and condemned the homebred historians who had allegedly sold themselves to the West by challenging the traditional parochial view of the war.[80]

Therefore, although there were significant changes for D-Day remembrance in other countries during this period, correspondents of at least two major Russian newspapers failed to notice any growing acceptance of the Soviet Union's role in the war, as well as exhibited no personal re-assessment of the event. Free from Party control, *Izvestiia*, for instance, limited itself to a single photo and a five-line caption about the commemoration ceremony that had taken place in France.[81] It appears that *Pravda*'s derisive remarks were not entirely unwarranted, though. Not only did the organizers of the commemoration ceremony fail to invite official representatives of the former Soviet Union, but they also managed to raise a few eyebrows even among Western historians by overlooking the massive Byelorussian offensive that "took enormous pressure off Americans, who still had not broken out of the Normandy Pocket."[82]

Although Vladimir Putin shared the limelight with other world leaders during the D-Day celebrations ten years later in 2004, *Pravda* continued to lament the fact that no one, except the French President, mentioned the Soviet military aid to the Allies.[83] Adopting a rather sarcastic tone in describing the ceremony, *Izvestiia* announced that despite the Russian delegation's sole aim to remind everyone that "the Second Front was just that, second," only the mayor of Caen acknowledged the Russian presence by adoring the City Hall with a Russian national tricolor together with other flags.[84] The clearly less sensitive Russian scholarly community, in the meantime, had displayed heightened interest toward the forthcoming events in France, organizing at least two separate international conferences in Moscow.[85] The following year, the capital witnessed the unveiling of a new monument to the wartime Alliance.

Nevertheless, despite a more objective view of the battles in the West, the timeworn reasoning remained constant in the mainstream Russian scholarly literature: while the opening of the Second Front had been prompted by the Allied desire "not to miss out," it had turned out to be too little, too late. By exhibiting excessive caution in Northern France the Western Allies had wasted precious time, as well as more Soviet lives, and eventually had to be rescued by the Red Army, which would have come out of the war victorious in any case.[86]

The last contention has preoccupied scholarly and public imagination since the dissolution of the Soviet Union. Although debates continue among historians, the Russian public eagerly shares the view that the Soviets would have slowly achieved victory over Germany, albeit with far greater military and civilian losses.[87] According to opinion polls carried out throughout the two post-Soviet decades, Russians retained a relatively constant perspective concerning the Red Army's chances of beating Nazi Germany on its own (See Table 1).

Table 1:
Do you think the Soviet Union could have won
the war without the Allied help?

	1991*	1997	2001	2003	2005	2006	2007	2008	2009	2010	2011	2013
Yes	62	71	71	67	60	65	64	64	63	57	60	61
No	26	21	21	26	32	28	28	26	27	30	32	32
Don't Know	12	8	8	7	8	7	8	10	10	13	8	7

Note: the figures are based on a Russia-wide poll of urban and rural population over 18 years of age on a representative sample of 1,600 people from 130 settlements and 45 regions of the country.
* based on a representative sample of 1,000 individuals.
Source: Yuri Levada Analytical Centre. I am grateful to Boris Dubin for providing these data.

This, of course, goes against the widespread opinion in the West, reflected in Barack Obama's speech during the sixty-fifth anniversary of D-Day, when the US president announced that "had the Allies failed [in Normandy], Hitler's occupation of this continent might have continued indefinitely."[88] Since at least in Western textbooks the term "Allies" generally refers to Great Britain and the United States, and very rarely to the Soviet Union, the latter is once again omitted from the virtuous struggle against Hitler.[89] Even though the Russians generally know who fought next to them in World War II, or the Great Patriotic War as many are still accustomed to think of it, in April 2000 only 40 percent of them believed that the Allied role in the war was significant, with 5 percent affording considerable credit to the Allies and 7 percent dismissing their input all together (See Table 2).

Table 2:
In your opinion, how important was our allies' contribution to the final victory?

Very important	5
Important	35
Insignificant	43
Marginal	7
Do not know	10

Source: Yuri Levada Analytical Centre. Data provided by Boris Dubin.

Considering the increasingly nationalistic tone of current Russian textbooks and political pronouncements, it is unlikely that the favorable perception of the Western Allies has taken a dramatic upward turn in the last decade. If anything, the current state-sponsored anti-Americanism that has a receptive audience among at least a third of Russians, residual Soviet pride in wartime achievements and the incessant cultivation of the feeling of duty before the war dead are probably widening the divide between the former allies.[90] The choice of a smaller font describing the opening of the Second Front in one official textbook is quite revealing and is certainly not conductive to any meaningful appreciation of the events.[91] In its bid for popularity, the current Russian government seems to be keeping up the tradition of the war, even if it means preserving its myths and accepting Soviet hypocrisy. Russian bookstores display an enviable array of war-related literature. Upon closer inspection, however, the majority of these studies suffer from familiar trappings of Soviet historiography. One even draws a parallel between World War II and current US policies abroad.[92]

Obviously, it is impossible to gauge the direct effect of this propaganda on the contemporary public. If electronic discussion boards can serve as any indicator, Russian Internet users are deeply divided in their attitude toward the Western Allies and specifically their landing in Normandy. Mutual accusations of hurrah-patriotism on the one hand, and of disloyalty and disrespect toward the war dead on the other are very common. So is the predominance of historic knowledge acquired in Soviet schools.[93] Any attack on the heroic epic often warrants aggression on the part of those who grew up with it. Opinion polls show that it is the older cohort of Russians from provincial towns, with higher education and conservative political leanings, that tend to dismiss the Allied contribution. Nevertheless, a rising number of younger Russians, in the twenty-five to forty age brackets, are beginning to give a more nuanced analysis of the events.[94] One discussion of the American blockbuster, *Saving Private Ryan* (1998), perhaps encapsulates the ambiguity and complexity of popular attitudes. Even though there is a minority view, which dismisses the Allied war effort as incomparable with that of the Soviet Union and feels that the film "has flushed the Russians down the toilet" by not mentioning the concurrent battles in the East, the overwhelming majority of spectators on this forum applaud the film's artistic as well as educational value.[95]

This is an important point, for, despite their vociferous irritation at what they perceive as the diminishing of their contribution to victory in World War II, Russians, like the Soviets before them, seem to be *unique* in actively promoting the memory of the Alliance, both as part of peaceful coexistence discourse, and as part of the national victory celebration.[96] Coverage of the Allied role in the war is still superficial in contemporary Russia, and where D-Day is concerned there seems to be little discontinuity between what has been said about it in the fifties, the eighties, or in recent years. This reflects problems of political legitimacy as well as a nationalist sentiment engendered by the traumatic war experience and reinforced by decades of the Cold War confrontation. What began as a premeditated manipulation of history and memory has overtime transformed into a kind of popular inertia. Nevertheless, Russian children, even more so than their parents before them, do not grow up in ignorance of the event. They simply pass what they learn through a filter of their own national history, one that seems proper to them, just like any other nation.[97] Despite strong ideological and cultural biases, the invasion of Normandy did go down in the Soviet/Russian version of history as one of the decisive battles of World War II that hastened the war's end, but its geographic and psychological remoteness makes it "their landing" and an "overdue" one at that.

1. State Archive of the Russian Federation (GARF) f.9518, op.1, d.373, ll. 104–6. I am grateful to Andrei Kozovoi for bringing this document to my attention. For more on *The Longest Day*, see Michael R. Dolski's chapter in this volume.

2. Fedor Razzakov, *Nashe liubimoe kino. Tainoe stanovitsia iavnym* (Moscow: Algoritm, 2004), 522–4, 540. See a letter from the Defense Minister and his colleagues, initiating the production of the film with the working title *Liberation of Europe* as an answer to Western cinematography and indicating that such a production should become a matter of state importance, in Russian State Archive of Literature and Art (RGALI) f.2944, op.24, d.60, ll. 46–47.

3. "Doklad Predsedatelia GKO na torzhestvennom zasedanii Moskovskogo soveta deputatov trudiashchikhsia s partiinymi i obshchestvennymi organizatsiiami g. Moskvy, 6 noiabria 1944," in *Vneshniaia politika Sovetskogo Soiuza v period Otechestvennoi voiny. Dokumenty i materialy: 1 ianvaria—31 dekabria 1944*, vol.2 (Moscow: OGIZ, 1946), 42.

4. The term was coined by Hayden White in his "Historiography and Historiophoty," *American Historical Review* 93 (December, 1988): 1193.

5. See David M. Glantz, "American Perspectives on Eastern Front Operations in World War II," Foreign Military Studies Office, US Army, Ft. Leavenworth, KS, accessed 10 February 2012, http://fmso.leavenworth.army.mil/documents/e-front.htm; Ronald Smelser and Edward J. Davies II, *The Myth of the Eastern Front: The Nazi-Soviet War in American Popular Culture* (Cambridge: Cambridge University Press, 2008).

6. It is a common misconception to think that the Soviets equated World War II with the Great Patriotic War. There was a very clear distinction between the two in Soviet historiography and military thought, although the two terms were, and still are, used interchangeably among lay audiences. Originally a symbolic phrase, "Patriotic War" was first mentioned in reference to the

conflict on the Eastern Front in June 1941. Intended to serve as an inspiration, the term was linked to the nineteenth-century French invasion of Russia. Considering its far more traumatic nature and scope, the ongoing conflict soon acquired the epithet "Great." Thus according to the official historiography, the Great Patriotic War was part of World War II, starting with the German invasion and ending on 9 May 1945 with Germany's unconditional surrender. Upon its attack on the Kwantung Army in Manchuria, the Soviet Union entered the final stage of World War II. Notably, neither the war with Japan, nor the 1939–1940 European campaigns have ever been included in the chronology of the Great Patriotic War. Even though the Soviet Union had temporarily allied itself with Germany in 1939, the Soviet leadership constantly maintained that, unlike the British and the French, they had had no other option but to sign a non-aggression pact with Germany because neither the Soviet Union nor the West felt prepared to contain German encroachments in Eastern Europe. From the Soviet point of view, the later partition of Poland—never mentioned directly in the agreement—was also borne out of military necessity, "internationalist duty," and pressure from German diplomats. Retrospectively, the trumpeting of the Soviet war experience might seem today as an attempt to whitewash the earlier collaboration with the Nazis; however, the Soviet leadership never publicly expressed any qualms regarding this unfortunate alliance. Instead, it presented the Soviet Union as a victim of German treachery and Western appeasement.

7.   It is tempting to see the Soviet propensity to overstate their own war effort as resulting from the lack of coverage of the European and Pacific War by the Soviet mass media. Indeed, newspaper editors allotted little space to foreign affairs, limiting their reporting to communiqués from foreign news agencies. Yet, even the children's press endeavored to inform its audience about the war raging beyond the Soviet borders, although it is impossible today to determine what effect these dry editorials had on their readers. Prior to the 1941 invasion, the media had treated the events with curious ambiguity: while the children's press, such as *Pionerskaia Pravda* (see esp. the rubrics "War in Western Europe" and "The World Telegraph"), as well as the two major newspapers *Pravda* and *Izvestiia* seemed sympathetic toward Germany fighting the war in Europe and Africa, its adversaries, Britain and France, were also represented in a fairly impartial manner. The press intended for soldiers, however, condemned the two countries for instigating "the second imperialist war" (see,

for instance January and February 1940 issues of *Vperiod k Pobede*). When Germany invaded, allegiances shifted and the Soviet mass media began to praise the military might of the new-found Allies. The latter's victories apparently helped sustain morale in the Red Army during the first years of the war, while the Allies' defeats were sometimes concealed by political officers in their inspirational discussions with soldiers. Besides separate articles on the Allied activities, *Pravda* ran a short rubric, called "The War in The Pacific Ocean," although battles in Africa and Italy would gradually elbow out the coverage of the war in the Far East. It is another matter, however, that after Stalingrad, Stalin had let it be known that nothing beyond this point could be of great military significance, so the Allied war effort became secondary by definition. For the "general line" in the Soviet press, see Karel C. Berkhoff, *Motherland in Danger: Soviet Propaganda during World War II* (Cambridge, MA: Harvard University Press, 2012), 20, 50; for the Allied successes as a morale sustaining factor see Boris Voyetekhov, *The Last Days of Sevastopol* (New York: Alfred A. Knopf, 1943), 218-19. I am grateful to Yan Mann for this reference.

8. For the discussion of the War's place in modern day Russia, see Olga Kucherenko, "That'll Teach 'em to Love their Motherland!: Russian Youth Revisit the Battles of World War II," *The Journal of Power Institutions in Post-Soviet Societies* 12 (2011), accessed 22 April 2012, http://pipss.revues. org/3866.

9. A 1994 poll, for instance, showed that 65 percent of Americans thought that their country played the main role in the Allied victory in World War II, and only one percent believed that all the Allies equally contributed. See *The Gallup Poll: Public Opinion 1994* (Wilmington: Scholarly Resources Inc., 1995), 93. For a discussion of American textbooks cultivating this perception whether deliberately or due to format constraints, see David R. Stone, "Vostochnyi front v amerikanskikh uchebnikakh istorii: vzgliad optimista" in *Rossiiai SShA na stranitsakh uchebnikov: Opyt vzaimnykh reprezentatsii*, eds. Victoria I. Zhuravliova and Ivan I. Kurilla (Volgograd: Izdatel'stvo Volgogradskogo Universiteta, 2009), 141-59; and Carole Fink, "Sovteskii Soiuz i Vostochnyi front v amerikanskikh uchebnikakh s 1990g," in *Vtoraia mirovaia i Velikaia Otechestvennaia voiny v uchebnikakh istorii stran SNG i ES: Problemy, podkhody, interpretatsii*, eds. T. S. Guzenkova and V. N. Filianova (Moscow: RISI, 2010) 45, 48-50. For a more general discussion of American war culture, see Smelser and Davies.

10. *Pravda*, 23 Feb. 1942, 1; see also Alexander Werth, *Russia at War, 1941-1945*, 2nd ed. (New York: Carroll & Graf Pubs., Inc., 2000), 381.

11. A. V. Fateev, *Obraz vraga v sovetskoi propagande, 1945-1954gg.* (Moscow: RAN, 1999), 18-19. See a Russian-language text of Konstantin Simonov's "Amerikantsy," *Publitsist i kaiocher kivoennykh let: Otsovetsko goinform-buro…1941-1945*, http://www.bibliotekar.ru/informburo/38.htm.

12. *Pravda*, 7 Nov. 1942, 1; 4 June 1943, 2; and 6 Aug.1943, 2; Timothy Johnston, *Being Soviet: Identity, Rumor, and Everyday Life under Stalin, 1939-1953* (Oxford: Oxford University Press, 2011), 47, 49, 55.

13. See, for instance, *Pravda*, 12 Nov.1942, 3; and 1 Oct.1943, 4.

14. Richard Overy, *Why the Allies Won* (London: Pimlico, 1995), 129.

15. See, for example, Averell Harriman quoted in Ibid., 253; also see Werth (2000), 485.

16. GARF, f.8581, op.1, d.114, ll.52-53ob; for other complaints, see Russian State Archive of Socio-Political History (RGASPI), f.17, op.125, d.248, ll.26, 29.

17. Quoted in Albert Axell, *Russia's Heroes* (London: Robinson, 2001), 109.

18. A similar sentiment was widespread among the French as well. See Robert Belot, "Nekommunisticheskoe dvizhenies coprotivleniia vo Frantsii i obraz SSSR: Henri Frenay i dvizhenie 'Combat'" in *SSSR iFrantsiia v gody Vtoroi mirovoi voiny: Sbornik nauchnykh statei*, eds. Mikhail Narinski et al., (Moscow: MGIMO-Universitet, 2006), 133.

19. Werth (2000), 486, 668-9, 727; Boris Gorbachevsky, *Through the Maelstrom: A Red Army Soldier's War on the Eastern Front, 1942-1945*, trans. Stuart Britton (Lawrence: University Press of Kansas, 2008), 269, 282-3; Johnston, *Being Soviet*, 65, 67, 70; The Harvard Project on the Soviet Social System (HPSSS), A.1, 2, 28 and A.3, 27, 15, http://hcl.harvard.edu/collections/hpsss/.

20. Published respectively by the British Embassy in Moscow and the United States Information Agency, *Britanskii Soiuznik* and *Amerika* (the latter appeared in circulation after the Normandy landings) enjoyed unprecedented popularity among Soviet intelligentsia. Reportedly, demand far exceeded supply and the Soviet authorities kept a close eye on the distribution. See Vladimir O. Pechatnov, "The Rise and Fall of *Britansky Soyuznik*: A Case Study in Soviet Response to British Propaganda of the mid-1940s," *The Historical Journal* 41 (1998), 293–4.

21. Werth (2000), 480–1.

22. Gorbachevsky, 189. This opinion was corroborated by other veterans interviewed in Elena Joly, ed., *Pobeda liuboi tsenoi* (Moscow: IAUZA, EKSMO, 2010), 104–5, 188.

23. Gorbachevsky, 189; Johnston, 67; Paul Winterton, *Report on Russia* (London: Cresset Press, 1945), 23.

24. For examples of the Allied effort to inform the Soviet public about Western material aid and military pressure on the Axis, see *Amerika*, 1 (1944): 44–5, 57–9, and 2 (1944): 8, 14–16, 17-23; *Britanskii Soiuznik*, 2 Jan. 1944, 3–6; 9 January 1944, 1; 30 January 1944, 3, 7; 6 February 1944, 1–2; 5 March 1944, 7; and 16 April 1944, 1–2. For later attempts by the Americans, see *Amerika*1 (1944), 44–5, 57-9; and 2 (1944), 8, 14–16, 17–23.

25. RGASPI, f.17, op.125, d.248, ll. 37–9, 45. In their propaganda to the occupied Europe all three Allies tended to give a fair appraisal of each other's role in the war, but Soviet ideologues seemed to be particularly resentful of their Western partners' insistence on equating the war efforts. See GARF, f.8581, op.2, d.98, ll.6, 25-6, 35; f.8581, op.2, d.101, l.9.

26. *Pravda*, 1 May 1944, 1.

27. Gorbachevsky, 189; John R. Deane, *The Strange Alliance: The Story of American Efforts at Wartime Cooperation with Russia* (London: John Murray, 1947), 150.

28. A. Ia. Livshin and I. B. Orlov, eds., *Sovietskaia propaganda v gody Velikoi Otechestvennoi voiny: "Kommunikatsiia ubezhdeniia" i mobilizatsionnye mekhanizmy* (Moscow: POSSPEN, 2007), 703; see also Overy (1995), 248.

29. Werth (2000), 746; for the veterans' opinion, see Joly, 84, 308. Also see Helene Keyssar and Vladimir Pozner, *Remembering War: A US-Soviet Dialogue* (New York: Oxford University Press, 1990).

30. This belief in Germany's eventual defeat has been encouraged by the Soviet mass media since the first days of the invasion in an attempt to help the defending nation retain courage and determination, and even anticipate victory as early as 1941. See Olga Kucherenko, *Little Soldiers: How Soviet Children Went to War, 1941–45* (Oxford: Oxford University Press, 2011), 131 and Anthony Beevor, *A Writer at War* (London: Harvill Press, 2006), 243. Some modern historians of the Eastern Front agree that although defeat could not be fully assured, by mid-1944 Germany was in no position to achieve victory, considering its losses, the strategic position of the Red Army, and the coming *Bagration* offensive. See, for instance, Alexander Hill, *The*

Great Patriotic War of the Soviet Union, 1941–45: A Documentary Reader (London: Routledge, 2009), 284; Beevor, 62.

31. Livshin and Orlov, 703 (quotation); Werth (2000), 853; Gorbachevsky, 190; Chris Bellamy, *Absolute War. Soviet Russia in the Second World War: A Modern History* (London: Macmillan, 2007), 612; Beevor, *A Writer at War*, 271; G.K. Zhukov, *Vospominaniiai Razmyshleniia*, Vol.3 (Moscow: APN, 1986), 137; HPSSS, A.23, 456, 60. For a much colder reception of the news, see Deane, *The Strange Alliance*, 151.

32. Livshin and Orlov, 694.

33. Werth (2000), 842. At the same time, the NKVD were on the lookout for those who were too critical of the Western Allies. See Johnston, 78.

34. *Pravda*, 7 June 1944, 3 (quotation), 4; see also a gleeful report in *Izvestiia*, 7 June 1944, 3.

35. Berkhoff, 264. According to an American officer, those in the Soviet military who saw the footage were greatly impressed. See Deane, 151.

36. *Pravda*, 7 June 1944, 3.

37. *Pravda*, 11 June 1944, 1; see also the 14 June issue, the first page of which featured Stalin's favorable analysis of the landing and on the second called it "historically unprecedented" and "exceptionally difficult."

38. Richard Overy, *Russia's War* (London: Penguin, 1997), 240.

39. Livshin and Orlov, 731.

40. Bellamy, 612; Werth (2000), 855–6.

41. On American newsreels, see Johnston, 59; on the Soviet complaints, see Soviet Information Bureau's meeting minutes in GARF, f.8591, op.2, d.93, ll.1–8; f.8591, op.2, d.94, l.1; f.8591, op.2, d.97, ll.2, 4–7, 67.

42. See a letter of complaint to Stalin in RGASPI, f.17, op.125, d.244, l.89.

43. Though according to the dominant view, the Cold War emerged gradually after Roosevelt's death, certain events taking place during World War II accelerated the former's onset. Thus, there is evidence that the "arms race," an essential element of the Cold War, had started already in 1942, when Stalin launched the Soviet atomic program. On the genesis of the Cold War, see Melvyn Leffler and Odd Arne Westad, eds., *Cambridge History of the Cold War*, vol. 1 (Cambridge: Cambridge University Press, 2010); on Soviet espionage, see John Earl Haynes, Harvey Klehr, and Alexander Vassiliev, *Spies: The Rise and Fall of the KGB in America* (New Haven, CT: Yale University Press, 2010); for the reassessment of Roosevelt's "atomic policy," see Martin

J. Sherwin. "The Atomic Bomb and the Origins of the Cold War," in *Origins of the Cold War: An International History*, eds. Melvyn J. Leffler and David S. Painter, 2d ed. (New York: Routledge, 1994), 64-5; for the roots of the "atomic policy" in the Soviet conduct in Eastern Europe, see Cambell Craig and Sergey Radchenko, *The Atomic Bomb and the Origins of the Cold War* (New Haven and London: Yale University Press), 21.

44. GARF, f.8581, op.1, d.114, l.40.

45. "DokladPredsedatelia GKO," 42-3.

46. Vladimir O. Pechatnov, "The Big Three after World War II: New Documents on Soviet Thinking about Post War Relations with The United States and Great Britain," *Cold War International History Project*, The Woodrow Wilson International Center for Scholars, Working Paper no. 13(May,1995): 3. http://www.wilsoncenter.org/sites/default/files/ACF17F.PDF.

47. On changing attitudes toward the Red Army in the West, see O. V. Rychkova, "Obraz Krasnoi Armii v amerikanskoi presse v kontse Vtoroi mirovoi voiny," *Voenno-Istoricheskii Zhurnal* (hereafter *VIZh*) 10 (2008): 33-6; Vladimir O. Pechatnov, "'Strel'ba kholostymi': Sovetskaia propaganda na Zapad v nachale kholodnoi voiny (1945-1947)," in *Stalinskoe desiatiletie kholodnoi voiny: fakty i gipotezy*, ed. A. O. Chubar'ian(Moscow: Nauka, 1999), 109.

48. Rósa Magnúsdóttir, "Keeping Up Appearances: How the Soviet State Failed to Control Popular Attitudes toward the United States of America, 1945-1959" (PhD diss., UNC Chapel Hill, 2006), 26-7, 36, 44, 68; D. G. Nadzharov, "Antiamerikanskie propagandistskie pristrastiia stalinskogo rukovodstva," in *Stalinskoe desiatiletie* 135, 137, 138.

49. Katharine Hodgson, *Written with the Bayonet: Soviet Russian Poetry of World War Two* (Liverpool: Liverpool University Press, 1996), 260-1.

50. Ibid., 271, 273; Matthew P. Gallagher, *The Soviet History of WWII: Myths, Memories, and Realities* (New York: Praeger, 1963), 28.

51. I. I. Mints, *Velikaia Otechestvenniaia voina Sovetskogo Soiuza* (Moscow: Nauka, 1947); also see Gallagher, 29.

52. Pechatnov, "'Strel'ba kholostymi,'" 111.

53. Gallagher, 48.

54. On the Soviet visual propaganda portraying American imperialists as new Nazis, see Andrei Kozovoi, "De Goebbels à Reagan: La Filation Nazie dans l'Antiaméricanisme Soviétique pendant la 'Nouvelle Guerre Froide' (1977-1985)," in eds., Christian Delporte et al., *La guerre après la guerre: Images*

et construction des imaginaires de guerre dans l'Europe du XXe siècle (Paris, 2009), 231-48.

55. RGASPI, f.17, op.125, d.436, ll.24-8, 41-2.

56. Pechatnov, "The Rise and Fall," 301.

57. Nadzharov, "Antiamerikanskie," 140.

58. D. G. Nadzhafov and Z.S. Belousova, eds., *Stalin i kosmopolitizm: 1945-1953* (Moscow: Demokratiia, 2005), 468-71.

59. Gallagher, *The Soviet History*, 145, 177-8, also ch.7. For an example of such conservative assessments, see V. Kurasov, "O kharaktere i periodizatsii vtoroi mirovoi voiny 1939-1945 godov," *VIZh* 1 (1959): 36.

60. E. Boltin, "O periodizatsii Velikoi Otechestvennoi voiny Sovetskogo Soiuza," *VIZh* 2 (1959): 21.

61. S. P. Platonov et al., eds., review of *Vtoraia mirovaia voina 1939-1945gg. Voenno-istoricheskii ocherk*, by V. Vorobiov et al., *VIZh* 5 (1959), 97, 102, 105. Perhaps much of this critique stemmed not only from the ideological requirements of the day, but also from the Soviet lack of familiarity with an amphibious operation of such a scale. Even though they had plenty of experience with this kind of warfare, the Soviets did nothing that mirrored D-Day. Moreover, considering a constant comparative assessment of casualties, they seemed to judge the effort put into use by losses taken, which Normandy presented little of, at least by Soviet standards.

62. Daniil Kraminov, *Pravda o Vtorom Fronte: Zapiski voennogo korrespondenta* (Petrozavodsk: GI Karelskoi ASSR, 1960), 5, 7-8.

63. Ibid., 71, 78-9, 82, 87, 125 (quotation); also see I. Zaitsev, "K voprosu ob otkrytii vtorogo fronta i ego roli vo Vtoroi mirovoi voine," *VIZh* 6 (1959): 63.

64. Kraminov, 103.

65. Kurasov, 23-4; V. Israelian, "O strategii SShA i Anglii v Evrope (obzor novoi amerikanskoi i angliiskoi literatury po strategii Vtoroi mirovoi voiny)," *VIZh* 3 (1959): 95, 100; Iu. Red'ko, "Ob otvetstvennosti zapadnykh derzhav za vtoruiu mirovuiu voinu (Obzor angliiskoi i amerikanskoi istoricheskoi literatury), *VIZh* 3 (1963): 49-57.

66. Kurasov, 26, 27; Zaitsev, 53.

67. *Pravda*, 27 March 1959, 1.

68. On two Norwegian films that were not allowed on the big screen in the Soviet Union, see a report in V. Iu. Afiani, ed., *Ideologicheskie komissii TsK KPSS, 1958-1964. Dokumenty* (Moscow: ROSSPEN, 2000), 265.

69. B. I. Marushkin, *Istoriia i politika. Amerikanskaia burzhuaznaia istoriografiia sovetskogo obshchestva* (Moscow: Nauka, 1969), 282. For a general discussion of the war as the legitimizing myth of the Brezhnev regime, see Ilya Kukulin, "Regulirovanie boli," in M. Gabovich, *Pamiat' o voine 60 let spustia: Rossiia, Germaniia, Evropa* (Moscow: NLO, 2005), 623-9.

70. Marushkin, 287, 294.

71. See, for instance, V. Poliakov, "Vtoraia mirovaia voina v osveshchenii angliiskogo istorika," *VIZh* 10 (1967), 109; V. Sekistov and G. Korotkov, "Otsenka angliiskimi istorikami voennoi strategii Anglii i SShA," *VIZh* 7 (1968), 102-9; Idem., "Pravda i vymysly o poslednei kampanii voiny v Evrope," *VIZh* 5 (1970), 45-51; I. Chelyshev, "Frantsuzskii istorik o vtoroi mirovoi voine," *VIZh* 11 (1970), 104-9; A. Iakushevskii, "Operatsii Sovetskoi Armii v 1944 godu v osveshchenii burzhuaznoi istoriografii," *VIZh* 6 (1974), 74-80.

72. G. Korotkov and A. Orlov, "O politike i startegii SShA i Anglii v Zapadnoi Evrope v 1944 g.," *VIZh* 8 (1974), 80, 85.

73. Iakushevskii, "Operatsii," 75, 79.

74. See a recent monograph by a veteran Cold Warrior, insisting that having liberated Europe, the Russian Federation has this right even today, L. I. Ol'shtynskii, *Razgrom fashizma: SSSR i anglo-amerikanskie soiuzniki vo Vtoroi mirovoi voine (politika i voennaia strategiia: fakty, vyvody, uroki istorii)* (Moscow: ITRK, 2010), 249; for contemporary Western assessments, see Gabriel Gorodetsky, ed., *Stafford Cripps in Moscow 1940-1942: Diaries and Papers* (London: Vallentine Mitchell, 2007), 171.

75. Ronald Reagan, "Normandy Speech: Ceremony Commemorating the Fortieth Anniversary of the Normandy Invasion," at Pont-du-Hoc, France, YouTube video, 13:22, televised 6 June 1984, posted by "Reagan Foundation," 16 April 2009, http://www.youtube.com/watch?v=eEIqdcHbc8I.

76. *Pravda*, 7 June 1984, 4, 5; see also A. Iakushevskii, "Kritika burzhuaznoi istoriographii sobytii 1944 goda na sovetsko-germanskom fronte 1944 godanasovetsko-germanskomfronte," *VIZh* 12 (1984): 70-1, 73.

77. *Izvestiia*, 7 June 1984, 3.

78. See, for instance, Aleksandr Girin, "Sovetskoe voennoe iskusstvo v Belorusskoi operatsii 1944 goda," *VIZh* 6 (1984), 11; for a pre-commemoration analysis, see V. Sekistov, "Pravda i vymysel ob otkrytii vtorogo fronta v Evrope," *VIZh* 5 (1984), 74-82.

79. I. I. Dolutskii, "Dr. Jekyll and Mr. Hyde: SShA v sovetskikh i rossiiskikh uchebnikakh istorii," in *Rossia i SShA,*, eds., Zhuravliova and Kurilla, 236; P. Bobipev, "V pomoshch' prepodavateliam istorii: Polnoe izgnanie vraga iz predelov Sovetskogo Soiuza. Osvobozhdenie narodov Evropy i okonchatel'nyi razgrom fashistskoi Germanii (ianvar' 1944–mai 1945)," *VIZh* 3 (1984), 83.

80. *Pravda*, 7 June 1994, 3.

81. *Izvestiia*, 7 June 1994, 3.

82. Smelser and Davies, 1.

83. *Pravda*, 8 June 2004, 3.

84. *Izvestiia*, 7 June 2004, 1-2.

85. See *Pravda*, 8 June 2004, 3 and *Novaia i Noveishaia Istoriia* 4 (2004).

86. See, for instance, a fairly balanced overview by A. S. Orlov, *Za kulisami vtorogo fronta* (Moscow: Veche, 2011). A linear progression of the parochial school of thought is evident in various editions of Soviet and Russian Encyclopedias. See *Bol'shaia Sovetskaia Entsiklopediia*, Vol. 9, 387–9 and Vol. 30, 176–7 (Moscow: Nauka, 1951 and 1954); Ibid., Vol. 5, 499, and Vol. 18, 130-1 (Moscow: Nauka, 1971); *Bol'shaia Istoricheskaia Entsiklopediia*, vol. 3, 902, and Vol. 10, 340 (Moscow: Nauka, 1963 and 1967); *Bol'shaia Entsiklopediia*, Vol. 10, 368, and Vol. 33, 41–2 (Moscow, 2006). For a discussion of Soviet legacy in modern Russian textbooks, see Dolutskii, "Dr. Jekyll," 261.

87. For scholarly arguments, see Russian historian Aleksei Isaev, interview by Vitaly Dymarsky, Radio Moscow, radio broadcast, 17 Sept. 2010, accessed 10 Feb.2012, http://www.echo.msk.ru/programs/victory/626273-echo/. Also see interviews of Soviet veterans in *Pobeda liuboi tsenoi*, 84, 308. For the corroboration of this idea by Western military historians, see David M. Glantz and Jonathan House, *When Titans Clashed: How the Red Army Stopped Hitler* (Edinburgh: Birlinn, 1995), 285.

88. Barack Obama, "Remarks by the President at D-Day Sixty-Fifth Anniversary Ceremony," at Normandy American Cemetery and Memorial, Normandy, France, 5 June 2009, http://www.whitehouse.gov/the_press_office/Remarks-by-the-President-at-D-Day-65th-Anniversary-Ceremony/.

89. On the content of British, German, and French textbooks, which are generally hostile toward the Soviet Union, see Holger Nehring, "Vtoraia mirovaia voina v nemetskikh i britanskikh shkol'nykh uchebnikakh istorii: mezhdu

Imperiei, Evropoi i gegemoniei liberalizma," 102, and Jean-Pierre Arrignon, "Sovetskii Soiuz vo frantsuzskikh uchebnikakh," 55-57, in *Vtoraia mirovaia i Velikaia Otechestvennaia voiny v uchebnikakh istorii stran SNG i ES: Problemy, podkhody, interpretatsii*, eds. T. S. Guzenkova and V. N. Filianova (Moscow: RISI, 2010).

90. For opinion polls, see:"Otnoshenie rossiyan k drugim stranam," Yuri Levada Analytical Center, 14 June 2012, http://www.levada.ru/14-06-2012/otnoshenie-rossiyan-k-drugim-stranam.

91. V. A. Shestakov, *Istoriia Rossii, XX-nachalo XXI veka. 11 klass* (Moscow: Prosveshchenie, 2010), 248.

92. Ol'shtynskii. Notably, a very balanced discussion of the Second Front, the Allied capabilities and the Soviet chances of winning the war on their own, appeared in a book by a young journalist Alexander Khramchikhin, *Russkienavoine* (Moscow: Kliuch-S, 2010), 132-5.

93. See, for instance,"Geroicheskaya vysadka soiuznikov v Normandii," *Voennoe Obozrenie*, 13 Jan. 2012,accessed 12 Apr. 2012, topwar.ru/10107-geroicheskaya-vysadka-soiuznikov-v-normandii.html.

94. For opinion polls, see: "Rossiyane o prazdnovanii Dnya Pobedy," Yuri Levada Analytical Center, 8 May 2013, accessed 15 May 2013, http://www.levada.ru/print/08-05-2013/rossiyane-o-prazdnovanii-dnya-pobedy.

95. "Saving Private Ryan," *Kinomania*, 20 Nov. 2008,http://www.kinomania.ru/movies/s/Saving_Private_Ryan/rev1.shtml.

96. Rósa Magnúsdóttir, "From the Meeting on the Elbe to Parading on Red Square: Discourses about the Soviet-American War Alliance, 1945–2010" (paper presented at the annual meeting of Association of Slavic, Eastern European and Eurasian Studies, Washington, DC, 17–20 November 2011), 15 (cited here with author's permission).

97. A survey of textbooks across six participant nations in World War II has found that each concentrates more on its own history than on others, sometimes distorting the historical record. See Susan P. Santoli and Andrew Weaver, "The Treatment of World War II in the Secondary School National History Textbook of the Six Major Powers Involved in the War," *Journal of Social Studies Research* 23 (1999): 34-44.

Conclusion

Michael Dolski, Sam Edwards,
John Buckley

A nation is a soul, a spiritual principle. Two things, which, in truth, are
really one, constitute this soul, this spiritual principle. One is the past,
the other is the present. One is the possession in common of a rich
legacy of memories; the other is the present day consent, the desire to
live together, the will to continue to value the undivided heritage one
has received . . . . To have the glory of the past in common, a shared
will in the present; to have done great deeds together, and want to do
more of them, are the essential conditions for the constitution of a
people.

–Ernest Renan, 1882

D-Day was a transnational event of obvious importance to those
involved. While those touched by the battle naturally reacted to it
in varying ways, what was not so obvious at first was the manner in
which the participant societies would conceive of the day's events.
It was by no means certain as to how politicians, press, and the
public would shape and structure the story of the "Longest Day."
Contests, disputes, and changing views over time aside, the most
striking thing, therefore, is that collective interpretations of D-Day
have tended to flow along national lines. Site specificity, as argued
above, heavily influences interpretations of the past.[1] Throughout
this work, the contributors have shown in ample detail how specificity in cultural, geographic, political, and social terms all shade our

views of history. Although, as some have argued, we may be entering a new era of globalization that gradually erodes the significance of national boundaries, when it comes to learning about, engaging with, and drawing upon the past, processes always performed for present purposes, many people still see the nation as the primary narrative framework. D-Day remembrance displayed this proclivity in stark relief. A transnational event quickly became a story shaped by national preferences, and it remains so almost seven decades later. As we have demonstrated here, there were and are many stories of D-Day, and in collective terms these stories reinforce national self-perceptions.

D-Day has come to transcend dusty "history" and has turned instead into somewhat contested terrain, something for politicians, writers, journalists, and film-makers to employ with startling regularity. D-Day did not always mean the same thing to all people. D-Day and its commemoration offered many potential stories. Nevertheless, this work has presented a few consistent themes about D-Day's perceived meaning—those that have dominated national conversations.

National Commemorative Frames

Overall, the dominant D-Day stories have represented a combination of choices, long-standing tendencies in a given society, reactions to global events, and personal, group, and national biases. As the world has turned, the past seeped into present conversations while present-orientated outlooks have always influenced understandings of the past. In the immediate postwar period, this past-present dynamic led many people to see new challenges and new developments with a set of Second World War blinkers framing the view—blinkers heavily dependent upon a few iconic moments like D-Day. During the Cold War, for instance, the events of D-Day were often cut loose from their moorings in history and tugged into the present as a means to make sense of the moment. For, in a world fractured by ideological divide, a D-Day story of Western Allied martial prowess in a quest for liberty provided, understandably, invaluable political capital to leaders in Washington, London, Ottawa, and Paris. In time, even the enemies of the Day—Germans and Austrians—found in this story something to meet the demands of their postwar experience. This liberation mantra affirmed the morality in the past and present as new battles and a twilight struggle for freedom took shape. These enduring constructions intensified during the Cold War and ultimately outlasted that confrontation. They emerged in many places at once, from popular to scholarly analyses, in political rhetoric and memorial services, in the form of monuments and ephemeral media productions. As the eminent historian Gerhard Weinberg remarked, "Interestingly, the passage of time makes the significance of the invasion as the basis for major postwar developments all the more, not the less, apparent."[2]

In the United States, the D-Day tale remained a story of America, of Americans, and of American perceptions of themselves. Casting D-Day as a costly yet decisive battle involving whitemen fighting and dying in the name of liberty tells us something about the society that scripted such constructed versions of the past. The day's service represented willing sacrifice and military strength in a "Great Crusade" to vanquish evil, save the world, and launch the American Century. These democratic heroes of D-Day then returned home, made America great, and became the "Greatest Generation" as a result. The striking thing is not the veracity of this tale, but its staying power over the decades since it first formed. This D-Day story represented nostalgia for an era before race riots, gender upheaval, Vietnam, and political-social-economic-religious crises that would shake America to its core, when the country was rising to the top not precariously tottering at the brink. While many actors and actions determined this narrative direction, the 1984 anniversary events stood in striking importance and acted as a key moment propelling the D-Day story into the realm of American myth.

A similar inclination, to draw on lauded glories while facing present challenges, characterizes much of the British commemorative approach to D-Day as well. D-Day formed the last dying gasp of Empire as Britain, along with its Allies, exerted decisive military force in a grand offensive against tyranny. This battle occupied a narrative position that redeemed Britain's earlier defeats in the war even as it turned the page toward a new, truncated role in global affairs for the Commonwealth. Sharing much with its transatlantic partners, both during the war and in the decades after, the British went through a cycle of limited-increasing-overt commemorative focus on the Normandy invasion as a hallmark of their military might and benevolent use of power. The primary difference here, however, is that, contrasting the Americans, the Second World War served as a capstone to any pretentions of a resurgent Britannia's claims on sole global leadership. Thus, D-Day served as the beginning of the end—the end of this particular war as well as of the British Empire.

Others among the Allies, such as the Canadians, had a more mixed engagement with D-Day. Canada had much to commemorate with its important role in this significant battle, yet its people have tended to disregard their martial past in the years since. While D-Day does not elicit scorn or derision, the fact is that Canadians as a whole lean toward eschewing celebrations of their military heritage. The lodestar that does tend to draw some public acknowledgement is the First World War with Vimy Ridge serving as the embodiment of Canada's role in the conflict. Relative neglect of D-Day, however, does not mean outright ignorance as some scholars, politicians, and media figures have struggled to increase public awareness of Canada's role in the Second World War in general and the Normandy invasion in particular. Significantly, most of these actions appeared after the great resurgence of American and British interested in D-Day that reared in the 1980s. In many respects, the efforts by Canadian memory activists to implant a D-Day memory in their country's public memory served as a corrective reaction to overshadowing engendered by these other nations' self-celebration.

The French relationship with D-Day has been complicated by divergent wartime and postwar military, political, and social experiences. Furthermore, by simple fact that the landings took place on French soil, with the resultant battles destroying French towns and lives, a reluctance to embrace this supposed day of liberation readily emerged. Seeking to unify a fractured body politic, national leaders emphasized a narrative of wartime suffering but also of coming together, of trials and tribulations brought to an end largely through *French* effort. Thus, the Normandy invasion played a lesser role in this story than did the activities of the Resistance—or indeed than did Operation Dragoon, the French-dominated invasion of southern France—as the French attempted to incorporate the recent past into a workable understanding of their world. As Cold War tensions and imperial decline drove the French further from the British and Americans, so did the distancing of D-Day remembrance follow suit. That is, a distancing became evident at the national level, particularly following the return to power of Charles de Gaulle in 1958; at the local level, however, people in Normandy readily held onto their memories of the invasion. Considering that their memories bespoke more of terror and loss than of joyous liberation, perhaps the stark difference in remembrance practices of the liberators and liberated stand out here most sharply. Yet it is important to keep in mind the commemorative influence that can be exerted by control of the sites of remembrance. Thus, despite persistent Gaullist frustrations with D-Day as event and icon, the French have nonetheless proved masterful hosts at the annual commemorations in Normandy, many of which had become large-scale galas by the 1980s. Of course, the French were not content to let the Western Allies simply bask in glory; they had their own story to tell too, as evidenced in the construction of the Caen Memorial that emphasized the suffering wrought by all wars. Despite the obvious differences in approach and purpose, the similarities in timing, selected themes, and transnational reactions draw our attention.

An even greater degree of uncertainty regarding D-Day was, perhaps, more understandable when reviewing German and Austrian commemorative practice in light of their unsuccessful opposition to the landings. In Germany, moreover, another degree of complexity to this matter was the postwar division of the country into competing entities, with each attempting to use the recent past in order to discredit the other. In both Germanys, the Second World War and the Nazi regime's terror acts remained dangerous topics that were best left unexplored, pushed away, or sanitized for popular consumption in the immediate postwar period. East Germans blamed the "capitalistic" West for all that went wrong, hailed the Soviets for defeating Hitler, and, therefore, wrote D-Day out of the national story. West Germans preferred to ignore, deny or neglect; or, if pushed to acknowledge the events of 1939-45, tended to focus on their own war-related suffering and loss. Significantly, this latter idea provides, even today, the framework employed by many Austrians to make sense of the landings, and of Austria's experience of the war.

By the 1950s, however, in a bid for rearmament and full inclusion into the NATO alliance, the leaders of Federal Republic of Germany did initiate a more engaged relationship with the wartime past. But the resultant refurbishment of the Second World War tended to stress German martial prowess despite Allied material advantages—and the grueling Normandy campaign served this agenda rather well. Of course, such an idea was often well-received by the Anglo-American military leaders of the West, many of whom still nursed a war-induced respect for German military ability, and many of whom also dreamed of the strategic advantage that might be gained if they had access to some "crack" German divisions that they could throw at the expected Soviet onslaught.

By the 1980s, however, as the Western Allies celebrated success in the Second World War and on D-Day in ever more grandiose terms, new-old wounds were reopened in a soon to be reunited Germany. As the attempts to "master" the Nazi past first subverted then delicately confronted the terror regime's actions, now Germans felt excluded from the international community of nations, at least in terms of Second World War remembrance. All the efforts by the Western Allies to hail the "good" war implicitly cast the Germans on the "bad" side of the contest. But through the work of several decades that spanned the end of the Cold War and reunification, culminating in the early 2000s, German politicians, journalists, and scholars began trumpeting a new idea. Thus, inspired by the D-Day commemorations of their European Union comrades in arms—the French—German leaders turned to depicting the invasion as the beginning of the end of their own impressment. D-Day, in short, began the liberation of Germany from the tyranny of Nazism.

The final country case study examined in this work displays the reactive or iterative approach to nationalistic memory politics in the starkest terms. Throughout the war, strained alliance politics between the Anglo-Americans and the Soviets fed a feeling of suspicion and even outright hostility. Thus, the Soviets declaimed the slow opening of the Second Front as an attempt to fight the Germans to the last Soviet soldier. When the Allies did land, after a brief moment of congratulatory goodwill, the official Soviet line turned to one of disdain for the small-scale, slow-going offensives in France, which came at a time of massive Red Army operations in the East. Rather quickly, then, the distant Normandy invasion became something of a non-event to the Soviets. This distancing only intensified in the postwar years as the Communist Party sought to take on the appearance of savior of the people, which would permit no other significant military heroics either in or outside of the Soviet Union. Suppression remained the norm for decades. By the 1970s and 1980s, more concerted attempts to deal with the growing cult of victory in the West led Soviet scholars and politicians to attack the one leg of self-celebration upon which these arguments most firmly rested: D-Day. At a time of late Cold War international tensions, D-Day remembrance formed one more realm of contestation with perceived propaganda value. Just as parochial as the other countries covered herein, even after the collapse of the Soviet Union the Russians retained pride in their nation's accomplishments, especially during the last big war. Of course, fixating on Second World War success was a way to pass over failure in Afghanistan, a subterfuge akin to American evasions of Vietnam. Nevertheless, the point remains that even in a post-Cold War order, the Russian people and their leaders continue to doubt, ignore, and at times reject outright the hyper-intensive celebration of D-Day.

THEMATIC SIMILARITIES

Despite the production and persistence of nationally specific D-Day narratives, this volume also demonstrates the often interlinked nature of the remembrance practices connected to the Normandy landings. Indeed, despite differences in approach and intent, the similar chronological evolution and commonality of key themes stands out in the preceding chapters. Thus, even as each nation's memory activists pursued D-Day commemoration in varied ways, the fact that these actions took place in an international setting, with developments in one country feeding those in another, ensured national specificity of remembrance practices within a larger context. The chronological nature of these developments, in fact, appears upon consideration of each individual nation's experience, as all covered herein shared the same five broad periods:

1. Initial exuberance and attention devoted to D-Day during and immediately after the battle; the performance of mourning rituals and the construction of memorials and burial grounds.
2. A fading of concern for D-Day as first the war, then the difficult postwar period (up to the early 1950s) demanded attention;
3. The growing embrace of D-Day by elite figures and the masses from the mid-1950s to the mid-1960s;
4. A distancing from military affairs, including D-Day remembrance, in light of Vietnam, imperial decline (Britain and France), economic uncertainty, and new transnational tensions through the early 1980s; and,
5. The return of widespread D-Day celebration in the mid-1980s, growing to immense proportions by the early 2000s. This was a response to various national/international events (Falklands conflict; end of Cold War; German reunification; the Gulf War) *and* a response to new socio-cultural circumstances (economic boom) *and* a product of human/psychological factors (especially issues connected to veterans' life-cycle).

The point here is not that every nation followed the same path of remembrance connected to D-Day; quite clearly, they diverged in telling ways. Rather, the point is that D-Day commemorative activity went through similar cycles that reflect commonalities in veteran or other interested party life expectancy, political developments, changes in historical consumption, and, of course, the reaction of one group/nation to the efforts of another when touting supposed historical credentials.

Aside from the interconnections in timing, the major themes that emerged in the national memory contexts also shared significant similarities. The two major themes drawn out of the analyses presented earlier in this work consist of "sacrifice" and "redemption." In the first case, each nation discussed herein stressed their own sacrifices above all others when commemorating the destructive Second World War. While a rather natural inclination when taken at first glance, the relationship between this emphasis on sacrifice and the other theme, redemption, warrants deep consideration. All nations involved lost a great deal in the war. With the D-Day stories, however, that sacrifice most clearly came to have a purpose: to end the war, to defeat tyranny, to set the world aright, or, in the case of the Soviets/Russians, to continue to attack perceived slights on the national past/present. Even the defeated, the Germans, came to appropriate this tale of D-Day redemption by placing it as the beginning of the end in a narrative of national suffering at the hands of the Nazis.

Of course, one should not lose sight of the peculiarities that also defined each nation's approach to D-Day remembrance. In fact, even thinking of each nation in singular terms, as if each were a solidly unified actor in its own right, carries the risk of glossing over the many differences evident within national boundaries. Here, however, we have explored the relationship between national identity and national remembrance patterns related to a major event. Thus, the difference is, in a way, a similarity in that each nation strove to interpret and present the D-Day story in its own parochial manner. The national divergences are just as interesting as their similarities in approaching D-Day. Most striking in the former regard stands the effort by each nation to place its own story at the forefront, to emphasize its own losses and experiences as the most significant.

Secondarily, the thrust of these remembrance activities also remained oriented toward divergent goals. For the Americans, for instance, D-Day remembrance served a self-congratulatory bent in nationally divisive times while also displaying for the world at large the super-power's supposed benevolent leadership role. The British cast D-Day as the end of Imperial greatness, the beginning of a new relationship with America, and even as an example to emulate in times of military challenge, such as in the Falklands. The Canadians have yet to engage fully with their martial past and recent attempts to do so tend to gravitate toward more conservative ends of the political spectrum at home. The French have jockeyed for honor in their stories, but still acknowledge the massive destruction wrought in the name of freedom. Meanwhile, the appropriation of D-Day by Germans, as a day of their own liberation, has demonstrated public memory's fluid nature. For the Russians, D-Day was first a distant event of little obvious import, then something to decry as Western propaganda, and only now something to assimilate into a broader understanding of the Second World War that still remains heavily oriented toward the Eastern Front.

D-Day + Seventy Years:
A Beginning? An End?

The late scholar Tony Judt has opined that, in Europe, with the Cold War's collapse, "What we are witnessing, so it seems to me, is a sort of interregnum, a moment between myths when the old versions of the past are either redundant or unacceptable, and new ones have yet to surface."[3] D-Day—as constructed and created by the national cultures explored in this volume—is just one of these myths; its place and purpose on the landscape of American, European, and Russian war memory is by no means certain or guaranteed. Indeed, if the political, social, and economic challenges of the early twenty-first century ensure that "old versions of the past" are in decline, the future of D-Day—like all the events of the Second World War—is also rendered precarious, or at the very least uncertain, by the fact that the actors of history are currently exiting the stage. To be sure, as these actors—the veterans—age and pass-on, collective memories of the Normandy landings will not disappear; the intense and sustained cultural activities of the past seventy years ensure that this is so, at least for the foreseeable future. Moreover, commentators have been anticipating this "end" for quite some time. Already by 1969, some journalists were suggesting that the age and infirmity of those who had commanded the D-Day landings ensured that an "end" was approaching. This was an idea frequently returned to, particularly by those reporting on the large-scale gatherings of 1984, 1994 and 2004. By the end of the twentieth century, it was assumed by many that the aging army of democracy, the Greatest Generation, had marched for the last time. As we near the seventieth anniversary of D-Day, these concerns will surely re-emerge, and old GIs and Tommies will no doubt be interviewed as the last of the frail few.

Yet the persistence of this concern is, paradoxically, reason to be optimistic. For despite nearly fifty years of concern regarding the "future" of D-Day, it remains an important event on the global commemorative calendar, or at least in Western Europe and the United States. Just as importantly, it stands more than ready to cross the bridge from the realm of "memory" into the land of "history." Indeed, many of the commemorative activities that have unfolded since the 1950s have taken this to be their mission, their task. For the memorials, monuments, museums, films, and histories of D-Day produced over the last seventy years are intended to be the bulwark against which the errors and inaccuracies of memory will crash. Standing as steadfast sentinels, they are designed to ensure that D-Day will not be "forgotten." Thus, whatever new understandings of the past assume primacy of place in the nations discussed in this volume, the present versions of D-Day likely will remain somewhat plastic—either adapted for contemporary concerns or, perhaps, faded away if deemed less relevant. Certainly, the example of the First World War suggests that something will "live on": only now has the living connection to this earlier global conflagration been broken, but it still remains alive in the imagination of Europeans. Similar grounds for optimism can be found in the place and position of the American Civil War—now almost 150 years distant—in the modern United States.

Nonetheless, if there is reason for optimism with regard to the future of the D-Day past, we must also acknowledge that, in other regards, the battle now occupies an uncertain place across the globe. With the tumultuous Sixties, Vietnam, European decline, and Cold War tensions, D-Day and the Second World War faded for a moment from international public conversations. The possibility of another remembrance recession has emerged with divisive military ventures and social fragmentation echoing the turbulent 1970s. Nevertheless, popular interest in D-Day, the effects of previous commemorations, and moral ascriptions that seem to relate to present struggles all suggest that D-Day and the Second World War may avoid such oblivion. A dichotomization between "good" and "bad" wars could, perhaps, intensify with D-Day serving as the key standard of the former.

Notes

1. See Kate Lemay's chapter in this volume.
2. Gerhard L. Weinberg, "D-Day: Analysis of Costs and Benefits," in *D-Day 1944*, ed. Theodore A. Wilson, fwd. John S. D. Eisenhower (Lawrence: University Press of Kansas, 1994), 337.
3. Tony Judt, "'The Past is Another Country: Myth and Memory in Post-War Europe," in *Memory and Power in Post-War Europe: Studies in the Presence of the Past*, ed. Jan-Werner Müller (New York: Cambridge University Press, 2002), 180.

Bibliography

Primary Sources

Archives, Select Memorials, and Museums

Army Heritage and Education Center, Carlisle Barracks, Pennsylvania, United States.
    Manuscript Collection.
    - Richard D. Winters Papers Collection.
    - Robert A. Rowe Papers Collection.
    - Thomas North Papers Collection.
Archives of the Comité du Débarquement, Bayeux, Normandy, France.
    Monuments Signaux.
Archives of the Mairie de Quibou, Quibou, Manche, France.
    Préfecture de la Manche, "Commandations à mort des militaires américains," No. 2820B.
Archives of the Mémorial de Caen.
    Questionnaire, "Les Français et le cinquantenaire du débarquement Allié de juin 1994," from *1994: 50e Anniversaire: Presse France*.
La Cambe German Military Cemetery, Normandy, France.
Commonwealth War Graves Commission Cemetery and Memorial, Bayeux, Calvados, Normandy, France.
D-Day Museum, Portsmouth, United Kingdom.

Dwight D. Eisenhower Library and Archives, Abilene, Kansas, United States.

    C. D. Jackson Papers Collection.

Library and Archives of Canada, Ottawa, Canada.

    Record Group 24.

- Volume 10.
- Volume 10790.

Margaret Herrick Library, The Academy of Motion Picture Arts and Sciences, Beverly Hills, California, United States.

    Core Collection.

- *D-Day, the Sixth of June* Material.
- Darryl F. Zanuck Material.
- *The Longest Day* Material.
- *Saving Private Ryan* Material.

Le mémorial de Caen, Calvados, Normandy, France.

Musée de Débarquement, Arromanches, Calvados, Normandy.

National Archives, Kew, London, United Kingdom.

    FO 371/112815: Celebration of Tenth Anniversary of D-Day Landings in Normandy: Opening of Mulberry Harbor Exhibition at Arromanches, 1954.

    FO 371/112818: Ceremonies to Celebrate the Tenth Anniversary of D-Day Landings in Normandy.

    FO 371/112819: Ceremonies to Celebrate the Tenth Anniversary of D-Day Landings in Normandy, 1954.

    FO 371/174341: Celebrations of Twentieth Anniversary of D-Day, 1964.

    CAB 21/3250: French Establishment of a Museum to Commemorate D-Day Landing: Request for Information about Units of British Army, 1952-53.

    PREM 11/671: Invitations to the Prime Minister and Lady Churchill to Visit Arromanches on June 6, 1952, for D-Day Celebrations Representation of the Prime Minister by Admiralty Staff, 1948-54.

    DEFE 25/399: Fortieth Anniversary of D-Day Celebrations, June 1984.

National Archives and Records Administration, College Park, Maryland, United States.

    Record Group 117, Records of the American Battle Monuments Commission [ABMC].

- Administrative History.

- General Records, 1923-65.
- Records Relating to Cemeteries and Memorials, 1918-93.
- Records Relating to Construction and Maintenance.
- Records Relating to Dedications.
- General Records.

Record Group 208, Records of the Office of War Information.

- Records of the News Bureau.

Record Group 331, Records of Allied Operational and Occupation Headquarters, World War II.

- Supreme Headquarters Allied Expeditionary Forces (SHAEF) Special Staff Adjutant General's Division Executive Section.

Record Group 338, Records of US Army Operational, Tactical, and Support Organizations (World War II and Thereafter).

- Records of European Theater of Operations US Army (ETOUSA)/ US Forces European Theater (USFET).

Record Group 407, Records of the Adjutant General's Office, 1917- [AGO].

- Reports Relating to World War II and Korean War Combat Operations and to Activities in Occupied Areas, 1940-54.

National D-Day Monument, Bedford, Virginia, United States.

Memorial Area.

National World War II Museum, New Orleans, Louisiana, United States.

Main Exhibit Hall.

Normandy American Cemetery, Colleville-sur-Mer, France.

Cemetery and Memorial Area.

Robert E. and Jean R. Mahn Center for Archives and Special Collections, Ohio University. Library, Athens, Ohio, United States.

Cornelius Ryan Collection of World War II Papers.

- The "Longest Day" Records.
- Miscellaneous Supplementary Material Records.

Russian State Archive of Socio-Political History (RGASPI), Moscow, Russia.

State Archive of the Russian Federation (GARF), Moscow, Russia.

Suffolk Records Office, Bury St. Edmunds, Suffolk, United Kingdom.

GB 554/B13/40: Programme of Commemorating the Fortieth Anniversary of the Normandy Landings, Bayeux.

Government Publications

von Bundeskanzler, Rede, and Wolfgang Schüssel. Europa-Forum Wachau, 6 June
2004. http://www.austria.gv.at/2004/6/9/g%C3%B6ttweig2004_final_k.pdf
(accessed August 21, 2012).
Canadian Senate Subcommittee on Veterans Affairs. "Guarding History." May
1998.
Schüssel, Wolfgang. Sixty-Fourth Session of Parliament, 4 June 2004, Stenographic
Protocol. Nationalrat, 22. GP, 64. Sitzung, 8.
US Government Accountability Office. *Battle of Normandy Foundation:
Uncertainties Surround Its Future Viability.* November 1994.
von Weizsäcker, Richard. "Speech in the Bundestag on 8 May 1985 during the
Ceremony Commemorating the Fortieth Anniversary of the End of War in
Europe and of National-Socialist Tyranny." Accessed 3 Sept. 2012. http://
www.mediaculture-online.de/fileadmin/bibliothek/weizsaecker_speech_
may85/weizsaecker_speech_may85.pdf.

Published Primary Sources

Eade, Charles, ed. *The War Speeches of the Right Honourable Winston S. Churchill.*
Vol. 3. London: Cassell, 1964.
Kulturreferat Landeshaupstadt München, ed. *Bilanz einer Ausstellung:
Dokumentation der Kontroverse um die Ausstellung "Vernichtungskrieg.
Verbrechen der Wehrmacht 1941 bis 1944."* Munich: Knaur, 1998.
Romeiser, John B., ed. *"Beachhead Don": Reporting the War from the European
Theater, 1942-1945.* New York: Fordham University Press, 2004.
*Vneshniaia politika Sovetskogo Soiuza v period Otechestvennoi voiny. Dokumenty i
materialy: 1 ianvaria – 31 dekabria 1944.* Vol. 2. Moscow: OGIZ, 1946.

Memoirs/Diaries/Contemporary Histories

Bohlen, Charles. *Witness to History.* New York: Norton, 1973.
Bradley, Omar N. *A Soldier's Story.* New York: Henry Holt and Company, 1951.
Capa, Robert. *Slightly out of Focus.* New York: Henry Holt and Company, 1947.

Deane, John R. *The Strange Alliance: The Story of Our Efforts at Wartime Co-Operation with Russia*. New York: Viking, 1947.

Eisenhower, Dwight D. *Crusade in Europe*. New York: Doubleday and Company, 1948.

———. *Crusade in Europe*. London: Heinemann Ltd., 1948.

Kortenhaus, Werner. *Die Schlacht um Caen 1944: Der Einsatz der 21. Panzer-Division*. 132-page-typescript in Günter Bischof's possession.

von Luck, Hans. *Panzer Commander: The Memoirs of Colonel Hans von Luck*. Fwd. Stephen E. Ambrose. New York: Praeger, 1989.

Mints, I. I. *Velikaia Otechestvenniaia voina Sovetskogo Soiuza*. Moscow: Nauka, 1947.

Montgomery, Field Marshal The Viscount of Alamein. *Normandy to the Baltic*. London: Hutchinson and Co., 1947.

Munro, Ross. *Gauntlet to Overlord: The Story of the Canadian Army*. Toronto: Macmillan, 1945.

Ryan, Cornelius. *The Longest Day: June 6, 1944*. New York: Simon and Schuster, 1959.

———. *The Longest Day: June 6, 1944*. Greenwich: Fawcett Publications, 1959.

Speidel, Hans. *Invasion 1944: Ein Beitrag zu Rommels und des Reiches Schicksal*. Tübingen and Stuttgart: Rainer Wunderlich Verlag Hermann Leins, 1949.

Stacey, C. P. *A Date with History: Memoirs of a Canadian Historian*. Ottawa: The Queen's Printer, 1948.

———. *Six Years of War: The Army in Canada, Britain, and the Pacific*. Ottawa: The Queen's Printer, 1955.

———. *The Victory Campaign: The Operations in North-West Europe*. Vol. 3. Ottawa: The Queen's Printer, 1960.

Terkel, Studs, with Sydney Lewis. *Touch and Go: A Memoir*. New York: The New Press, 2007.

Turner, John Frayn. *Invasion '44: The Full Story of D-Day*. London: George G. Harrap & Co. Ltd., 1959.

Voyetekhov, Boris. *The Last Days of Sevastopol*. New York: Alfred A. Knopf, 1943.

Wilmot, Chester. *The Struggle for Europe*. London: Collins, 1952.

Winterton, Paul. *Report on Russia*. London: Cresset Press, 1945.

Novels

Holland, Steve, ed. *No Surrender, a War Picture Library Anthology*. London: Prion, 2010.

Lowe, George. *Commando: Fight or Die: The Ten Best Commando D-Day Comic Books Ever.* London: Carlton Books Ltd., 2011.

Ryan, Jonathan. *After Midnight.* London: Review, 2005.

Shapiro, Lionel. *The Sixth of June: A Novel of World War II.* New York: Doubleday, 1955.

———. *D-Day: Sixth of June.* London: Collins, 1955.

News Media and Journals

American Heritage

Amerika

The Bedford Democrat

Britanskii Soiuznik

Chicago Daily Tribune

Courrier de l'ouest

Daily Boston Globe

Daily Mail

Daily Mirror

L'Eveil de Lisieux

Foreign Affairs

Globe and Mail

Guardian

International Herald Tribune

Izvestiia

Kleine Zeitung

Kurier

Le Lexovien

Liberté de Normandie

Look

London Times

Los Angeles Times

Mail on Sunday

National Post

New York Herald Tribune

New York Times

New York Times Magazine

Newsweek

Nice-Matin

Novaia i Noveishaia Istoriia

The Observer

Ouest-France

Paris-Presse

Philadelphia Inquirer

Pionerskaia Pravda

Pravda

Die Presse

Profil

Publishers Weekly

La Renaissaince

Salzburger Nachrichten

Der Spiegel

Südetusche Zeitung

Sun

Time

Toronto Star

Variety

Vperiod k Pobede

Die Welt

Wiener Zeitung

Der Zeit

Veterans' Association Newsletters

Bridgehead Sentinel
Dagwood Dispatches
Der Kamerad

Films, Documentaries, and Television Shows

Band of Brothers. Dirs. David Frankel, Mikael Salomon, Tom Hanks, David Leland, Richard Loncraine, David Nutter, Phil Alden Robinson, and Tony To. HBO in association with DreamWorks Pictures, 2001. 10 eps.

Battle of Britain. Dir. Guy Hamilton. Perfs. Michael Caine, Laurence Olivier, and Christopher Plummer. Spitfire Productions, 1969. 132 min.

Breakthrough. Dir. Lewis Seiler. Warner Brothers Pictures, 1950. 91 min.

The Bridge on the River Kwai. Dir. David Lean. Perfs. William Holden, Sir Alec Guinness, and Jack Hawkins. Columbia Pictures Corporation, 1957. 161 min.

D-Day: 6.6.44 (2004). Dir. Richard Dale. British Broadcasting Corporation, Discover Channel, ProSieben, France 2, Telfrance, Dangerous Films, 2004; British Broadcasting Corporation, DVD. 120 min.

D-Day: As It Happens. Dirs./Prods. Martin Gorst and Joe Myerscough. Windfall Films and Channel 4, 2013.

D-Day Plus 20 Years: Eisenhower Returns to Normandy. CBS Reports, Columbia Broadcasting Systems, Inc., 1964. 123 min.

"D-Day…The Normandy Invasion." *World War II: The War Chronicles.* Dir. Don Horan. A&E Television Networks, 1983. A&E Home Video, 2000. DVD, 25 min.

D-Day the Sixth of June. Dir. Henry Koster. Twentieth Century Fox, 1956. 106 min.

D-Day to Berlin. Dir. Andrew Williams. 150 mins. British Broadcasting Corporation, 2005.

Dunkirk. Dir. Leslie Norman. Ealing Studios, 1958. 134 min.

It Ain't Half Hot Mum. Created by Jimmy Perry and David Croft. British Broadcasting Corporation, 1974-1981. 56 eps.

La face cachée des libérateurs. Dir. Patrick Cabouat and Alain Moreau. 54 min. France 3, 2006. 54 min.

The Longest Day. Dir. Ken Annakin, Andrew Marton, Bernhard Wicki, and Darryl F. Zanuck. 178 min. Darryl F. Zanuck Productions, Inc. and Twentieth Century

Fox Film Corporation, 1962. Twentieth Century Fox Home Entertainment, 2006. DVD, 178 min.

"The Making of the National D-Day Museum," *Save Our History*. A&E Television, 1996. 50 min.

News of the Day, Invasion Extra! (15, no. 280). Metro-Goldwyn-Mayer, 1944. 10 min.

Overlord (1975).Dir. Stuart Cooper. Joswend and Imperial War Museum, 1975. 83 min.

Saving Private Ryan. Dir. Steven Spielberg. DreamWorks Pictures and Paramount Pictures, 1998. 169 min.

Ten Days to D-Day. Dir. Marione Milne. 3BM Television, 2004. 90 min.

The True Glory. Dir. Garson Kanin. Ministry of Information and US Office of War Information, 1945. 87 min.

Video Games

Call of Duty 2. Dirs. Keith Arem, Jason West, and Vince Zampella. Perfs. Michael Cudlitz, Rick Gomez, Frank John Hughes, James Madio, David Rees Snell, Ross McCall, Rene L. Moreno, J. Matthew Morton, Stephen Saux, Richard Speight, Jr., and Joshua Gomez. Activision, Aspyr, and Konami, Video Game, 2005.

Call of Duty 2: Big Red One. Dir. Christian Busic. Perfs. Michael Cudlitz, Frank John Huges, Richard Speight, Jr., Davis Rees Snell, J. Matthew Morton, and Mark Hamill. Activision and Konami, Video Game, 2005.

Medal of Honor. Dirs. Peter Hirschmann and Steven Spielberg. Electronic Arts and Sony, Video Game 1999.

Select Websites

American Battle Monuments Commission: http://www.abmc.gov/home.php.

Commonwealth War Graves Commission: http://www.cwgc.org.

German War Graves Commission: http://www.volksbund.de/volksbund.html.

Memorial des Victimes Civiles : http://www.crhq.cnrs.fr/1944/Basse-Normandie. php.

Normandy Veterans Association (UK): http://www.nvafriends.nl/index. php?cid=36.

Normandie Mémoire : http://www.normandiememoire.com.

Books

Addison, Paul, and Jeremy A. Crang, eds. *The Burning Blue: A New History of the Battle of Britain*. Pimlico: London, 2000.

Afiani, V. Iu., ed. *Ideologicheskie komissii TsK KPSS, 1958-1964. Dokumenty*. Moscow: ROSSPEN, 2000.

Allen, H. C. *The Anglo-American Relationship since 1783*. London: A & C Black, 1959.

Allen, Michael J. *Until the Last Man Comes Home: POWs, MIAs, and the Unending Vietnam War*. Chapel Hill: University of North Carolina Press, 2009.

Ambrose, Stephen E. *Band of Brothers: E Company, 506th Regiment, 101st Airborne from Normandy to Hitler's Eagle's Nest*. New York: Simon and Schuster, 1992.

———. *D-Day: June 6, 1944*. London: Pocket Books, 1994.

———. *D-Day, June 6, 1944: The Climactic Battle of World War II*. New York: Simon and Schuster, 1994.

———. *Pegasus Bridge: June 6, 1944*. New York: Simon and Schuster, 1985.

Anderson, Benedict. *Imagined Communities: Reflections on the Origin and Spread of Nationalism*. Rev. ed. New York: Verso, 1991.

Assmann, Aleida. *Cultural Memory and Western Civilization: Functions, Media, Archive*. Cambridge: Cambridge University Press, 2011.

Axell, Albert. *Russia's Heroes*. London: Robinson, 2001.

Azema, Jean-Pierre, Robert O. Paxton, and Philippe Burrin. *6 juin 44*. Caen: Editions Perrin/Le Mémorial de Caen, 2004.

Baldwin, Peter, ed. *Reworking the Past: Hitler, the Holocaust and the Historians' Debate*. Boston: Beacon Press, 1990.

Balkoski, Joseph. *Beyond the Beachhead: The 29th Infantry Division in Normandy*. Fwd. Stephen E. Ambrose. 1989. Repr., Mechanicsburg, PA: Stackpole Books, 1999.

———. *Omaha Beach: D-Day: June 6, 1944*. Mechanicsburg, PA: Stackpole Books, 2004.

———. *Utah Beach: The Amphibious Landing and Airborne Operations on D-Day*. Mechanicsburg, PA: Stackpole Books, 2005.

Bando, Mark. *Vanguard of the Crusade: The 101st Airborne Division in World War II*. Bedford, PA: Aberjona Press, 2003.

Barcellini, Serge, and Annette Wiewiorka. *Passant, souviens-toi! Les lieux du souvenir de la Seconde Guerre mondial en France*. Paris: Plon, 1995.

Barthes, Roland. *Mythologies*. Ed. and trans. Annette Lavers. Paris: Editions du Seuil, 1957; New York: Noonday Press, 1972.

Bartlett, C. J. *"The Special Relationship": A Political History of Anglo-American Relations since 1945*. London: Longman, 1992.

Basinger, Jeanine. *The World War II Combat Film: Anatomy of a Genre*. With an updated filmography by Jeremy Arnold. New York: Columbia University Press, 1986; Middletown, CT: Wesleyan University Press, 2003.

Beevor, Anthony. *D-Day*. London: Viking, 2009.

———. *A Writer at War*. London: Harvill Press, 2006.

Beidler, Philip D. *The Good War's Greatest Hits: World War II and American Remembering*. Athens: University of Georgia Press, 1998.

Bellamy, Chris. *Absolute War. Soviet Russia in the Second World War: A Modern History*. London: Macmillan, 2007.

Bercuson, David J., and S. F. Wise. *The Valour and the Horror Revisited*. Montreal: McGill-Queen's University Press, 1994.

Berkhoff, Karel C. *Motherland in Danger: Soviet Propaganda during World War II*. Cambridge, MA: Harvard University Press, 2012.

Biess, Frank. *Homecomings: Returning POWs and the Legacies of Defeat in Postwar Germany*. Princeton: Princeton University Press, 2006.

Bischof, Günter, and Wolfgang Krieger, eds. *Die Invasion in der Normandie 1944*. Innsbruck: Studien Verlag, 2001.

Bischof, Günter, and Fritz Plasser, eds. *The Schüssel Era in Austria*. Contemporary Austrian Studies. Vol. 18. New Orleans/Innsbruck: UNO Press/Innsbruck University Press 2010.

Blight, David W. *Race and Reunion: The Civil War in American Memory*. Cambridge, MA: Harvard University Press, 2001.

Bliven, Bruce, Jr. *The Story of D-Day: June 6, 1994*. Fiftieth Anniversary ed. 1956. Repr., New York: Random House, 1994.

Bodnar, John E. *The "Good War" in American Memory*. Baltimore: The Johns Hopkins University Press, 2010.

———. *Remaking America: Public Memory, Commemoration, and Patriotism in the Twentieth Century*. Princeton: Princeton University Press, 1992.

Boivin, Michel, and Bernard Garnier. *Les victimes civiles de la manche dans la bataille de Normandie*. Caen: Éditions du Lys, 1994.

Bol'shaia Entsiklopediia. Vols. 10 and 33. Moscow : 2006.

Bol'shaia Istoricheskaia Entsiklopediia. Vols. 3 and 10. Moscow : Nauka, 1971.

Bol'shaia Sovetskaia Entsiklopediia. Vols. 5, 9, 18, and 30. Moscow : Nauka, 1951, 1954, and 1971.

Bourdin, Michel, and Bernard Garnier. *Les victimes civiles du Calvados dans la bataille de Normandie.* Caen: Éditions du Lys, 1995.

Brinkley, Douglas. *The Boys of Pointe du Hoc: Ronald Reagan, D-Day, and the US Army 2nd Rangers Battalion.* New York: HarperPerennial, 2005.

Brinkley, Douglas, and Ronald J. Drez. *Voices of Valor: Day: June 6, 1944,* including two audio CDs. New York: Bulfinch Press, 2004.

Brokaw, Tom. *The Greatest Generation.* New York: Random House, 1998.

———. *The Greatest Generation.* New York: Random House, 2004.

Brown, Gordon, and Terry Copp. *Look to Your Front: Regina Rifles 1944-45.* Waterloo: LCMSDS Press 2001.

Buckley, John, ed. *The Normandy Campaign 1944: Sixty Years On.* New York: Routledge, 2006.

———, ed. *The Normandy Campaign 1944: Sixty Years On.* Abingdon, Oxon: Routledge, 2006.

Budreau, Lisa M. *Bodies of War: World War I and the Politics of Commemoration in America, 1919-1933.* New York: New York University Press, 2010.

Burke, Kathleen. *Old World, New World: The Story of Britain and America.* London: Abacus, 2009.

Calder, Angus. *The Myth of the Blitz.* London: Cape, 1991.

———. *The People's War: Britain, 1939-1945.* London: Jonathan Cape, 1969.

Campbell, Duncan. *The Unsinkable Aircraft Carrier: American Military Power in Britain.* London: Paladin, 1986.

Campbell, Ian S. *Murder at the Abbaye: The Story of Twenty Canadian Soldiers Murdered at the Abbaye d'Ardenne.* Ottawa: The Golden Dog Press, 1966.

Campbell, Joseph. *The Hero with a Thousand Faces.* 3d ed. New York: Pantheon Books, 1949; Novato, CA: New World Library, 2008.

Campion, Garry. *The Good Fight: Battle of Britain Propaganda and the Few.* Basingstoke: Palgrave Macmillan, 2009.

Capdevila, Luc, and Danièle Voldman. *War Dead: Western Societies and the Casualties of War.* Edinburgh: Edinburgh University Press, 2002.

Cappelletto, Francesca, ed. *Memory and World War II: An Ethnographic Approach.* New York: Berg Publishers, 2005. "

Carrell, Paul. *"Invasion! They're Coming!"* New York: Dutton, 1963.

————. *Sie Kommen: Der deutsche Bericht über die Invasion und die 80 tägige Schlacht um Frankreich*. Oldenbourg: Gerhard Stalling Verlag, 1961.

Chambers, John Whiteclay, II, and David Culbert, eds. *World War II: Film and History*. New York: Oxford University Press, 1996.

Chubar'ian, A. O. *Stalinskoe desiatiletie kholodnoi voiny: fakty i gipotezy*. Moscow: Nauka, 1999.

Clark, Peter. *The Last Thousand Days of the British Empire*. New York: Bloomsbury Press, 2012.

Connelly, Mark. *The Great War, Memory and Ritual: Commemoration in the City and East London, 1916-1939*. London: Royal Historical Society, 2001.

————. *Reaching for the Stars: A New History of Bomber Command in World War II*. London: I. B. Tauris, 2001.

————. *We Can Take It!: Britain and the Memory of the Second World War*. New York: Pearson, 2004.

————. *We Can Take It! Britain and the Memory of the Second World War*. London: Pearson, 2004.

Copp, Terry. *A Canadian's Guide to the Battlefields of Normandy*. Ontario: Laurier, 1994.

————. *Fields of Fire: The Canadians in Normandy*. Toronto: University of Toronto Press, 2003.

————. *No Price Too High: Canadians in the Second World War*. Toronto: McGraw-Hill Ryerson, 1994.

————, ed. *Montgomery's Scientists: Operational Research in Northwest Europe*. Waterloo: Wilfrid Laurier University Press, 2001.

Copp, Terry, and Robert Vogel. *Maple Leaf Route: Caen*. Alma: Maple Leaf Route, 1983.

Craig, Cambell, and Sergey Radchenko. *The Atomic Bomb and the Origins of the Cold War*. New Haven: Yale University Press, 2008.

Danchev, Alex. *On Specialness: Essays in Anglo-American Relations (St. Anthony's Series)*. London: Palgrave Macmillan, 1998.

Dear, I. C. B. *The Oxford Companion to the Second World War*. Oxford: Oxford University Press, 1995.

Delporte, Christian, Isabelle Veyrat-Masson, Denis Maréchal, and Caroline Moine. *La guerre après la guerre: Images et construction des imaginaires de guerre dans l'Europe du XXe siècle*. Paris : Noveau Monde, 2009.

D'Este, Carlo. *Decision in Normandy*. Old Saybrook, CT: Konecky and Konecky, 1983; New York: HarperPerennial, 1994.

————. *Warlord: A Life of Churchill at War, 1874-1945.* London: Allen Lane, 2009.

Doherty, Thomas. *Projections of War: Hollywood, American Culture, and World War II.* Revised and updated. New York: Columbia University Press, 1999.

Drez, Ronald J., ed. *Voices of D-Day: The Story of the Allied Invasion Told by Those Who Were There.* Fwd. Stephen E. Ambrose. Baton Rouge: Louisiana State University Press, 1994.

Duke, Simon. *US Defence Bases in the United Kingdom: A Matter for Joint Decision?* London: Macmillan, 1987.

Dumbrell, John. *A Special Relationship: Anglo-American Relations from the Cold War to Iraq.* London: Palgrave Macmillan, 2006.

Echternkamp, Jorg, and Stefan Martens, eds. *Experience and Memory: The Second World War in Europe.* Oxford: Berghahn, 2010.

Ehrman, John. *The Eighties: America in the Age of Reagan.* New Haven, CT: Yale University Press, 2005.

Ellis, L. F. *Victory in the West.* Vol. 1. *The Battle of Normandy.* London: Her Majesty's Stationery Office, 1962.

Embacher, Helga, ed. *Umkämpfte Erinnerung: Die Wehrmachtsausstellung in Salzburg.* Salzburg: Residenzverlag, 1999.

Engelhardt, Tom. *The End of Victory Culture: Cold War America and the Disillusioning of a Generation.* New York: Basic Books, 1995.

English, John. *Just Watch Me.* Toronto: Knopf Canada, 2009.

Evans, Martin, and Ken Lunn, eds. *War and Memory in the Twentieth Century.* Oxford: Berg, 1997.

Farmer, Sarah. *Martyred Village: Commemorating the 1944 Massacre at Oradour-sur-Glane.* Berkeley: University of California Press, 2000.

Fateev, A.V. *Obraz vraga v sovetskoi propagande, 1945-1954gg.* Moscow: RAN, 1999.

Fischer, Pete. *Highway of Heroes: True Patriot Love.* Toronto: Dundurn, 2011.

Fotheringham, William. *Roule Britannia: Great Britain and the Tour de France.* London: Yellow Jersey Press, 2012.

Francis, Martin. *The Flyer: British Culture and the Royal Air Force, 1939-1945.* Oxford: Oxford University Press, 2008.

Frei, Norbert. *1945 und Wir: Das Dritte Reich im Bewusstsein der Deutschen.* Munich: C. H. Beck, 2005.

Gabovich, M. *Pamiat' o voine 60 let spustia: Rossiia, Germaniia, Evropa.* Moscow: NLO, 2005.

Gallagher, Matthew P. *The Soviet History of WWII: Myths, Memories, and Realities.* New York: Praeger, 1963.

The Gallup Poll: Public Opinion 1994. Wilmington: Scholarly Resources Inc., 1995.

Gibb, Robin, Steve Darlow, and Jim Dooley. *The Bomber Command Memorial: We Will Remember Them.* London: Fighting High, 2013.

Gilbert, Martin. *D-Day.* London: John Wiley & Sons, 2004.

Gillis, John R., ed. *Commemorations: The Politics of National Identity.* Princeton: Princeton University Press, 1994.

Gilzmer, Mechtild. *Mémoires de Pierre: Les monuments commémoratifs en France après 1944.* Trans. German into French by Odile Demange. Pref. Serge Barcellini. Paris: Éditions Autrement, 2009.

Glantz, David, and Jonathan House. *When Titans Clashed: How the Red Army Stopped Hitler.* Lawrence: University Press of Kansas, 1995.

Goebel, Stefan. *The Great War and Medieval Memory: War, Remembrance and Medievalism in Britain and Germany, 1914-1940.* Cambridge: Cambridge University Press, 2007.

Good, David F., and Ruth Wodak, ed. *From World War to Waldheim: Culture and Politics in Austria and the United States.* New York: Berghahn, 1999.

Gorbachevsky, Boris. *Through the Maelstrom: A Red Army Soldier's War on the Eastern Front, 1942-1945.* Trans. Stuart Britton. Lawrence: University Press of Kansas, 2008.

Gorodetsky, Gabriel, ed. *Stafford Cripps in Moscow 1940–1942: Diaries and Papers.* London: Vallentine Mitchell, 2007.

de Groot, Jerome. *Consuming History: Historians and Heritage in Contemporary Popular Culture.* New York: Routledge, 2009.

Gussow, Mel. *Don't Say Yes until I Finish Talking: A Biography of Darryl F. Zanuck.* New York: Doubleday, 1971; Repr. New York: Pocket Books, 1972.

Guzenkovoi, T. S., and V. N. Filianovoi, eds. *Vtoraia mirovaia i Velikaia Otechestvennaia voiny v uchebnikakh istorii stran SNG i ES: Problemy, podkhody, interpretatsii.* Moscow: RISI, 2010.

Hagopian, Patrick. *The Vietnam War in American Memory: Veterans, Memorials, and the Politics of Healing.* Amherst: University of Massachusetts Press, 2009.

Halbwachs, Maurice. *On Collective Memory.* Ed. and trans. Lewis Coser. Chicago: University of Chicago Press, 1992.

Hamburger Institut für Sozialforschung, ed. *Krieg ist ein Gesellschaftszustand: Reden zur Eröffnung der Ausstellung "Vernichtungskrieg. Verbrechen der Wehrmacht 1941 bis 1944."* Hamburg; Hamburger Edition, 1998.

Harrison, Gordon A. *Cross Channel Attack.* United States Army in World War II. Washington, DC: United States Army Center of Military History, 1951; New York: BDD, Inc., 1993.

Harrison, Richard. *The Russian Way of War: Operational Art, 1904-1940.* Lawrence: University Press of Kansas, 2001.

Hart, Russell A. *Clash of Arms: How the Allies Won in Normandy.* Boulder, CO: Lynne Rienner, 2001.

———. *Clash of Arms: How the Allies Won in Normandy.* Norman, OK: University of Oklahoma Press, 2004.

Hartcup, Guy. *Code Name Mulberry: The Planning, Building and Operation of the Normandy Harbours.* New York: Hippocrene Books, Inc., 1977.

Hastings, Max. *Overlord: D-Day and the Battle for Normandy.* New York: Simon and Schuster, 1984.

———. *Overlord: D-Day and the Battle for Normandy.* London: Pam Books, 1999.

Hayes, Geoffrey, Mike Bechthold, and Matt Symes, eds. *Canada and the Second World War.* Waterloo: Wilfrid Laurier University Press, 2012.

Haynes, John Earl, Harvey Klehr, and Alexander Vassiliev. *Spies: The Rise and Fall of the KGB in America.* New Haven, CT: Yale University Press, 2010.

Herf, Jeffrey. *Divided Memory: The Nazi Past and the Two Germanies.* Cambridge, MA: Harvard University Press, 1997.

Hitchcock, William I. *The Bitter Road to Freedom: A New History of the Liberation of Europe.* New York: The Free Press, 2008.

Hill, Alexander. *The Great Patriotic War of the Soviet Union, 1941-45: A Documentary Reader.* London: Routledge, 2009.

Hodgson, Katharine. *Written with the Bayonet: Soviet Russian Poetry of World War Two.* Liverpool: Liverpool University Press, 1996.

Hogan, Michael, ed. *The Ambiguous Legacy: US Foreign Relations in the "American Century."* New York: Cambridge University Press, 1999.

Holland, Steve, ed. *No Surrender.* London: Prion, 2010.

Holt, Tonie, and Valmai Holt. *Normandy Landing Beaches: Battlefield Guide.* Barnsley: Leo Cooper, 1999.

Howard, Michael. *Strategic Deception in the Second World War: British Intelligence Operations against the German High Command.* New York: W. W. Norton & Company, 1995.

Howarth, David. *Dawn of D-Day: These Men Were There, 6 June 1944.* London: Collins, 1959; London: Greenhill, 2001; Mechanicsburg, PA: Stackpole Books, 2001.

Hurd, Geoff, ed. *National Fictions: World War II in British Films and Television.* London: BFI Books, 1984.

Immerman, Richard H. *Empire for Liberty: A History of American Imperialism from Benjamin Franklin to Paul Wolfowitz.* Princeton, NJ: Princeton University Press, 2010.

Irwin-Zarecka, I. *Frames of Remembrance: The Dynamics of Collective Memory.* New Brunswick, NJ: Transaction Publishers, 1994.

Jacobsen, Hans-Adolf, and Jürgen Rohwer, eds. *Decisive Battles of World War II: The German View.* Trans. Edward Fitzgerald. Intro. Cyril Falls. Frankfurt am Main: Verlag für Wehrwesen Bernard & Graefe, 1960; New York: G. P. Putnam's Sons, 1965.

Johnson, R., G. McLennan, B. Schwarz, and D. Sutton, eds. *Making Histories: Studies in History-Writing and Politics.* London: Hutchinson, 1982.

Johnston, Timothy. *Being Soviet: Identity, Rumor, and Everyday Life under Stalin, 1939-1953.* Oxford: Oxford University Press, 2011.

Joly, Elena, ed. *Pobeda liuboi tsenoi.* Moscow: IAUZA, EKSMO, 2010.

Kammen, Michael G. *Mystic Chords of Memory: The Transformation of Tradition in American Culture.* New York: Vintage Books, 1991.

Kaplan, Alice Yaeger. *The Interpreter.* New York: Free Press, 2005.

Keegan, John. *Six Armies in Normandy: From D-Day to the Liberation of Paris.* New York: Viking Penguin, 1982.

———. *Six Armies in Normandy: From D-Day to the Liberation of Paris.* With a new introduction for the fiftieth anniversary of D-Day. New York: Penguin Books, 1994.

———. *Six Armies in Normandy: From D-Day to the Liberation of Paris.* London: Pimlico, 2004.

Keren, Michael and Holger H. Herwig, eds. *War Memory and Popular Culture: Essays on Modes of Remembrance and Commemoration.* Jefferson, NC: McFarland and Company, 2009.

Kershaw, Alex. *The Bedford Boys: One American Town's Ultimate D-Day Sacrifice.* Cambridge, MA: Da Capo Press, 2003.

Kershaw, Robert. *D-Day: Piercing the Atlantic Wall*. Annapolis, MD: Naval Institute Press, 1994.

Keyssar, Helene, and Vladimir Pozner. *Remembering War: A US-Soviet Dialogue*. New York: Oxford University Press, 1990.

Khramchikhin, Alexander. *Russkie na voine*. Moscow: Kliuch-S, 2010.

King, Alex. *Memorials of the Great War in Britain: The Symbolism and Politics of Remembrance*. New York: Berg, 1998.

Kraminov, Daniil. *Pravda o Vtorom Fronte: Zapiski voennogo korrespondenta*. Petrozavodsk: GI Karelskoi ASSR, 1960.

Kucherenko, Olga. *Little Soldiers: How Soviet Children Went to War, 1941–45*. Oxford: Oxford University Press, 2011.

Kuretsidis-Haider, Claudia, and Winfried R. Garscha, eds. *Keine "Abrechnung": NS-Verbrechen, Justiz, und Gesellschaft in Europa nach 1945*. Leipzig-Vienna: Akademische Verlagsanstalt, 1998.

Laborie, Pierre. *Le chagrin et le venin: La France sous l'occupation, mémoire, et idées reçues*. Paris: Bayard, 2011.

Lackenbauer, P. Whitney, and C. W. Madsen. *Kurt Meyer on Trial: A Documentary Record*. Kingston: Canadian Forces Leadership Institute, 2007.

LaFeber, Walter. *The American Age: US Foreign Policy at Home and Abroad, 1750 to the Present*. London: W. W. Norton & Company, 1994.

Lamâche, Stéphane. *La Normandie Américaine*. Paris: Larousse, 2010.

Lawrence, John Shelton, and Robert Jewett. *The Myth of the American Superhero*. Grand Rapids, MI: William B. Eerdmans Publishing Company, 2002.

Lebow, Richard Ned, Wulf Kansteiner, and Claudio Fogu, eds. *The Politics of Memory in Postwar Europe*. Durham, NC: Duke University Press, 2006.

Leffler, Melvyn, and David S. Painter. *Origins of the Cold War: An International History*. 2d ed. New York: Routledge, 1994.

Leffler, Melvyn, and Odd Arne Westad, eds. *Cambridge History of the Cold War*. Vol. 1. Cambridge: Cambridge University Press, 2010.

Leuchtenburg, William E., ed. *American Places: Encounters with History*. New York: Oxford University Press, 2000.

Lewis, Adrian R. *Omaha Beach: A Flawed Victory*. Chapel Hill, NC: University of North Carolina Press, 2001.

Lilly, J. Robert. *Taken By Force: Rape and American GIs in Europe during World War II*. New York: Palgrave Macmillan, 2007.

Livshin, A. Ia., and I. B. Orlov, eds. *Sovietskaia propaganda v gody Velikoi Otechestvennoi voiny: "Kommunikatsiia ubezhdeniia" i mobilizatsionnye mekhanizmy.* Moscow: POSSPEN, 2007.

Lloyd, D. W. *Battlefield Tourism: Pilgrimage and the Commemoration of the Great War in Britain, Australia and Canada, 1919-1939.* New York: Berg, 1998.

Longworth, Philip. *The Unending Vigil: A History of the Commonwealth War Graves Commission, 1916-1967.* London: Constable, 1967.

Louis, W. R., and H. Bull. *The Special Relationship: Anglo-American Relations Since 1945.* New York: Oxford University Press, 1986.

Lowenthal, David. *The Heritage Crusade and the Spoils of History.* Cambridge: Cambridge University Press, 1998.

———. *The Past is a Foreign Country.* Cambridge: Cambridge University Press, 1990.

Lucas, W. S. *Divided We Stand: Britain, the US and the Suez Crisis.* London: Hodder and Stoughton, 1991.

MacDonald, Bruce. *The Trial of Kurt Meyer.* Toronto: Clarke, 1954.

Maier, Charles S. *The Unmasterable Past: History, Holocaust, and German National Identity.* Cambridge, MA: Harvard University Press, 1988.

Marushkin, B. I. *Istoriia i politika.Amerikanskaia burzhuaznaia istoriografiia sovetskogo obshchestva.* Moscow: Nauka, 1969.

Michaelis, David. *Schulz and Peanuts: A Biography.* New York: HarperCollins, 2007.

Miller, Russell. *Nothing Less Than Victory: An Oral History of D-Day.* London: William Morrow and Company, 1993.

Milner, Marc. *From D-Day to Carpiquet: The North Shore Regiment and the Liberation of Europe.* Fredericton, NB, Canada: Goose Lane Editions, 2007.

Moeller, Robert G. *War Stories: The Search for a Usable Past in the Federal Republic of Germany.* Berkeley: University of California Press, 2001.

Mönch, Winfried. *Entscheidungsschlacht "Invasion" 1944? Prognosen und Diagnosen.* Stuttgart: Franz Steiner Verlag, 2001.

Morgan, Gerald, and Gavin Hughes. *Southern Ireland and the Liberation of France.* Bern: Peter Lang AG, 2011.

Morrison, James W. *Bedford Goes to War: The Heroic Story of a Small Virginia Community in World War II.* 2d ed. Lynchburg, VA: Warwick House Publishing, 2006.

Mosse, George. *Fallen Soldiers: Reshaping the Memory of the World Wars.* New York: Oxford University Press, 1990.

Müller, Jan-Werner, ed. *Memory and Power in Post-War Europe: Studies in the Presence of the Past.* New York: Cambridge University Press, 2002.

Murray, Williamson, and Allan R. Millett. *A War to be Won: Fighting the Second World War.* Cambridge, MA: Harvard University Press, 2000.

Nadzhafov, D. G., and Z. S. Belousova, eds. *Stalin i kosmopolitizm: 1945-1953.* Moscow: Demokratiia, 2005.

Narinskiæi, Mikhail M., et al., eds. *SSSR i Frantsiia v gody Vtoroi mirovoi voiny: Sbornik nauchnykh statei.* Moscow: MGIMO-Universitet, 2006.

Nargolian, Howard. *Conduct Unbecoming: The Story of the Murder of Canadian Prisoners of War in Normandy.* Toronto: University of Toronto Press, 1998.

Neillands, Robin. *D-Day, 1944: Voices from Normandy.* London: Orion Books, 1993.

Neisser, Ulric, and Ira Hyman. *Memory Observed: Remembering in Natural Contexts.* San Francisco: W. H. Freeman and Company, 1982.

Newhouse, John. *De Gaulle and the Anglo-Saxons.* London: Andre Deutsch, 1970.

Ninkovich, Frank. *The Wilsonian Century: US Foreign Policy since 1900.* Chicago: University of Chicago Press, 1999.

Noakes, Lucy. *War and the British: Gender, Memory, and National Identity.* London: I. B. Tauris, 1998.

Noakes, Lucy, and Juliette Pattison. *British Cultural Memory and the Second World War.* London: Continuum, 2013.

Nora, Pierre, ed. *Realms of Memory: Rethinking the French Past.* 3 vols. Ed. Lawrence Kritzman. Trans. Arthur Goldhammer. New York: Columbia University Press, 1996-1998.

Ol'shtynskii, L. I. *Razgrom fashchizma: SSSR i anglo-amerikanskie soiuzniki vo Vtoroi mirovoi voine (politika i voennaia strategiia: fakty, vyvody, uroki istorii).* Moscow: ITRK, 2010.

Orlov, A. S. *Za kulisami vtorogo fronta.* Moscow: Veche, 2011.

Ostcow, Robin, ed. *(Re)Visualizing National History: Museums and National identities in Europe.* Toronto: University of Toronto Press, 2003.

Overy, Richard. *Russia's War.* London: Penguin, 1997.

———. *Why the Allies Won.* London: Pimlico, 1995.

Paris, Michael. *Warrior Nation: Images of War in British Popular Culture, 1850-2000.* London: Reaktion Books, 2000.

Pelinka, Anton, and Erika Weinzierl, eds. *Das grosse Tabu: Österreichs Umgang mit seiner Vergangenheit.* Vienna: Verlag der österreichischen Staatsdruckerei, 1987.

Penrose, Jane, ed. *The D-Day Companion: Leading Historians Explore History's Greatest Amphibious Assault*. Osceola, WI: Osprey Publishing for the National D-Day Museum, New Orleans, 2004.

Piehler, G. Kurt. *Remembering War the American Way*. 1995. Repr., Washington, DC: Smithsonian Institution Press, 2004.

Poupard, Jean, ed. *Témoignages des Saint Lois de 1944*. Saint Lô: Association « Saint Lô 44 » Responsable éditions, Octobre 1994.

Prados, Edward F., and US Navy Memorial Foundation, eds. *Neptunus Rex: Naval Stories of the Normandy Invasion, June 6, 1944*. Novato, CA: Presidio Press, 1998.

Quellien, Jean. *La Normandie au coeur de la geurre*. Rennes: Éditions Ouest-France, 1992.

———. *Les Victimes Civiles de Basse-Normandie dans la Bataille de Normandie*. Caen: Éditions-Diffusion du Lys, 2009.

Ramsey, W. G., ed. *D-Day: Then and Now*. Vol. 2. London: After the Battle, 1995.

Razzakov, Fedor. *Nashe liubimoe kino. Tainoe stanovitsia iavnym*. Moscow: Algoritm, 2004.

Richler, Noah. *What We Talk About, When We Talk About War*. Fredericton: Goose Lane, 2012.

Roberts, Mary Louise. *What Soldiers Do: Sex and the American GI in WWII Europe*. Chicago: University of Chicago Press, 2013.

Robin, Ron. *Enclaves of America: The Rhetoric of American Political Architecture Abroad, 1900-1965*. Princeton, NJ: Princeton University Press, 1992.

Rosenberg, Bruce. *Custer and the Epic of Defeat*. State College: Pennsylvania State University Press, 1974.

Rosenberg, Emily S. *A Date Which Will Live: Pearl Harbor in American Memory*. Durham, NC: Duke University Press, 2003.

Rousso, Henri. *The Vichy Syndrome: History and Memory in France since 1944*. Trans. Arthur Goldhammer. Cambridge, MA: Harvard University Press, 1991.

Roy, Reginald. *1944: The Canadians in Normandy*. Ottawa: Macmillan, 1984.

Ruggero, Ed. *The First Men In: U.S. Paratroopers and the Fight to Save D-Day*. New York: HarperCollins, 2006.

Schivelbusch, Wolfgang. *The Culture of Defeat: On National Trauma, Mourning, and Recovery*. Trans. J. S. Chase. London: Granta Books, 2004.

Sebald, W. G. *On the Natural History of Destruction*. London: Hamish Hamilton, 2003.

Sherman, Daniel. *The Construction of Memory in Interwar France*. London: University of Chicago Press, 1999.

Shestakov, V. A. *Istoriia Rossii, XX-nachalo XXI veka. 11 klass*. Moscow: Prosveshchenie, 2010.

Shomon, Joseph James. *Crosses in the Wind: The Unheralded Saga of the Men in the American Graves Registration Service in World War II*. New York: Stratford House, 1947.

Slotkin, Richard. *Regeneration through Violence: The Mythology of the American Frontier, 1600-1860*. Middletown, CT: Wesleyan University Press, 1973.

Small, Ken. *Forgotten Dead*. London: Bloomsbury, 1999.

Smelser, Ronald, and Edward J. Davies II. *The Myth of the Eastern Front: The Nazi-Soviet War in American Popular Culture*. New York: Cambridge University Press, 2008.

Smith, Malcolm. *Britain and 1940: History, Myth, and Popular Memory*. London: Routledge, 2000.

Stafford, David. *Ten Days to D-Day: Countdown to the Liberation of Europe*. London: Little, Brown, 2003.

Steinhoff, Johannes, Peter Pechel, Dennis Showalter, eds. *Voices from the Third Reich: An Oral History*. New York: Da Capo Press, 1994.

Stoffer, Jeff. *Mother of Normandy: The Story of Simone Renaud*. China: Iron Mike Entertainment, 2010.

Sturken, Marita. *Tangled Memories: The Vietnam War, the AIDS Epidemic, and the Politics of Remembering*. Berkeley: University of California Press, 1997.

Suid, Lawrence H. *Guts and Glory: The Making of the American Military Image in Film*. Rev. ed. Lexington: University Press of Kentucky, 2002.

Suleiman, Susan R. *Crises of Memory and the Second World War*. Cambridge, MA: Harvard University Press, 2006.

Summerfield, Penny, and Corinna Peniston-Bird. *Contesting Home Defence: Men, Women, and the Home Guard in the Second World War*. Manchester: Manchester University Press, 2007.

Tatum, James. *The Mourner's Song: War and Remembrance from the Iliad to Vietnam*. Chicago: University of Chicago Press, 2003.

Terkel, Studs. *"The Good War": An Oral History of World War II*. New York: The New Press, 1984.

Tobin, James. *Ernie Pyle's War: America's Eyewitness to World War II*. Lawrence: University Press of Kansas, 1997.

Todman, Daniel. *The Great War, Myth and Memory*. London: Hambledon , 2005.

Torgovnick, Marianna. *The War Complex: World War II in Our Time*. Chicago: University of Chicago Press, 2005.

Torgovnik, Marianna. *The War Complex: World War II in our Time*. London: University of Chicago Press, 1998.

Tulving, E., ed. *The Oxford Handbook of Memory*. Oxford: Oxford University Press, 2000.

Virilio, Paul. *Bunker Archeology*. Princeton: Princeton University Press, 1984.

Voldman, Daniéle. *La Reconstruction des villes Françaises de 1940 à 1954*. Paris: L'Harmattan, 1997.

Wagner, Sarah E. *To Know Where He Lies: DNA Technology and the Search for Srebernica's Missing*. Berkeley: University of California Press, 2008.

Wahnich, Sophie, Barbara Lášticová, and Andrej Findor, eds. *Politics of Collective Memory: Cultural Patterns of Commemorative Practices in Post-War Europe*. London: Lit Verlag, 2009.

Watson, Janet S. K. *Fighting Different Wars: Experience, Memory and the First World War in Britain*. Cambridge: Cambridge University Press, 2007.

Weigley, Russell F. *Eisenhower's Lieutenants: The Campaign of France and Germany, 1944-1945*. Bloomington: Indiana University Press, 1981.

Werth, Alexander. *Russia at War, 1941-1945*. New York: E. P. Dutton & Co., Inc., 1964.

Werth, Alexander. *Russia at War, 1941-1945*. 2d ed. New York: Carroll & Graf Pubs., Inc., 2000.

Whelan, Richard. *Robert Capa*. New York: Alfred A. Knopf, 1985.

Whitlock, Flint. *The Fighting First: The Untold Story of the Big Red One on D-Day*. Boulder, CO: Westview Press, 2004.

Wieviorka, Olivier. *Histoire du débarquement en Normandie: Des origins à la liberation de Paris, 1941-1944*. Paris: Éditions du Seuil, 2007.

————. *La mémoire désunie: Le souvenir politique des années sombres, de la libération à nos jours*. Paris: Éditions du Seuil, 2010.

————. *Normandy: The Landings to the Liberation of Paris*. Trans. M. B. DeBevoise. Cambridge, MA: Harvard University Press, 2008.

Williams, Andrew. *D-Day to Berlin*. London: Hodder, 2004.

Willmott, H. P. *June 1944: In France, Italy, Eastern Europe, and the Pacific, Allied Armies Fought Momentous Battles Which Decided the War and the Future of the World Itself*. London: Grub Street, 1999.

Wilson, Charles Reagan. *Baptized in Blood: The Religion of the Lost Cause, 1865-1920*. Athens: University of Georgia Press, 1982.

Wilson, Theodore A., ed. *D-Day 1944*. Fwd. John S. D. Eisenhower. Lawrence: The University Press of Kansas, 1994.

Winter, Jay. *Remembering War: The Great War between Memory and History in the Twentieth Century.* New Haven: Yale University Press, 2006.

————. *Sites of Memory, Sites of Mourning: The Great War in European Cultural History.* Cambridge: Cambridge University Press, 1995.

Winter, Jay, and Emmanuel Sivan, eds. *War and Remembrance in the Twentieth Century.* Cambridge: Cambridge University Press, 1999.

Wippermann, Wolfgang. *Wessen Schuld? Vom Historikerstreit zur Goldhagen Kontroverse.* Berlin: Elefanten Press, 1997.

Wood, Nancy. *Vectors of Memory: Legacies of Trauma in Postwar Europe.* New York: Berg Publishers, 1999.

Young, James, ed. *The Art of Memory: Holocaust Memorials in History.* New York: Prestel, 1994.

————. *The Texture of Memory: Holocaust Memorials and Meaning.* New Haven: Yale University Press, 1993.

Zhukov, G. K. *Vospominaniia i Razmyshleniia.* Vol. 3. Moscow: APN, 1986.

Zhuravliova, Victoria I., and Ivan I. Kurilla, eds. *Rossiia i SShA na stranitsakh ucheb-nikov: Opyt vzaimnykh reprezentatsii.* Volgograd: Izdatel'stvo Volgogradskogo Universiteta, 2009.

Ziegler, Meinrad, and Waltraud Kannonier-Finster. *Österreichs Gedächtnis: Über Erinnern und Vergessen der NS-Vergangenheit.* Vienna: Böhlau Verlag, 1993.

Articles

Ambrose, Stephen E. "*The Longest Day* (1962): "Blockbuster" History." *Journal of Film, Radio, and Television* 14 (1994): 421-31.

Barcellini, Serge. "Diplomatie et commémoration: Les commémorations du 6 juin 1984: Une bataille de mémoire." *Guerres Mondiales et conflits contemporains* 47, no. 186 (1997): 121-46.

Bischof, Günter. "Die Instrumentalisierung der Moskauer Erklärung nach dem 2. Weltkrieg." *Zeitgeschichte* 20 (Nov.-Dec. 1993): 345-66.

————. "Victims? Perpetrators? 'Punching Bags' of European Historical Memory? The Austrians and Their World War II Legacies." *German Studies Review* 27 (Feb. 2004): 17-32.

Bobipev, P. "V pomoshch prepodavateliam istorii: Polnoe izgnanie vraga iz predelov Sovetskogo Soiuza. Osvobozhdenie narodov Evropy i okonchatel'nyi razgrom fashistskoi Germanii (ianvar' 1944-mai 1945)." *Voenno-Istoricheskii Zhurnal* 3 (1984): 83.

Boltin, E. "O kharaktere i periodizatsii vtoroi mirovoi voiny 1939-1945 godov." *Voenno-Istoricheskii Zhurnal* 1 (1959).

Buckely, John. "Victory or Defeat? Perceptions of the British Military in Northwest Europe, 1944-5." *Global War Studies* (forthcoming).

Chapman, James. "Television and History: The World at War." *Historical Journal of Film, Radio, and Television* 31, no. 2 (2011): 247-75.

————. "'The Yanks Are Shown to Such Advantage': Anglo-American Rivalry in the Production of *The True Glory* (1945)." *Historical Journal of Film, Radio, and Television* 16, no. 4 (1996): 533-54.

Chelyshev, I. "Frantsuzskii istorik o vtoroi mirovoi voine," *Voenno-Istoricheskii Zhurnal* 11 (1970).

Confino, Alon. "Collective Memory and Cultural History: Problems of Method." *American Historical Review* 102 (Dec. 1997): 1386-1403.

Connelly, Mark. "The Longest Days: A Personal View of the Television Coverage of the Fiftieth Anniversary of D-Day." *Contemporary Record* 8 (1994): 602-09.

Conway, M., and M. Ross. "Getting What You Want by Revising What You Had." *Journal of Personality and Social Psychology* 47 (1984): 738-48.

Copp, Terry. "Workers and Soldiers: A Memoir." *Canadian Historical Review* 93 (Sept. 2012): 463-86.

Crane, Susan. "Writing the Individual Back into Collective Memory." *American Historical Review* 102 (1997): 1372-85.

Dehays, Antonin. "'Blosville': Un cimetière américain provisoire en Normandie." *39-45 Magazine*. Bayeux: Éditions Heimdal, 2011: 46-51.

Delaney, Kate. "The Many Meanings of D-Day." *European Journal of American Studies*, Special Edition (2012): Doc. 13. http://ejas.revues.org/9544.

Eley, Geoff. "Finding the People's War: Film, British Collective Memory, and World War II." *American Historical Review* 106 (2001): 818-38.

Fitzpatrick, Meagan. "Feds Launch War of 1812 Anniversary Plans" *CBC News*, 11 October 2011.

Gedi, N. and Y. Elam. "Collective Memory – What Is It?" *History and Memory* 8 (1996): 30-50.

Girin, Aleksandr. "Sovetskoe voennoe iskusstvo v Belorusskoi operatsii 1944 goda." *Voenno-Istoricheskii Zhurnal* 6 (1984): 11.

Gough, Paul. "A Difficult Path to Tread." *Canadian Military History* 8 (1999): 75-80.

Griffiths, Nan. "The Canadian Memorial Garden Caen, Normandy, France: Two Views—Memory, Monuments, and Landscapes." *Canadian Military History* 8 (1998): 75-81.

Hutton, Patrick. "Recent Scholarship on History and Memory." *History Teacher* 33 (2000): 533-48.

Iakushevskii, A. "Kritika burzhuaznoi istoriographii sobytii 1944 goda na sovetsko-germanskom fronte." *Voenno-Istoricheskii Zhurnal* 12 (1984): 70-71, 73.

———. "Operatsii Sovetskoi Armii v 1944 godu v osveshchenii burzhuaznoi isto-riographii." *Voenno-Istoricheskii Zhurnal* 6 (1974): 109.

Israelian, V. "O strategii SSHA i Anglii v Evrope (obzor novoi amerikanskoi i angliiskoi literatury po strategii Vtoroi mirovoi voiny)." *Voenno-Istoricheskii Zhurnal* 3 (1959): 95, 100.

Kansteiner, Wulf. "Finding Meaning in Memory: A Methodological Critique of Collective Memory Studies." *History and Theory* 4 (2002): 179-97.

Korotkov, G., and A. Orlov. "O politike i startegii SShA i Anglii v Zapadnoi Evrope v 1944g." *Voenno-Istoricheskii Zhurnal* 8 (1974): 80, 85.

Kucherenko, Olga. "That'll Teach 'Em to Love their Motherland!: Russian Youth Revisit the Battles of World War II." *Journal of Power Institutions in Post-Soviet Societies* 12 (2011). http://pipss.revues.org/3866.

Kurasov, V. "O kharaktere i periodizatsii vtoroi mirovoi voiny 1939-1945 godov." *Voenno-Istoricheskii Zhurnal* 1 (1959): 36.

Kwon, Miwon. "One Place after Another: Notes on Site Specificity." *October* 80 (Spring 1997): 85-110.

Lemay, Kate C. "The American War Cemeteries in Normandy and the Politics of Grief." *Winterthur Portfolio* (under review).

Maier, Charles S. "A Surfeit of Memory? Reflections on History, Melancholy and Denial." *History & Memory* 5 (Fall/Winter 1993): 136-52.

McDougall, Walter A. "American Exceptionalism...Exposed." Foreign Policy Research Institute E-Notes, October 2012. http://www.fpri.org/articles/2012/10/american-exceptionalism-exposed.

McMackin, Vanessa. "Rearranged Snowdrops: The Construction of Memory at the Abbaye d'Ardenne." *Canadian Military History* 20 (2011): 30-42.

Moeller, Robert G. "War Stories: The Search for a Usable Past in the Federal Republic of Germany." *American Historical Review* 101 (Oct. 1996): 1008-48.

Olick, Jeffrey. "Collective Memory: the Two Cultures." *Sociological Theory* 17 (1989): 333-48.

Paris, Michael. "Picturing D-Day." *History Today* 54 (2000): 10-16.

Pechatnov, Vladimir O. "The Big Three after World War II: New Documents on Soviet Thinking about Post War Relations with The United States and Great Britain." *Cold War International History Project*. The Woodrow Wilson Center for Scholars. Working Paper no. 13 (May,1995): i-iii, 1-26. http://www.wilson-center.org/sites/default/files/ACF17F.PDF.

————. "The Rise and Fall of *Britansky Soyuznik*: A Case Study in Soviet Response to British Propaganda of the mid-1940s." *Historical Journal* 41 (1998): 293-301.

Petersen, Judith. "How British Television Inserted the Holocaust into Britain's War Memory in 1995." *Historical Journal of Film, Radio, and Television* 21, no. 3 (2001): 255-72.

Pitt, Andrew. "A Changing Anglo-Saxon Myth: Its Development and Function in French Political Thought, 1860-1914." *French History* 14 (2000): 150-73.

Platonov, S. P. et al., eds. Review of *Vtoraia mirovaia voina 1939-1945gg. Voenno-istoricheskii ocherk*. By V. Vorobiov et al., *Voenno-Istoricheskii Zhurnal* 5 (1959).

Poliakov, V. "Vtoraia mirovaia voina v osveshchenii angliiskogo istorika." *Voenno-Istoricheskii Zhurnal* 10 (1967): 109.

Red'ko, Iu. "Ob otvetstvennosti zapadnykh derzhav za vtoruiu mirovuiu voinu (Obzor angliiskoi i amerikanskoi istoricheskoi literatury)." *Voenno-Istoricheskii Zhurnal* 3 (1963): 49-573.

Reynolds, David. "Rethinking Anglo-American Relations." *International Affairs* 65 (Winter, 1988-1989): 89-111.

Roediger, H. L. "Memory Metaphors in Cognitive Psychology." *Memory and Cognition* 8 (1980): 231-46.

Rychkova, O. V. "Obraz Krasnoi Armii v amerikanskoi presse v kontse Vtoroi mirovoi voiny." *Voenno-Istoricheskii Zhurnal* 10 (2008): 33-6.

Santoli, Susan P., and Andrew Weaver. "The Treatment of World War II in the Secondary School National History Textbook of the Six Major Powers Involved in the War." *Journal of Social Studies Research* 23 (1999): 34-44.

Schofield, John. "D-Day Sites in England: An Assessment." *Antiquity* 75 (2001): 77-83.

Schröder, Hans Joachim. "Die Vergegenwärtigung des Zweiten Weltkrieges in biographischen Interviewerzählungen." *Militärgeschichtliche Mitteilungen* 1 (1991): 9-37.

Sekistov, V. "Pravda i vymysel ob otkrytii vtorogo fronta v Evrope." *Voenno-Istoricheskii Zhurnal* 5 (1984): 74-82.

Sekistov, V., and G. Korotkov. "Otsenka angliiskimi istorikami voennoi strategii Anglii i SShA." *Voenno-Istoricheskii Zhurnal* 7 (1968): 102-9.

———. "Pravda i vymusly o poslednei kampanii voiny v Evrope." *Voenno-Istoricheskii Zhurnal* 5 (1970): 45-51.

Sherman, Daniel. "Bodies and Names: The Emergence of Commemoration in Interwar France." *American Historical Review* 103 (1998): 443-66.

———. "Objects of Memory: History and Narrative in French War Museums." *French Historical Studies* 19 (1995): 49-74.

Summerfield, Penny. "Divisions at Sea: Class, Gender, Race, and Nation in Maritime Films of the Second World War, 1939-60." *Twentieth Century British History* 22 (2011): 330-53.

———. "Dunkirk and the Popular Memory of Britain at War, 1940-58." *Journal of Contemporary History* 45 (2010): 788-811.

Twomey, Steve. "Soldiers of Germany Return for D-Day, Too." *Philadelphia Enquirer* (5 June 1984). NewsBank (accessed 5 June 2008).

White, Hayden. "Historiography and Historiophoty." *American Historical Review* 93 (Dec. 1988): 1193-99.

Wills, Henry. "Archaeological Aspects of D-Day: Operation Overlord." *Antiquity* 68 (1994): 843-45.

Zaitsev, I. "K voprosu ob otkrytii vtorogo fronta i ego roli vo Vtoroi mirovoi voine." *Voenno-Istoricheskii Zhurnal* 6 (1959): 63.

Unpublished Papers, Dissertations, and Presentations

Dolski, Michael. "'To Set Free a Suffering Humanity': D-Day in American Remembrance." PhD diss., Temple University, 2012.

Edwards, Sam. "War and Collective Memory: American Military Commemoration in Britain and France, 1943 to the Present." PhD diss., Lancaster University, 2007.

Hill, Roger H. "Memorializing Community Grief: Bedford, Virginia, and the National D-Day Memorial." DA diss., George Mason University, 2006.

Lemay, Kate C. "Forgotten Memorials: The American Cemeteries in France from World War II." PhD diss., Indiana University, 2011

de Loizellerie, Jacquemine. "Les lieux de mémoire de la Seconde Guerre mondiale dans la manche." Mémoire de maitrise, Université de Caen, 1998.

Magnúsdóttir, Rósa. "From the Meeting on the Elbe to Parading on Red Square: Discourses about the Soviet-American War Alliance, 1945-2010." Paper presented at the Annual Meeting of Association of Slavic, Eastern European, and Eurasian Studies, Washington, DC, November 17-20, 2011.

—————. "Keeping up Appearances: How the Soviet State Failed to Control Popular Attitudes toward the United States of America, 1945-1959." PhD diss., UNC Chapel Hill, 2006.

Pizy, Pierre-Laurent. "Commémorations du débarquement de la bataille de Normandie à travers le journal *Ouest-France* (1954-1994)." Mémoire de Maitrise, Université de Caen, 2003.

Rodriguez, L. "Mémoire(s) et commémorations de la Seconde Guerre mondiale en Basse-Normandie de 1945 à nos jours." Mémoire de Maitrise, Université de Caen, 2003.

Seitz, David. "Grave Negotiations: The Rhetorical Foundations of American World War I Cemeteries in France." PhD diss., University of Pittsburgh, 2011.

Contributors' Biographies

GÜNTER BISCHOF is the Marshall Plan Professor of History and the Director of Center Austria at the University of New Orleans; he was appointed a university "research professor" in June 2011. He served as a visiting professor at the Universities of Munich, Innsbruck, Salzburg, Vienna, the *Wirtschaftsuniversität Wien*, the Economics University of Prague (VSR), and the "Post-Katrina" Visiting Professor at LSU in the fall of 2005. Bischof is the author of *Austria in the First Cold War, 1945/55: The Leverage of the Weak* (1999), and *Relationships /Beziehungsgeschichten: Austria and the United States in the Twentieth Century* (forthcoming 2013); he is co-editor of *Contemporary Austrian Studies* (22 vols.) and the co-editor of another twenty books on topics of international contemporary history (World War II and the Cold War in Central Europe), among them with Stephen E. Ambrose, *Facts against Falsehood: Eisenhower and the German POWs* (1992), *Eisenhower: A Centenary Assessment* (1995), and with Saki Dockrill, *Cold War Respite: The Geneva Summit of 1955* (2000), all published by LSU Press. He also published with Wolfgang Krieger, eds., *D-Day: Die Normandieinvasion 6. Juni 1944: Eineinternationale Perspective* (2001). Bischof serves as a "Presidential Counselor" for the National World War II Museum.

JOHN BUCKLEY is a Professor of Military History at the University of Wolverhampton. Buckley's research interests focus upon twentieth-century military and strategic studies, particularly air power. He has published on British maritime air power in the interwar era and in World War Two, most notably a study of RAF Coastal Command, and on many other broader aspects of air power such as strategic bombing, British defence policy in the 1930s, and air power and total war. In addition, Buckley has researched and published on the Normandy campaign of 1944. In 2004 he published *British Armour and the Normandy Campaign 1944*, an in-depth study of the role, development and performance of the British armoured arm in the summer of 1944. Moreover, 2006 saw the publication of *The Normandy Campaign 1944: Sixty Years On*, an edited collection derived from the highly successful conference held at the University of Wolverhampton in 2004 by History and Governance Research Institute (HAGRI) and co-ordinated by Buckley. He is now working on the British tank industry in World War Two and *Monty's Men: The British Army and the Liberation of Northwest Europe 1944–5*, to be published by Yale University Press, a broader study of the performance of the British Army in the final stage of World War Two.

TERRY COPP is Professor Emeritus and Director of the Laurier Centre for Military Strategic and Disarmament Studies at Wilfred Laurier University. He is the author or co-author of fourteen books and numerous articles on Canadian, social, labour, and military history. Recent publications include *Fields of Fire: The Canadians in Normandy* (2003), which won the Society for Military History Distinguished Book Award in 2004, and *Cinderella Army: The Canadians in Northwest Europe 1944–45* (2006). Copp was the founding editor of the quarterly journal *Canadian Military History* and is well known to Canadians for his role in the television series *No Price Too High* and his regular feature articles in *Legion Magazine*. Edited works include *Montgomery's Scientists: Operational Research in 21 Army Group* (2000), *Guy Simonds and the Art of Command* (2007), and *Combat Stress: The Commonwealth Experience* with Mark Humphries (2010).

MICHAEL R. DOLSKI is a historian with the Joint Prisoner of War-Missing in Action Accounting Command's Central Identification Laboratory. Michael earned a PhD from Temple University in 2012. His focus area was American military history and particularly that of the twentieth century. His dissertation, "'To Set Free a Suffering Humanity': D-Day and American Remembrance," explored American public remembrance of the Normandy landings in Northwest France, June 1944, in the Second World War, and specifically highlighted patterns of commemoration and their ties to political as well as personal matters of evolving present-day concerns.

Sam Edwards is a Lecturer in American History at Manchester Metropolitan University (MMU). He was awarded his PhD in History by Lancaster University in 2008. His doctoral research explored the discourses and dynamics of American commemoration of World War II, particularly that which has unfolded in Britain and France over the past sixty-five years. His first monograph, titled *Allies in Memory: World War II and the Politics of Transatlantic Commemoration, c. 1941-2001*, is forthcoming with Cambridge University Press in 2014. Edwards has previously published essays discussing various aspects of American war commemoration and transatlantic relations, most recently in the *Journal of Transatlantic Studies* (March 2013), in C. Pearson, P. Coates and T. Cole (eds,) *Militarized Landscapes: From Gettysburg to Salisbury Plain* (2010), and in M. Keren and H. Herwig (eds.) *War Memory and Popular Culture* (2009). To date, Edwards' research has been funded by grants and awards from the Economic and Social Research Council (UK), the United States Army Military History Institute, the British Association of American Studies, and the US-UK Fulbright Commission. Prior to taking up his post at MMU, Edwards was a Fulbright Distinguished Scholar at the University of Pittsburgh. Edwards' current research is concerned with British commemoration of D-Day, transatlantic relations, and the cultural history of conflict.

Olga Kucherenko is a Research Fellow at St. John's College, Cambridge. Her research focuses on the social and cultural history of the Second World War, specifically Soviet experience of the war and its legacy in modern-day Russia. Kucherenko is particularly interested in conflict-based propaganda, legal history, and military anthropology. Her recent book, *Little Soldiers: How Soviet Children Went to War, 1941–1945* (OUP, 2011), taps the mentality of Soviet child-soldiers, as well as the role Stalinist culture played in their mobilisation for war.

Kate C. Lemay is Assistant Professor of Art History at Auburn University–Montgomery, where she teaches courses on Modern and Contemporary Art.

Her research interests include the study of American memorial art and architecture in France dedicated to World War II. Her projects have been supported by fellowships from IIE Fulbright, the Terra Foundation in American Art, the Smithsonian American Art Museum,the Centre nationale pour les recherches scientifiques,the Mémorial de Caen, and the Emily Landau Research Center at the Georgia O'Keeffe Museum. Her current book project addresses the evolution of postwar French memory relative to the American cemeteries in France from World War II. She has presented papers addressing the role of art and architecture in the memory of the American fallen soldier.

MICHAEL MAIER is a doctoral candidate at the Department of Economic and Social History, University of Vienna, and former Ministry of Science Fellow at Center Austria, University of New Orleans. His oral history-based University of Vienna dissertation deals with the metamorphoses and social (re)constructions of individual male identities ("remasculinization") of former Austrian *Wehrmacht* soldiers and prisoners of war in the aftermath of World War II. Currently he works as a museum guide at Hofburg Palace in Vienna and as a research fellow for the oral history project "MenschenLeben" at the Österreichische Mediathek (The Austrian Media Library). He has published a number of articles, including with Günter Bischof, "Reinventing Tradition and the Politics of History: Schüssel's Restitution and Commemoration Policies," in *Contemporary Austrian Studies*. Vol. 18, *The Schüssel Era in Austria*, eds. Günter Bischof and Fritz Plasser (New Orleans: University of New Orleans Press, 2010).

MATT SYMES is the editor of canadianmilitaryhistory.ca, the Publications Manager for the Laurier Centre for Military Strategic and Disarmament Studies, and a PhD Candidate (ABD) at Wilfrid Laurier University. He is the co-editor, with Geoff Hayes and Mike Bechthold, of *Canada and the Second World War: Essays in Honour of Terry Copp*. He has co-written and worked on five military history guidebooks:*1812: A Guide to the War and its Legacy, Canadian Battlefields 1915–1918: A Visitor's Guide,* and three on the Canadians in Italy during the Second World War. He is currently working with Jonathan Vance, Kellen Kurschinski, Steven Marti, and Alicia Robinet on a collection of First World War essays: *The Great War: From Memory to History*, set to be published with Wilfrid Laurier University Press in 2014.

Index